THE FIRST COMPLETE HOME DECORATING CATALOGUE

by the same authors

DECORATING AMERICAN STYLE
DECORATING WITH CONFIDENCE
COLOR IN DECORATION
DECORATING DEFINED
DECORATION USA

THE FIRST
COMPLETE HOME DECORATING
CATALOGUE

with 1,001 mail-order sources and ideas to help you
furnish and decorate your home

by
José Wilson and Arthur Leaman, ASID

HOLT, RINEHART AND WINSTON
NEW YORK

Prepared and produced by Vineyard Books, Inc., 159 East 64th Street, New York, N.Y. 10021
Published simultaneously in Canada by Holt, Rinehart and Winston
of Canada, Limited.

Library of Congress Cataloging in Publication Data
Wilson, José
    The first complete home decorating catalogue.

    Includes index.
    1. House furnishings—Catalogs. I. Leaman, Arthur,
joint author. II. Title.
TX311.W54   747'.8'802573   75-5474
ISBN Hardbound: 0-03-015106-6
ISBN Paperback: 0-03-014646-1

Designer: Helen Barrow

Printed in the United States of America

10 9 8 7 6 5 4 3 2

ACKNOWLEDGMENTS

We gratefully acknowledge the kind cooperation of the many companies who sent us their catalogues and photographs.

We particularly want to express our thanks to Helen Barrow for her advice, counsel, and patience; to Martin Kreiner for gathering and collating the catalogues; to Helen Gregutt and Duane Hampton for assistance with the manuscript; to Helene Dorn and Yvonne Yaw for typing the manuscript; and to Otto Maya for special photography.

Without their help this catalogue could not have been completed.

J.W. and A.L.

CONTENTS

FOREWORD

Like most good ideas, *The First Complete Home Decorating Catalogue* came about by both accident and necessity.

By accident, because while working with José Wilson on a do-it-yourself decorating book I wrote away for several catalogues and booklets. As an interior designer, I was, frankly, amazed at the wealth of information they provided and, even more so, by the array and variety of products for the home these books offered. I became curious, started clipping catalogue offers from magazines, writing for more catalogues, seeing the range and quality of ideas and merchandise available for the price of a postage stamp or a small charge, often refundable with the first purchase. It was only then that the necessity of this book hit home. Here was a perfect, new, and easy way for homemakers, the would-be decorator, and the casual browser to shop, to develop their decorating ideas, to plan their purchases wisely and economically, saving time and money.

Our catalogue is not just a book of sources for furniture, accessories, hardware— the simple everyday household items and the major furniture and appliances—but a book of ideas. In fact, you'll find sections on nothing but decorating ideas, how to mix furniture styles, how to make the most of space, unusual window treatments. There are booklets on remodeling and home improvement, home decorating courses that save you money by teaching you to do the job yourself, saving labor costs, invariably the biggest expense. There are do-it-yourself-kit catalogues for everything from needlepoint pillows to spiral staircases.

Inevitably, there are certain unavoidable omissions, though not, we hope, too many. Some manufacturers or companies to whom we wrote for a catalogue and up-to-date information never replied, despite follow-up letters. Others, fearful of being overwhelmed by a flood of inquiries, asked not to be included. Undoubtedly, there are all manner of small companies that we haven't heard of. We'd appreciate your suggestions for inclusion in future editions. Please send them to Complete Home Decorating Catalogue, c/o Arthur Leaman, 110 West 15th Street, New York, N.Y. 10011.

To make an item-by-item index of each catalogue would be impossible, due to the tremendous variety of products, ideas, and services offered. Instead, we have grouped catalogues in their general categories and then, within each category, listed as many of the outstanding offerings as was feasible. So, if you are looking for a serving cart but do not find it mentioned in our list of furniture catalogues, simply send for those catalogues that feature the style or period that interests you. Most likely you will be rewarded with a good selection.

Buying furniture represents a considerable investment. If you are not sure what you want or what is available, it makes sense to send for a slew of catalogues of the type you are searching for—traditional or contemporary—and look through until you find the likely sofa, table, or storage piece. You'll be able to check out all the specifications, finishes, choice of fabrics (most companies will send you fabric swatches and finish samples on approval), and dimensions. Many catalogues come with miniature furniture cutouts and graph paper so that you can plan the furniture arrangement in your room before ordering.

So, if you are contemplating anything from a one-room decorating job to remodeling your home, and if you like to browse and take your time making a decision, you will find that this book provides you with a wealth of information. I have, and I'm sure you will, too.

ARTHUR LEAMAN, ASID

PREFACE

When you are decorating or remodeling your home, one of the most time-consuming, wearisome, and often frustrating experiences you are likely to have is trying to find exactly what you have in mind—the right piece of furniture, the perfect fabric pattern, lamp, or hardware.

If you live in a big city like New York or Chicago, you can spend days, even weeks, casing one store after another. Should you live in a small town, forget it. You are stuck with what the local shopping centers and building centers have to offer, and that's not much. As a saleslady in a big department store once told me, when I asked why they didn't carry a certain sheet pattern I wanted, which was then being nationally advertised in magazines and newspapers, "It's not everybody's taste." Everybody's taste, the mass common demoninator, is what you are likely to encounter across the country.

I know whereof I speak, because for the past six years I have gone through various stages of redecorating and remodeling a house in the country. Although I knew just what I wanted, I was unable to get it locally, not even in the nearest big city, Boston. It seemed that I was eternally dashing down to New York for a footsore couple of shopping days, just to find something as simple as a plain white hanging globe fixture for the bathroom, good-looking brass handles for a French door, tile for the kitchen floor, even the color of deck paint I needed.

This book, then, is designed to save you time, money, and headaches by providing a handy catalogue of home furnishings that you can go through at your leisure. Despite the fact that my colleague, Arthur Leaman, and I have considerable knowledge of the field, even we were amazed, when we started going through the catalogues we had amassed, to discover some of the absolutely marvelous sources for offbeat things that could be ordered by mail. It seems there is almost nothing anyone could want, from a cigar-store Indian to Louis XV *boiserie*, that someone, somewhere, doesn't sell.

Of course, in such a huge and specialized market as home furnishings, not everything is, or can be, sold by mail. After each listing you'll find a group of letters that indicate how the furniture, floor covering, fabric, appliance, or other merchandise can be ordered—by mail **(MO)**, through a retail source such as a dealer or store **(RS)**, or through an interior designer **(ID)**. Most major furniture manufacturers sell through stores and interior designers, whereas smaller companies, usually those with imported, handcrafted, unfinished, or butcher-block furniture, do a large part of their business by mail. On the other hand, there are many companies that have both mail-order and retail operations. Some sell all three ways—mail order, retail, and through interior designers. On the relatively few occasions when merchandise is ID (available only through an interior designer), that presents no problem. You can use the decorating department of your nearest big department store, provided they carry that particular line, or you can contact the local chapter of the ASID (American Society of Interior Designers) for the names of professionals in your area. You don't pay any more, because the designer's fee represents the difference between the price you pay (retail) and the price at which he or she buys (wholesale, or trade discount).

Apart from well-known companies in the home-furnishings field whose products are familiar to us, we had no way of judging the quality of the merchandise. offered, other than by the catalogue descriptions and photographs, so this book should be regarded as a guide to what is available, not as a recommendation or endorsement. We have included approximate prices for merchandise, but in these days of spiraling inflation they are subject to change, as are the prices of new editions of the catalogues themselves. Catalogues are frequently issued seasonally or updated periodically when old merchandise is dropped and new added. The things we have picked out as worthy of mention will serve as an indication of what the company offers and the price range.

To get the best service out of this catalogue, let us offer you a few pointers, learned from personal experience, that may save you time, money, and unnecessary frustration.

Before ordering, always write for the catalogue first. Once you have received it (there may be some delay due to a revised edition of the catalogue), look through it carefully and ask yourself what information not included in the catalogue should be considered. For instance, if you are going to buy something that must be installed, such as an appliance, a ceiling fan, or wood flooring, find out from your electrician, plumber, or carpenter what you need to check out regarding such matters as installation, weight, wiring, size, or plumbing connections. There is no point in buying something you can't use without going to enormous expense or tearing your house apart.

If the catalogue costs $1.00 or more, the safest way to send the money is by check. Should you find it more convenient—for a 25-cent or 50-cent brochure—to send coins, wrap them and tape them to your letter. Often the price of the catalogue is refunded as a credit on your purchase. Out-of-state sales, incidentally, carry no sales tax, but if you live in the state from which you order merchandise, you'll have to add it on to the purchase price.

Ascertain before you order how the merchandise will be shipped—parcel post, United Parcel Service (UPS), or by motor or air freight—and whether shipping charges are included in the price or extra. UPS does not ship collect, so their charges must be prepaid with the order. Some freight companies will ship collect, which makes it even more advisable to find out ahead of time how your order will be dispatched and how much the charges will be.

Parcel post has a restriction on the weight and size of packages. Parcels can weigh up to 40 pounds, provided they are not more than 84 inches in length and girth (girth meaning the circumference of the parcel). Larger parcels, weighing up to 70 pounds and 100 inches in length and girth, will be delivered to towns with second-class post offices. The problem with parcel post is that you have no way of knowing how long a parcel will take to get to you, and nowadays speed is not the word.

United Parcel Service and similar delivery companies take parcels of up to 50 pounds, with size stipulation of 108 inches, length and girth combined, and are invariably faster than parcel post. Because they require a signature, you must be at home to receive the package; otherwise, after three attempts to deliver (they leave a notice if you aren't home), they return the package to the sender. That's true of parcel post, too, unless you give the post office specific instructions to hold the package or go there in person to collect it. It is always advisable, if you are going to be away from home during the day, to arrange about receipt of any merchandise you order. For UPS you can leave a note on the door redirecting delivery to a friend's house, though a safer thing to do is to inform their local office.

Freight lines handle heavier packages of from 50 to 500 pounds and deliver either by truck or air express.

Most mail-order houses have their regular shipping methods and usually do their best to spare you unnecessary expense, but it is always smart to find out first how the merchandise will be sent.

It is advisable to keep a record of your orders, the name and address of the company, the description and catalogue number of the merchandise, the date ordered, and so on. Include in your records any required sales tax and handling and shipping charges with your payment and the number of your personal check or money order, which will provide proof of payment.

Many mail-order companies now let you charge merchandise on a credit card such as American Express, Master Charge, or Bank Americard. The buy-now, pay-later routine is seductive, but our advice is don't do it. Once the mail-order house has passed the charge on to the credit-card company, you'll have a devil of a time straightening things out should you have to return the merchandise for some reason, or should it arrive damaged. Furthermore, if the company from whom you ordered happens to be handling a lot of business or has temporarily run out of stock, your order may not be shipped immediately. Chances are you will not only be billed for it but if you don't pay right away (and who would for undelivered goods?), a finance charge will be slapped on the following month. I made this unpleasant discovery when I ordered something on a charge card in April, was billed in May, and didn't receive the order until the first part of June. Finding the merchandise unsatisfactory, I returned it immediately by registered mail, return receipt requested. At the same time I wrote to the local branch of the credit-card company, giving them full details and asking them to see that I was credited for the returned merchandise and not debited with a finance charge. In reply I got a form asking for proof the merchandise had been returned, which I duly sent off, along with the credit slip from the mail-order company. All of this was well within the 30-day limit for notice of statement errors stipulated by the credit-card company. I finally got the credit, but I am now being billed every month with a mounting finance charge on what they claim to be an "unpaid balance." I have been assured that this will be corrected on my next bill, but after six months I'm still waiting. Had I paid by personal check this could never have happened.

While we don't anticipate any such problems, there is always the possibility that your order will arrive damaged, too late, or prove in some way unsatisfactory. You can always return it, provided there isn't a no-return policy, as there often is on special sale items. Some companies have a time limit for returns, ranging from 10 to 30 days; others don't mention this in their literature. Make a point of checking the company policy on returns, substitutions, and guarantees. In any case, it is always advisable to return damaged or unsatisfactory goods within 10 days of receipt. Write a letter (keeping a carbon or Xerox) stating clearly and precisely what was wrong with the order and whether you want a replacement, exchange, or refund. If you don't hear from the company within 30 days after returning the merchandise, write to them by registered mail, return receipt requested.

If the contents of the package arrive damaged or broken, first write to the company explaining the problem and ask what they want you to do with the package. Be sure not to throw away the original packaging, as this is necessary to prove that damage occurred in transit and not through any fault of yours.

If your order is delayed and arrives too late to be of any use, don't open the package. Write on the outside "Refused—return to sender" and send it back. If you open the package, you must pay the return postage. Here again, it is wise to send it by registered mail and request a return receipt as proof of delivery.

Let's say you are ordering something that you absolutely must have on or before a certain date, such as Christmas or a birthday. Write on your check "This order is canceled if the merchandise cannot be delivered by . . . " and give a date.

In the unlikely event that you don't receive a reply, refund, or replacement, here are some consumer agencies to which you can refer a complaint with a request that they look into the matter:

Mail Order Action Line Service of the Direct Mail Advertising Association, 230 Park Avenue, New York, NY 10017.

US Postal Service's Consumer Affairs Office, Washington, DC 20260.

Council of Better Business Bureaus, 1150 17th Street, Washington, DC 20036 (watchdog for illegal or unethical business practices and false or misleading advertising of national retailers and manufacturers).

Before you complain to any agency or association, however, it is advisable to make every attempt to settle the matter with the manufacturer or company concerned. If you don't get an answer from a representative of the company, a letter to the president (whose name you can get by calling the company or consulting a business directory in your public library) will often bring immediate results. The president of the firm, after all, has the biggest stake in the reputation of his product!

Happy shopping!

JOSÉ WILSON

IDENTIFICATION OF ABBREVIATIONS

MO—mail-order sales
RS—retail stores
ID—through an interior designer

Throughout the book the official U.S. Postal Service abbreviations for each state have been used. Call your local post office for the complete, correct zip code.

STATE ABBREVIATIONS AND ZIP CODE PREFIXES

AL	350-369	Alabama	NB	680-693	Nebraska
AK	995-999	Alaska	NV	890-898	Nevada
AZ	850-999	Arizona	NH	030-038	New Hampshire
AR	716-729	Arkansas	NJ	070-089	New Jersey
CA	900-969	California	NM	870-884	New Mexico
CO	800-816	Colorado	NY	100-149	New York
CT	060-069	Connecticut	NC	270-289	North Carolina
DE	197-199	Delaware	ND	580-588	North Dakota
DC	200-205	District of Columbia	OH	430-458	Ohio
FL	320-339	Florida	OK	730-749	Oklahoma
GA	300-319	Georgia	OR	970-979	Oregon
HI	967-968	Hawaii	PA	150-196	Pennsylvania
ID	832-838	Idaho	PR	006-009	Puerto Rico
IL	600-629	Illinois	RI	028-029	Rhode Island
IN	460-479	Indiana	SC	290-299	South Carolina
IA	500-528	Iowa	SD	570-577	South Dakota
KS	660-679	Kansas	TN	370-385	Tennessee
KY	400-427	Kentucky	TX	750-799	Texas
LA	700-714	Louisiana	UT	840-847	Utah
ME	039-049	Maine	VA	220-246	Virginia
MD	206-219	Maryland	VT	050-059	Vermont
MA	010-027	Massachusetts	WA	980-994	Washington
MI	480-499	Michigan	WV	247-268	West Virginia
MN	550-567	Minnesota	WI	530-549	Wisconsin
MS	386-397	Mississippi	WY	820-831	Wyoming
MO	630-658	Missouri	VI	008	Virgin Islands
MT	590-599	Montana			

Historic Charleston Reproductions

TREASURES FROM HISTORIC CHARLESTON
A UNIQUE AMERICAN HERITAGE
FAITHFULLY REPRODUCED
FOR TODAY'S LIVING

GENERAL, GIFT, AND MUSEUM SOURCES

Hall tree, *Montgomery Ward*

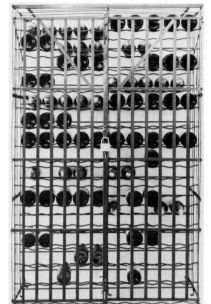

Wine jailhouse, *Hammacher Schlemmer*

THE GIANT STORES AND MAIL-ORDER HOUSES

ALDEN'S
Dept. CHC
Box 6167
Chicago, IL 60680

Color catalogue, $1.00, published spring, summer, fall, winter.

Though not as large as Sears or Montgomery Ward, this is a big mail-order house, primarily noted for clothing but with some home furnishings, such as furniture, lamps, kitchenware, and brand-name appliances.
MO

HAMMACHER SCHLEMMER
Dept. CHC
147 East 57th Street
New York, NY 10022

"Hammacher Schlemmer Catalogue," no charge, published five times a year, 64 pages, black and white, illustrated.

This famous, old-established New York store specializes in comforts, aids, and luxuries for the home, chiefly in the categories of bed and bath, outdoor living and entertaining, kitchen equipment, and tableware. They have good-looking cast-aluminum garden furniture, hammocks, and garden umbrellas; a "wine jail" for around $90 that holds 50 bottles behind bars (the 300-bottle size is around $240); feather-light mohair throws from England for $45; electrically heated towel stands ($120 to $130); and an electric unit that vibrates the mattress and massages away your tensions for around $40. A very wide range of prices.
MO/RS

MONTGOMERY WARD
Dept. CHC
Montgomery Ward Plaza
Chicago, IL 60681

General catalogues, Spring/Summer and Fall/Winter, Anniversary catalogue, Lawn and Garden catalogue, and Sale catalogues throughout the year. To get on the catalogue list you must make a purchase, either at the catalogue counter of a Ward's store or from a borrowed catalogue, and to stay on the list you have to make at least two sizable purchases every six months.

In addition to the usual array of home furnishings found in these enormous catalogues, Montgomery Ward has in its latest edition such offbeat items as an Edwardian hat rack, the classic bentwood rocker and side chairs, a 19th-century reproduction rolltop desk, bamboo blinds and shades, all kinds of shelving, and even an old-fashioned ceiling fan.
MO/RS

J.C. PENNEY COMPANY, INC.
Dept. CHC
1301 Avenue of the Americas
New York, NY 10019

Spring and fall catalogues, summer and Christmas supplements, no charge (but to receive them regularly you must buy regularly), color, illustrated.

Everything you would expect to find in home furnishings from this huge mail-order house, from furniture and fabrics to equipment and appliances, at competitive prices.
MO/RS

QUELLE, INC.
Dept. CHC
6050 Kennedy Boulevard East
West New York, NJ 07093

"Quelle International," $4.00 (refundable with first order), 850 pages, color, illustrated.

Would you like to browse through a European department store? You can by purchasing Quelle's "Shopping Advisor." Choc-a-bloc full of 40,000 amazing offers from all over Europe in curtains and bedding, gift items, as well as jewelry and fashions, all of tested quality at bargain prices.
MO

SEARS, ROEBUCK AND COMPANY
Dept. 139-CHC
4640 Roosevelt Boulevard
Philadelphia, PA 19132
         or
SEARS, ROEBUCK AND COMPANY
Dept. 139-CHC
2650 Olympic Boulevard
Los Angeles, CA 90051

Spring catalogue, January; fall catalogue, June. Supplemental home-furnishings catalogues: Carpet, Wonderful World of Wall Coverings, Home Improvement Catalogue, Accessories for Mobile Home and Recreation Vehicles Catalogue, Home Care and Convalescent Needs Catalogue, Craft Center, Power and Hand Tool Catalogue—all free, but to stay on the list you must buy at least $50 worth of merchandise every three months.

The general catalogues have a large selection of home furnishings, from carpets and rugs, wallcoverings and window treatments to furniture, lamps, china, and glassware.
MO/RS

Rocking chairs, *J. C. Penney*

GENERAL AND GIFT

SPIEGEL
Dept. CHC
1061 West 35th Street
Chicago, IL 60609

"Spiegel Catalogue," no charge, 139 pages, some color.

An all-inclusive mail-order catalogue with many inexpensive home-furnishing items, such as ready-made curtains and bedspreads, ready-to-hang four-panel shutters in stock sizes (about $15 a set), some room-size nylon rugs, any size under $80, moderately priced appliances, phono and stereo sets, and a few sets of upholstered living-room furniture.
MO

AMERICAN EXPRESS COMPANY
Dept. CHC
Special Offer Headquarters
P.O. Box 757
Great Neck, NY 11025

"First Choice," no charge to card holders, published biannually, 41 pages, color, illustrated.

The issue we received, called "First Choice for All Your Sun Days," was full of lovely things for summer living. A Brazilian hammock, white and lacy, was $36, a 13½"-high hurricane shade with silver-plated base about $22; an interesting hexagonal aquarium, 58" tall, complete with purification system, $250.
MO

AMERICAN HERITAGE PUBLISHING
   COMPANY
Dept. CHC, Catalogue Department
P.O. Box 1776
Marion, OH 43302

"The American Heritage Catalogue," no charge, published annually, 32 pages, color, illustrated.

In addition to the handsome collection of American Heritage Press books, this catalogue offers an unusual selection of household items of historical significance, including a faithful reproduction of an 18th-century Sheraton bookstand on casters for $185, (the original sold for $3,400); an antique Chinese blue-and-white cachepot from the Tong Chih period (1862–1873), originally to hold joss sticks, now for flowers, at $75; a graceful pewter chamberstick copied from the 1850 original by Henry Hopper at $20; and a magnificent reproduction of a Ming table of black-and-red lacquer carving, 26" x 13⅛" x 9½" high, for $295. As a catalogue subscriber, you benefit from the discount prices, which are extended only to catalogue customers, and you pay no postage or packing charges, which add up to quite a savings.
MO

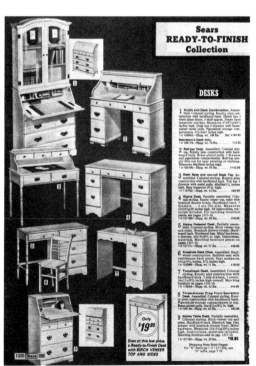

Unpainted furniture, *Sears, Roebuck*

22

Catalogue cover, *The Gallery*

Bird and animal collections, *Helen Gallagher*

**DOWNE MERCHANDISING
CORPORATION**
Dept. CHC
P.O. Box 1776
West Des Moines, IA 50265

*"The Great American Gift Catalogue,"
no charge, 23 pages, color, illustrated.*

In case you haven't picked up a copy
on an American Airlines plane, you can
send for their latest catalogue which
celebrates the Bicentennial with a vast
array of handsome items for the home,
such as a hand-engraved crystal
hurricane shade with eagle motif for
$27.50, an Americana Schoolhouse
clock (with cordless electronic
movement) for $65, or amusing bobbin
candlesticks from $12.50 to $15 the pair.
If your taste tends more to the
contemporary, there's a white molded
plastic-and-chrome bar that holds
bottles, glasses, dips, and built-in ice
bucket for $67.50, or a plastic terrarium
sphere kit for $14.95. Purchases can be
charged on credit cards, and there's a
toll-free telephone number for
ordering.
MO

DOWNS & COMPANY
Dept. CHC
1014 Davis Street
Evanston, IL 60204

*"Your Catalogue of Unusual Gifts," 25
cents, published three times a year, 64
pages, black and white, illustrated.*

Typical mail-order offerings, with some
interesting things for the home. A
portable folding checkers table for
games or snacks is only $16.99. A rolling
white steel wire cart for house plants,
with three 6" x 20" tiers, is $14.50. For
$8.25 you can get a folding reversible
paper fireplace fan that opens to 40"
wide by 20" high. A 15"-high brass-
and-glass pyramid from Mexico for
your collectibles is $19.95. Sizes, prices,
and order form are included.
MO

**THE HELEN GALLAGHER GALLERY
COLLECTION**
Dept. CHC
6523 North Galena Road
Peoria, IL 61632

*"The Helen Gallagher Gallery
Collection," no charge, 48 pages, color,
illustrated.*

A collection of well-selected gifts with
great variety, including many home-
furnishings items. A pierced tin hanging
shade, à la Tiffany, 20" wide x 14" deep,
ready to install, is under $30. From the
Oriental collection, a nest of three
bamboo plant stands in three sizes,
from 9" x 7" x 8" high up to 14" x 12½"
x 10" high, costs under $35. There are
some unusual pieces of furniture, too—
a fruitwood curio table, velour-lined,
glass top and sides, 20" diameter x 22"
high, about $125; a 53"-high cheval
glass with fruitwood frame; even a
reproduction of an antique bedwarmer
in solid brass and copper with wood
handle, 36" long, about $37. The Gallery
Aviary collection features bisque
porcelain birds, hand-painted in true-
to-life colors; The Gallery Menagerie,
handcrafted earthenware animals.
MO

Beflowered mailbox, *Greyhound Gift House*

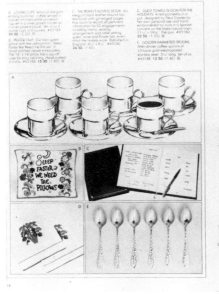

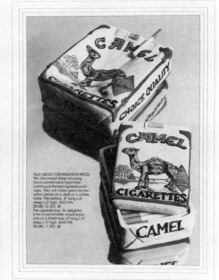

Unusual gifts, *Horchow Collection*

THE GALLERY
Dept. CHC
Amsterdam, NY 12010

"The Gallery," no charge, 32 pages, some color.

For over 76 years this company has been offering a select group of mail-order items. In this issue, for the home, there are two of tomorrow's telephones in clear acrylic plastic—the Apollo, about $125, and the Periscope, under $200; a collection of reproductions of old saloon mirrors, from about $20 for Schlitz or White Label mirror to $60 for the large Falstaff Beer mirror. For the bath, a level-beam floor scale is under $60, and for the garden a handsome "Exeter" sundial with a compass rose base is about $65. You'll find many other unusual items.
MO

THE GREYHOUND GIFT HOUSE
Dept. CHC
1201 N.W. 72nd Avenue
Miami, FL 33126

"The Greyhound Gift House," no charge, published annually, 47 pages, color, illustrated.

"In Pursuit of Excellence" is Greyhound's slogan. It seems justified, as the items shown have originality at a good price. A delightful beflowered mailbox for a suburban or city dweller (city people use them as catch-alls or planters) is under $25, a 16" plasticized fiberboard cube with six gameboards, which can double as end or coffee table, is under $12; a wall clock that indicates time all over the world, with electric movement, 17½" high, 24" wide, 4½" deep, is under $100.
MO

HAVERHILL'S
Dept. CHC
137 Utah Avenue
South San Francisco, CA 94080

Catalogue, no charge, 64 pages, some color, illustrated.

A general catalogue of many good-looking contemporary gift items, some made especially for Haverhill's. Many gadgets, but also a few pieces of modern furniture of the cube, end-table, and storage type.
MO

HERTER'S, INC.
Dept. CHC
Waseca, MI 56093

"Herter's Catalogue," $1.00 (refundable with $10 purchase), 100 pages, some color, illustrated.

Herter's big outdoors catalogue (there is a four-page index) has some amazing home-decorating finds, if you look hard enough. In addition to the expected weathervanes, bird feeders, garden bells, and the like, there are pages of antiques and reproductions. Old wooden decoys of such rare birds as the passenger pigeon are under $7. Reproductions of pressed-glass candy dishes with covers shaped like ducks, rabbits, or lovebirds are from $5 to $7. There are lamp kits, carved boxes, trays and tables of Indian shisham wood, brass candlesticks, ship models, ship decanters, and cut-crystal stemware, all at moderate prices.
MO

THE HORCHOW COLLECTION
Dept. CHC
P.O. Box 34257
Dallas, TX 75234

"The Horchow Collection," $1.00 for six issues a year, 65 pages, color, illustrated, plus special-interest mailings: "The Horchow Collection Pamper Book," 35 pages, color, illustrated; "The Horchow Collection Book for Cooks," 25 pages, some color, illustrated.

This is the Cartier of gift catalogues, with a surprising number of home furnishings that change with each issue—examples are a nest of bamboo tables for $27.50 and a one-of-a-kind Coromandel screen for $60,000 (don't rush to write; it may have been sold by now). In between these extremes are flower-shaped cradles, brass floor lamps, Eames chairs, bar carts, and foldaway tables. The Horchow buyers select an international array of top-quality gifts (with price tags to match), which is constantly updated and enlarged. This catalogue might be subtitled "Temptations Unlimited." Purchases can be charged to credit cards, and there's a toll-free telephone number for ordering direct, as well as an order form.
"The Pamper Book," one of the special mailings, is dedicated to renewing and refreshing your senses—the usual five plus your sense of well-being. There are such little luxuries as a video intercom, Canadian red fox throw, velour-covered hotwater bottle, and waterproofed chintz umbrellas from England.
"The Horchow Collection Book for Cooks" assembles some pretty classy equipment for cooking, dining, and entertaining, everything down to potholders, which are, as you might expect, out of the ordinary.
MO

24

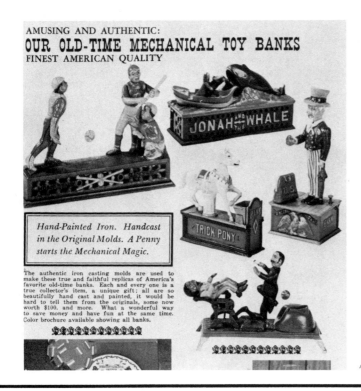

Antique metal banks, *New Hampton General Store*

Rose bowl, *Shopping International*

JENNIFER HOUSE
Dept. CHC
Great Barrington, MA 01230

"Jennifer House," no charge, published annually, 64 pages, some color, illustrated.

Jennifer House calls itself New England's Americana Marketplace, and it is just that. All kinds of Colonial items from a reproduction brass student lamp for under $130 to a white ironstone pitcher-and-bowl set for about $18. There are braid rugs, spatterware china, authentic pewter reproductions—even an Anne Adams swing cradle in maple, about $45. An interesting catalogue of nostalgia.
MO

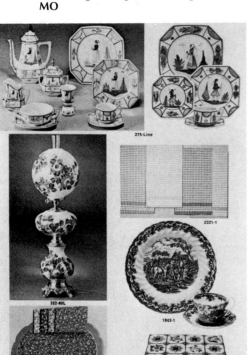

KREBS
Dept. CHC
U.S. Route #1
Westerly, RI 02891

"KREBS Gift & Home Catalog," no charge, published annually, 64 pages, some color, illustrated.

A well-rounded catalogue of gifts, items for the home, and a selection of specialized books for cooks, animal lovers, and collectors. This issue features Krebs' red, white, and blue Bicentennial quilt, 108" x 108", made entirely of corduroy, available custom-made for $375 or in kit form for $95. For cat lovers there's a collection of life-size ceramic cats from $14.95 for a Chocolate or Seal Point Siamese to $29.95 for a hand-painted floral Calico. For country-look bathrooms, accessories of cherry-finished pine or "wrought iron" strap hinge motif include towel bars and rings, robe hooks, and toothbrush and glass holders at moderate prices. There is even a full-sized reproduction of a wooden-handled brass bed warmer for only $29.50. The great variety of well-selected offerings makes this an interesting catalogue.
MO

MILES KIMBALL COMPANY
Dept. CHC
104 Bond Street
Oshkosh, WI 54901

"Miles Kimball Catalogue," no charge, 196 pages, published semiannually, color.

In this general mail-order catalogue of gifts, toys, and housewares are a few items for the home decorator, such as a planter-pole in chrome or brass to fit ceilings up to 8' 4", with four swivel arms that can be positioned at any height (under $13).
MO

HOUSE OF MINNEL
Dept. CHC
Deerpath Road
Batavia, IL 60510

"House of Minnel," 25 cents, 40 pages, some color, illustrated.

Gifts, gadgets, and gimmicks by the hundreds are illustrated in this gift-house catalogue. Among the more unusual items is a collection of reproductions of sand-cast iron mechanical banks, from about $20 for the Royal Elephant Bank to $40 for Uncle Sam. A hooded Dutch wall-hung clock from Barwick is under $300, a very good-looking contemporary molded plastic battery-operated perpetual-calendar clock under $35.
MO

Americana collection, *Jennifer House*

China, pottery, and crystal, *Shannon Free Airport*

Catchalls and storage pieces, *Nordiska*

NEW HAMPTON GENERAL STORE
Dept. CHC
RFD
Hampton, NJ 08827

"Spring/Summer and Fall/Winter Gazette," no charge, issued biannually, 63 pages, some color, illustrated.

The catalogue from this old-time general store reflects the great variety of its stock, everything from old-fashioned rock candy at $3.25 a pound to authentic 36"-wide Early American calicos at $2.35 a yard; a set of swatches is only 50 cents. Other unusual items for the home include a 45-piece set of English ironstone china in blue or green with white for only $59.95, three patchwork design pillows at $14.95 each, charming copies of 19th-century ironstone soap dishes from England in a choice of three colors at $3.95 each, or a collection of 28 replicas of cast-iron mechanical toy banks in a wide range of prices.
MO

NORDISKA
Dept. CHC
299 Westport Avenue
Norwalk, CT 06850

"Nordiska Catalogue," no charge, 22 pages, black and white, illustrated.

Along with a wide variety of kitchen and housekeeping implements, the catalogue includes clamp-on lamps, both plastic and metal, for wall, shelf, or desk, about $15; catch-all bins that become either storage walls or tables, about $6; and children's play furniture of colorful heavy-duty plastic—a stool and two chairs cost under $12.
MO/RS

ROMBINS' NEST FARM
Dept. CHC
Fairfield, PA 17320

Catalogue, 25 cents, published annually, 40 pages, black and white, illustrated.

The Rombinses refer to it as your "wish book" and describe it as "leaning heavily toward Early American and nostalgia." Every page is packed with items that cover just about everything that would go inside or outside a house. Along with "cute" gifts, replicas, and miniatures are some real finds, such as a hand-blown South Jersey Clevenger glass sunflower jug, $7, or an octagonal pressed-glass covered dish, under $8.
MO

SHANNON FREE AIRPORT
Dept. CHC
590 Fifth Avenue
New York, NY 10022

"Shannon Catalogue," 60 cents, 68 pages, color, illustrated.

In addition to watches, perfumes, Irish linens, and jewelry, this duty-free shop at Ireland's Shannon Airport has some lovely things for the home. There are beautiful Waterford crystal chandeliers from about $200 to $350 with matching wall sconces or an all-crystal Victorian courting lamp, under $80, plus a selection of Waterford tableware. From Holland, blue Delft from "De Porceleyne Fles," made since 1653; bone china from Royal Worcester, Coalport, and Spode; Wedgwood, Portland or Jasper blue earthenware or Wedgwood clocks, about $140. Two reproductions of 17th-century porcelain herb burners, the Village Church and Masters House, are each under $30. Air or surface mail charges are listed with the convenient mail-order form.
MO

SHOPPING INTERNATIONAL, INC.
Dept. CHC
800 Shopping International Building
Norwich, VT 05055

"Shopping International," 25 cents, published three times yearly, 48 pages, color, illustrated.

This mail-order catalogue is unusual in that it concentrates on imports from abroad that reflect the cultures of the countries, from clothing and jewelry to pottery, glassware, and decorative accessories. From Morocco, a Marmoucha blanket of hand-loomed fibranne in gray/brown/black is about $36. From Denmark, orange or white polystyrol Kalmen stools, 18" high, are under $15. From Mexico, Guerrero farmers' hand-painted barkcloth paintings are under $9. And from Japan, a miniature *tansu* chest of mahogany with hand-wrought brass fittings and four velvet-lined drawers, 12" x 8" x 6½", is under $60. Many other unusual items are offered.
MO

SLEEPY HOLLOW GIFTS
Dept. CHC
6651 Arlington Boulevard
Falls Church, VA 22042

"Quality Gifts by Mail," no charge, published annually, 79 pages, black and white, illustrated.

Gadgets and gifts from all over, with a smattering of items for the home. A personalized director's chair, your name embroidered on the back, with a choice of sling and frame colors, is under $35. A revolving desk-top book stand, just 11½" square, that holds up to 20 books costs under $25 in maple or walnut. For the garden, there is a purple martin mansion of from four to 20 apartments, made with snap-together plastic units, $13 to $46, the three-piece mounting pole about $30.
MO

Indian bedspreads and pillows, *Windfall*

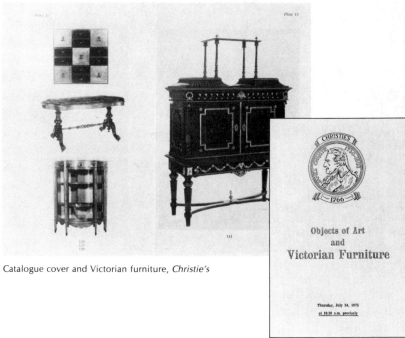

Catalogue cover and Victorian furniture, *Christie's*

AUCTION CATALOGUES

MUSEUM SOURCES

THE WESTON TRADING COMPANY
Dept. CHC
P.O. Box 165
Bethpage, NY 11804

"The Weston Trading Company Catalogue," no charge, published triannually, 33 pages, color, illustrated.

Every issue has different merchandise, but the eyecatchers in the most recent are a mirror with a silver-toned frame and a clipper ship hand-painted in reverse on the back of the glass, $65; a wicker basket of shells to decorate a desk or table, $10; a handsome folding walnut-finish luggage rack with needlework straps, $22.50; and a nest of four bamboo planters, 6½" to 9½" long, with galvanized liners, $37.50. There's a convenient post-paid order form.
MO

WINDFALL
Dept. CHC
Main Street
Sharon Springs, NY 13459

"Windfall," no charge, 62 pages, some color, illustrated.

The Lindstroms have assembled a nice collection of gift items for everyone, with several things for the home. From Pawleys Island, off the South Carolina coast, come handwoven cotton hammocks, from $50 to $60, depending on size. From India, hand-blocked spreads in classic designs and colors— "Tree of Life," "Bird of Paradise," or "Peacock," 72" x 108", under $10, or brightly colored cotton pillows embroidered with silk and inset with bits of mirror, 16" square, washable covers, about $12.50. There is also a large collection of well-made miniatures for doll houses or for the collector.
MO

CHRISTIE'S
Dept. CHC
Catalogue Department
867 Madison Avenue
New York, NY 10021

List of annual catalogue subscription rates and price lists, no charge.

Christie's international auction rooms are famous the world over, and their sales catalogues make wonderful reference books. By ordering catalogues in the categories that interest you, such as "English and Continental Furniture and Works of Art" or "Objects of Art and Vertu, Gold Boxes, and Works by Carl Fabergé," you can obtain a presale price estimate and make your bid by mail, cable, or telephone. With each subscription you will receive a monthly "Forthcoming Sales" pamphlet.
MO

SOTHEBY PARKE-BERNET INC.
Dept. CHC
980 Madison Avenue
New York, NY 10021

List of annual subscription rates for catalogues and price lists, no charge.

If you are too far away or too busy to attend the fascinating auction sales at Sotheby Parke-Bernet, the New York combination of the two famed London and New York auction houses, you can subscribe to a year of catalogues, ask for an estimate of what the item you are interested in will bring, then bid by mail or phone. Price lists sent after each sale give you a good idea of how prices are running. There are tremendous sales of art, antiques and antiquities, decorative objects, rugs, and carpets, usually grouped by design periods such as English or French 18th century, Art Deco, and so on.
MO

BOSTON MUSEUM OF FINE ARTS
Dept. CHC
465 Huntington Avenue
Boston, MA 02115

"Christmas Catalogue," 50 cents, published annually, color, illustrated.

This catalogue of objects, items, and gifts, all reproductions of the museum's collection, includes sculpture, 19th-century pewter and glass, Shaker furniture kits, needlework kits (needlepoint and crewel), and even a peacock weathervane. Wide range of prices.
MO

GALLERY SHOP
Brooklyn Museum
Dept. CHC
Brooklyn, NY 11238

"Gallery Shop Catalog," folder, 25 cents, some color, illustrated.

The Brooklyn Museum's Gallery Shop specializes in handcrafts, objects, and textiles from all over the world. Typical examples might be a Syrian copper jug, a delightful miniature chair from Haiti (about $6), a carved and painted Bolivian flute that would be handsome on a wall, or a colorful Indian spread for bed or wall hanging for about $20.
MO

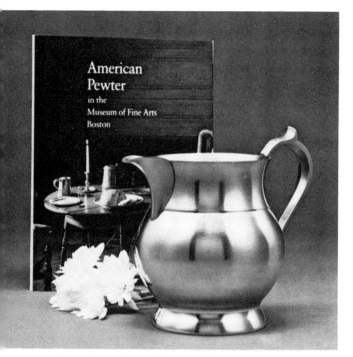

Pewter pitcher, *Boston Museum of Fine Arts*

Original furnishings, *Greenfield Village and Henry Ford Museum Collection*

THE J. PAUL GETTY MUSEUM
Dept. CHC
17985 Pacific Coast Highway
Malibu, CA 90265

Bookstore price list, no charge.

This little-known museum has some interesting books and publications for sale, such as "Ardabil Oriental Carpets" for $3.95, "Royal Pieces of Furniture" (from the museum collection) for 15 cents, and a "Handbook of Decorative Arts" for 80 cents.
MO

GREENFIELD VILLAGE AND HENRY
** FORD MUSEUM**
Reproductions Department
Dept. CHC
Dearborn, MI 48121

"Greenfield Village and Henry Ford Museum Catalogue," $1.50, 48 pages, some color, illustrated.

A handsome catalogue of all the reproductions of museum pieces. There is furniture from Colonial and Bartley; hooked rugs from Mountain Rug Mills, which can be ordered in your own colors; unusual lanterns and candlesticks from Sarreid, Ltd.; mirrors by LaBarge; pressed glass from Fostoria; lamps from Norman Perry; fabrics from the S. M. Hexter Company; interesting pewter pieces from Woodbury Pewterers. All prices are included with an order form.
MO/RS

HISTORIC CHARLESTON
** REPRODUCTIONS**
Dept. CHC
105 Broad Street
Charleston, SC 29401

"Historic Charleston Reproductions," $3.00, 24 pages, color, illustrated.

As part of the Historic Charleston Foundation's fund-raising efforts, reproductions of heirloom furniture, silver, porcelains, paintings, and other home furnishings have been commissioned and are shown in this color catalogue, both individually and in some of the original room settings. Each piece, which bears the hallmark of a palmetto tree in an oval, the official authorization seal of the Foundation, is accompanied by a brief history of the Charleston life-style it represents, with dimensions and price. Inside the front cover is a brief history of the various furniture styles that predominate in Charleston. Inside the back cover are swatches of paint colors and fabrics. For the collector of period furniture and reproductions, this is a most valuable handbook.
MO/RS

MEKANISK MUSIK MUSEUM
Dept. CHC
Vesterbrogade 150
Copenhagen, Denmark

"Mekanisk Musik Museum Review of Automatic Musical Instruments for Sale," $2.00, published annually, 100 pages, black and white, illustrated. Subscription rate, $10 for six issues.

A most unusual, specialized museum with a unique collection of automatic musical instruments of many types—pianos, organs, music boxes, symphonions, etc.—all illustrated, described, priced, and offered for sale. The catalogue has information about the museum and other subjects of interest to the musically minded collector.
MO

Ceremonial mask, *Gallery Shop, Brooklyn Museum*

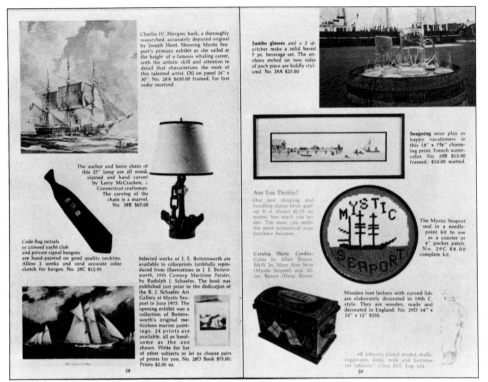

Nautical collection, *Mystic Seaport Museum Store*

THE METROPOLITAN MUSEUM OF ART
Dept. CHC
Box 255 Gracie Station
New York, NY 10028

Museum Shop catalogues and announcements, $1.00, color and black and white, illustrated.

Superb reproductions of fine china, silver, pewter and brass objects, ancient sculpture and jewelry, glassware, Early American miniature table pieces, tumblers, and other objects from the museum's collection; the copies are so precise that they are marked with the museum's monogram to distinguish them from the originals. Descriptions, historical background, and prices are given. The fall catalogue also has a very wide selection of Christmas cards, many with religious motifs taken from works of art, Christmas ornaments, needlework kits, engagement and wall calendars, Book of Hours. Complete with descriptions and prices. Separate booklets on Early American glass and Delft plates are available from the museum.
MO

MYSTIC SEAPORT MUSEUM STORE
Dept. CHC-A5
Mystic, CT 06355

"Mystic Seaport Stores, Inc.," 50 cents for two-year subscription to the catalogue, 22 pages, color, illustrated.

Photographed against backgrounds of the restored buildings and old ships of this historic New England port, the items have a definite nautical flavor. There are blown-glass captain's decanters with crystal stoppers, about $10; a welded black metal flight of seagulls, $115; pillows covered with seaport fabric by Greef of the *Emma C.*

Berry and *Charles W. Morgan*, with sails accented by trapunto padding, each $19; an adaptation of a nautical theme in a double block lamp with natural linen shade, 23" high, $47.50. Mystic Seaport reproductions include candlesticks, mess bowls, plates and mugs in pewter, solid mahogany ship's wheel tables (low and dining height) or wall pieces, which are available finished or as a kit. All prices and weights are given, and there is an order form.
MO

NEW-YORK HISTORICAL SOCIETY
Dept. CHC
170 Central Park West
New York, NY 10024

Christmas catalogue, no charge, black and white, illustrated.

Cards, prints, postcards, and publications about New York State and City, with some interesting reproductions of old prints.
MO

NORWEGIAN-AMERICAN MUSEUM
Dept. CHC
502 Water Street
Decorah, IA 52101

Norwegian-American Museum flyer, no charge.

As national interest in early crafts burgeons, museum shops are wisely combining both business and education by selling craft kits. The Norwegian-American Museum offers embroidery kits priced from $6 to $10 (which includes canvas, yarn, needle, pattern, and instructions), adapted by volunteers from early textiles in the museum collection. These designs can be fashioned into bell pulls, pillows, tote bags, and wall hangings in the traditional Norwegian *Klostersom* style of needlework.
MO

THE PEABODY MUSEUM OF SALEM
Dept. CHC
161 Essex Street
Salem, MA 01970

List of publications, no charge, published at random.

In addition to the books on historical subjects listed by the museum, there are also reproductions of ship prints from their collection, ranging in price from about $10 for lithographs to $30 for limited-edition, hand-colored prints and a set of 12 Wedgwood commemorative plates showing Salem sailing vessels.
MO

THE PHILADELPHIA MUSEUM OF ART
Dept. CHC
P.O. Box 7646
Philadelphia, PA 19101

"Christmas Catalogue," 25 cents, published annually, color, illustrated.

Among the museum's offerings are delightful needlepoint kits of Martha and George Washington dolls (or wall plaques) adapted from a Pennsylvania-German birth and baptismal certificate of 1779 and a stuffed cat, white with black spots and green eyes, inspired by a 19th-century Pennsylvania-German cast-iron door stop. There are stained-glass reproductions from 15th- and 16th-century English and Dutch originals to be used as ornaments for window or tree, some lovely prints from the museum originals, and *Treasures of the Philadelphia Museum of Art*, a handsome 112-page tome showing the period rooms and art objects.
MO

The following museums either publish catalogues for Christmas and sometimes at other seasons, or they will send you price lists of the prints or other objects they offer for sale.

The American Museum of Natural History, New York, NY
Chicago Art Institute, Chicago, IL
Cincinnati Museum of Art, Cincinnati, OH
City Art Museum, St. Louis, MO
The Corcoran Gallery of Art, Washington, DC
The Delaware Museum of Natural History, Greenville, DE
The Denver Art Museum, Denver, CO
The De Young Memorial Museum, San Francisco, CA
The Henry Francis Du Pont Winterthur Museum, Winterthur, DE
The Los Angeles County Museum of Art, Los Angeles, CA
Milwaukee Art Center, Milwaukee, WI
The Museum of American Folk Art, New York, NY
The Museum of Fine Arts, Houston, TX
Museum of Fine Arts, Seattle, WA
Museum of Fine Arts, San Francisco, CA
The Museum of Modern Art, New York, NY
Museum of New Mexico, Santa Fe, NM
The National Gallery of Art, Washington, DC
Newark Museum of Fine Art, Newark, NJ
The Smithsonian Institution, Washington, DC
The Walker Art Center, Minneapolis, MN
The Whitney Museum of American Art, New York, NY

Sandwich-glass epergne, *Metropolitan Museum of Art*

Needlepoint kits, *Philadelphia Museum of Art*

GIFTS TO STITCH

46. **Martha and George Washington.** Dolls or wall plaques adapted in needlepoint from a Pennsylvania-German birth and baptismal certificate of 1779. Includes hand-painted canvas, yarn, needle, and complete working instructions.

A. **Martha Plaque** (frame not included)   **$22.00**
B. **Martha Doll** (backing included; not shown)   **$20.00**
C. **George Plaque** (frame not included; not shown)   **$22.00**
D. **George Doll** (backing included)   **$20.00**

FURNITURE

Catalogue cover, *Ethan Allen*

Handcrafted table, *Berea College Student Craft Industries*

ANTIQUES   EARLY AMERICAN AND SHAKER

THE COASTAL TRADER, INC.
Dept. CHC
423 15th Avenue East
Seattle, WA 98112

"Presentations from the Coastal Trader," 25 cents, published annually, black and white, illustrated.

The only major furniture piece stocked by The Coastal Trader is a handsome antique Japanese two-section *tansu* (chest) made of kiri wood with heavy iron hardware, the type traditionally used to store clothes, bedding, and personal items. The chest illustrated, which costs $650, is circa 1880, but Coastal Trader claims to have a good selection of similar *tansu*.
MO

WAKEFIELD-SCEARCE GALLERIES
Dept. CHC
Shelbyville, KY 40065

"Wakefield-Scearce Galleries," $2.00, published annually, 56 pages, black and white, illustrated.

This interesting catalogue of 18th- and 19th-century English antiques, mostly Georgian or early Victorian, has some unusual pieces, such as a Chinese Chippendale collector's cabinet on stand and a mahogany bagatelle table. There are also rustic English items, a paneled Bacon settle, wheelback Windsor chairs, and a Welsh dresser. Among the reproductions is a serpentine-front chest-cum-television cabinet (the front lifts up and slides under the top, revealing a color TV inside). Most items are one of a kind, and you must write for prices.
MO

ETHAN ALLEN, INC.
Dept. CHC
Ethan Allen Drive
Danbury, CT 06810

"The Treasury of Ethan Allen American Traditional Interiors," $7.50 (no charge at showrooms), published every two years, 408 pages, color, illustrated.

An elaborate, lavishly illustrated color catalogue of Ethan Allen's enormous range of coordinated home furnishings from furniture to crafts. The furniture adaptations in the four collections cover a variety of traditional styles, such as Early American, Tudor and William and Mary, 18th century and Federal, painted and stenciled pieces, all of which can be bought in retail stores and the 250 Ethan Allen Galleries, or showrooms. There's also a 40-page decorating guide with examples of color schemes and room arrangements, a design history and glossary, furniture vocabulary, an American book section, a shopping guide for furniture, and advice on the care of furniture surfaces and upholstery, rugs, and various metals. A detailed pictorial index helps to identify the furniture pieces, with specifications and page numbers.
RS

BEREA COLLEGE STUDENT CRAFT INDUSTRIES
Dept. CHC
CPO #2347
Berea, KY 40403

Furniture catalogue, $1.00, 24 pages, black and white, illustrated.

The students of this college are required to work their way through school by producing and selling handcrafted furniture and objects, all part of the extensive craft program by which they pay for their education. The furniture they build reproduces Early American designs in such large pieces as corner cupboards and secretaries, as well as smaller tables, chairs, and stools. All pieces are handcrafted in either walnut, cherry, or mahogany and can be made to the customer's specifications—even to changes in design. In addition to reproductions of early designs, the students will make contemporary furniture to the buyer's specifications. Berea also markets a number of chestnut wood pieces under the Handex label. Most of this furniture tends to have a more basic, almost Shaker look. Be sure to request Handex information by name, since it comes in a separate free leaflet. Prices range from $100 to $1,000.
MO

Shaker reproductions, *Guild of Shaker Crafts*

Bay Colony dining group, *Cochrane*

BROYHILL FURNITURE INDUSTRIES
Dept. CHC
Lenoir, NC 28633

"Americana Decorating Guide," $1.00,
80 pages, black and white and color,
illustrated.

Suggestions on how to decorate with
Broyhill's Americana Collections of
furniture in pine, maple, and oak, with
color illustrations of room settings,
advice on choosing color schemes, and
a two-page feature on floor planning,
complete with scale drawings of
furniture pieces to cut out and arrange
on a sheet of graph paper.
RS

COCHRANE FURNITURE
Dept. CHC
P.O. Box 220
Lincolnton, NC 28092

"Bay Colony Scrapbook," $1.00,
updated semiannually, black and white,
illustrated.

Among the more interesting
reproduction Early American furniture
made by Cochrane are the cupboards
(buffets with open or closed decks) in a
variety of sizes and styles. No particular
wood is mentioned. Fine hardwoods
are used, and one finish, "Browntique,"
is offered. Dimensions and style
numbers are given but no prices. When
writing, ask for the nearest dealer.
RS

CORNUCOPIA, INCORPORATED
Dept. CHC
43 Waltham Street
Lexington, MA 02173

"The Second Cornucopia Catalogue,"
$1.25, published as necessary, price lists
published quarterly and mailed on
request, 19 pages, black and white,
illustrated.

Early American furniture made of solid
pine, screwed, bolted, pegged, and
hand-finished, in custom finishes and
stains, or unfinished, at savings of up to
20 percent. The catalogue shows tables,
chairs, beds, lamps, clocks, rugs in a
wide price range, up to $1,000.
MO

GUILD OF SHAKER CRAFTS
Dept. CHC
401 Savidge Street
Spring Lake, MI 49456

"Guild of Shaker Crafts Catalogue,"
$2.50, 28 pages, color, illustrated.

Shaker authority Mrs. Edward Deming
Andrews started this guild with local
craftsmen, who make careful and
meticulous copies of Shaker furniture.
A pine blanket chest, 49½" long x 18½"
deep x 23" high, is around $135, and a
one-slat dining chair with padded tape
seat is about $52. Plain and modest is
the keynote of the furniture,
accessories, and hand-sewn items in
this catalogue. The Guild also offers
chair tapes and a number of paints and
stains in such Shaker colors as heavenly
blue, ministry green, meetinghouse
blue, burnt orange, saffron, and Shaker
red.
MO

HAGERTY CO.
Dept. CHC
38 Parker Avenue
Cohasset, MA 02025

"Cohasset Colonials by Hagerty," 50
cents, published annually, 32 pages,
some color, illustrated.

Knocked-down kits for Colonial
furniture, with all the necessary items
such as glue, screws, hardware,
sandpaper, stain, and instructions.
Some of the pieces offered are Windsor
chairs, sleigh seats, blanket chests,
Shaker tables, desks, hutch cabinets,
and beds.
MO

HEYWOOD-WAKEFIELD CO.
Dept. CHC
Gardner, MA 01440

*"The Registered Collections of
Heywood-Wakefield Furniture,"* $2.50,
187 pages, some color, illustrated.

Heywood-Wakefield's various
collections—The Old Colony, The
Man's Castle, Academy Hill, and
Publick House—are shown in room
settings and individual pieces. The
furniture, including occasional and
accent pieces, is thoroughly illustrated,
with line drawings of details,
descriptions of finishes, special
construction features, and suggested
uses. There are also copious quotations
from early American writings to spice
the catalogue: recipes for New England
clam chowder, a rose potpourri, and
words of wisdom and humor.
RS

34

Catalogue cover, *Thomas Moser*

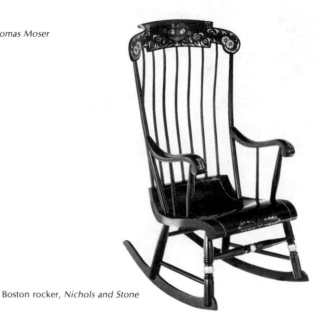

Boston rocker, *Nichols and Stone*

JENNIFER HOUSE
Dept. CHC
New Marlboro Stage
Great Barrington, MA 01230

Catalogue, no charge, 64 pages, color, illustrated.

This catalogue has a little bit of everything for the house, including reproductions of Early American furniture. In among the other items are captain's chairs, deacon's benches, rockers, high chairs, heirloom swing cradles, silent valet chairs, crewel wing chairs, Early American wagon seats, musical rockers for children, and combination étagère and music stands. Prices range from $18.95 for the smallest musical rocker to $270 for the wing chair.
MO

MARJON WOODWORKING
Dept. CHC
Box 41
Mountain Falls Rte.
Winchester, VA 22601

Leaflet offered on request, no charge, 2 pages, black and white, illustrated.

Marjon's prime piece is a "faithful handmade reproduction of an Early American cobbler's bench" for use as a coffee or end table. Each is handmade by one man of Ponderosa pine, hand-finished and authentic down to the tool marks. The bench, which includes five hand-fitted drawers and a "dished out" seat, is priced around $100. Marjon also produces a variety of Early American and Shaker reproductions, miniature chests, and fireside stools in three sizes. Prices are moderate.
MO

THOMAS MOSER
Dept. CHC
26 Cobb's Bridge Road
New Gloucester, ME 04260

"Thomas Moser Cabinet Maker," $1.00, 29 pages, black and white, illustrated.

Superbly crafted tables, beds, desks, chests, and grandfather clocks in the Pennsylvania Dutch and Shaker traditions, at home in either traditional or contemporary settings. The catalogue explains the crafting process and how Thomas Moser, a former English professor, perfected his own unique building patterns, based on simple Shaker lines. Custom work to your specifications is available. Order form and price list included. Prices from $56 to $830.
MO

NICHOLS AND STONE
Dept. CHC
232 Sherman Street
Gardner, MA 01440

"How to Choose the Right Colonial Chair," 50 cents, 40 pages, black and white, illustrated.

This little handbook of Early American chairs first delineates seven basic styles—through Boston rockers to Hitchcocks and from ladderbacks to comb backs, bow backs, and rod backs—and then proceeds, with photographs, sketches, and detailed descriptions, to explain the salient features and historical uses of over 50 reproductions of Colonial chairs manufactured by the Nichols and Stone company. The book is not, however, a mail-order catalogue, since the manufacturer's products must be bought through dealers, but the company will send you, on request, the name of a dealer in your area.
RS

Cobbler's bench reproduction, *Marjon Woodworking*

Colonial bedroom group, *Pennsylvania House*

Sugar Hill Pine dining set, *Plymwood Furniture*

PENNSYLVANIA HOUSE
Dept. CHC
North 10th Street
Lewisburg, PA 17837

"The Collector's Book," $7.50, published annually, currently the Bicentennial Edition, 287 pages, color, illustrated.

This elaborate catalogue, lavishly illustrated in full color, shows Pennsylvania House's seven different Early American collections: Upholstery, Independence Hall, Richmond, Stone House, Bucks County, Cushman, and Homestead. Each collection has a distinctive, beautiful, and broad range of furniture. Complete room settings, as well as individual pieces, are illustrated and described in detail. Also included are six "Decorator's Notebooks" of hints and tips on Windows, Walls, Floors, Fireplaces, Happy Hang-ups, and How to Use Color.
RS

PLYMWOOD FURNITURE CORP.
Dept. CHC
Lisbon, NH 03585

"Sugar Hill Pine," $1.00, published annually, 60 pages, some color, illustrated.

Reproductions of Early American pine furniture for dining room, bedroom, living room, plus some occasional pieces. The catalogue gives the history of the company, describes how the furniture is made, offers decorating hints, and includes a planning chart with graph paper and cutouts. Prices on request.
MO/RS

ROMBINS' NEST FARM
Dept. CHC
Fairfield, PA 17320

Catalogue, 25 cents, published annually, 40 pages, black and white, illustrated.

A small selection of furniture, mostly replicas of old designs—Colonial or Pennsylvania Dutch, among them a solid cherry Pennsylvania cradle. Moderate prices.
MO

SHAKER WORKSHOPS, INC.
Dept. CHC
P.O. Box 710
Concord, MA 01742

"Shaker Furniture," 50 cents, published semiannually, 30 pages, some color, illustrated.

Faithful reproductions of beautiful, functional Shaker furniture may be ordered in kit form from the Workshops. The kits contain all the materials needed to finish the pieces, which come ready to assemble with screwdriver and hammer, down to hardware, glue, sandpaper, and light or dark stain, with easy step-by-step instructions. A comfortable rocker with taped back and seat, typical of Shaker craftsmanship, is $65 in kit form; a drop-leaf table with mortise and tenon joinery is just $95. As little as $15 buys a four-bar standing towel rack. A more expensive kit for the compact chest with drop-leaf at back, based on the 1830 piece from Hancock, Massachusetts, is $250. You can also buy boards with pegs, the Shaker "wall system" in lengths from 12" to 48," from about $4 to $7 a length.
MO

Shaker reproductions to assemble, *Shaker Workshops*

Catalogue cover, *Sturbridge Yankee Workshop*

"American Classics" furniture, *Baker Furniture*

PERIOD STYLES

STURBRIDGE YANKEE WORKSHOP
Dept. CHC
Sturbridge, MA 01566

"Sturbridge Yankee Workshop Handbook and Catalogue," 50 cents, published annually, 64 pages, color, illustrated.

The subtitle of the catalogue from this famous Colonial restoration village— "1,000 Basic Items for Furnishing an Early American Home"—really speaks for itself. About 100 of the items are furniture—around 15 sizes of Hitchcock chairs and side tables, a number of wing chairs, cabinets, a dry sink or two, a spinning wheel, a crib, tea carts— even a TV stand in Colonial styling— and all are reasonably priced.
MO

VERMONT FAIR
Dept. CHC
P.O. Box 338
Brattleboro, VT 05301

"Vermont Fair," no charge, 30 pages, color, illustrated.

The New England heritage of making strong, functional furniture is still carried on by this 90-year-old Vermont store. Four pieces of Vermont pine are offered; an adaptation of a Colonial dough box roomy enough for games or knitting, with an ample side rack for magazines, is just $89.95, including shipping anywhere in the continental U.S. A coffee table, 24" x 50" x 14½" high, also of Vermont pine, is only $59.95. All measurements and prices are included with an order blank.
MO

ETHAN ALLEN, INC.
Dept. CHC
Ethan Allen Drive
Danbury, CT 06810

"Getting Beauty and Value for Your Decorating Dollars," 50 cents, 96 pages, some color, illustrated.

Ethan Allen's useful and informative little book is a decorating and shopping guide with several different sections covering furniture, its history, French, English, and American styles, upholstered furniture, and furniture care.

BAKER FURNITURE CO.
Dept. CHC
474 Merchandise Mart
Chicago, IL 60654

"The American Classics," 25 cents, 28 pages, some color, illustrated.

The catalogue shows the Baker American Classics Collection— reproductions of selected American antiques, most of them originally crafted when America began to trade with England, continental Europe, and the Orient. The Collection includes a variety of styles fashioned in a number of different woods, among them a William and Mary highboy in chinoiserie, a "turkey-breast" cabinet in pine with Chippendale influence, a delicately executed Chippendale tea table in mahogany. Each piece is illustrated and described. An index is provided.

"Baker Book," two volumes, $15, 400 pages, some color, illustrated.

More than just a catalogue, the two-volume Baker Book is hard-covered and printed on glossy paper. Volume One covers the French Collection and the Palladian Collection; Volume Two, the English and American Collection, the

Far East Collection, and the Executive Collection. Each volume has its own numerical index (by pattern number). A separate, visual, 63-page index groups the furniture by categories (beds, secretaries, etc.). The Baker Book is a comprehensive and detailed reference "of particular interest to those who share a special appreciation for choice examples of authentic design and expressive craftsmanship," which includes the Baker philosophy about furniture along with information about woods, upholstery, and finishes. Each Collection has a brief introduction and is subdivided into furniture for living rooms, dining rooms, and bedrooms and contains drawings of stacking unit components with dimensions.

"Milling Road Country French Furniture," 25 cents, color, illustrated.

Beautiful country French pieces in mellowed woods and delightful painted finishes, inspired by those of the chateaux of the provinces of France but scaled for today's rooms. There's a charming armoire with provincial carving detail, 52" wide x 20" deep and 70" high, in either wood or painted finishes, and a handsome three-drawer bombé chest, 33" wide by 18 ¾" deep by 25" high. The craftsmanship of Milling Road is a tradition in itself.
RS/ID

Butler's tray table, *Bartley Collection*

Williamsburg reproduction Federal sideboard, *Craft House*

THE BARTLEY COLLECTION, LTD.
Dept. CHC
747 Oakwood Avenue
Lake Forest, IL 60045

"Antique Furniture Reproductions,"
$1.00, 16 pages, black and white,
illustrated.

Exact replicas and careful adaptations
of original 18th-century furniture,
including five pieces from the Henry
Ford Museum. Each reproduction is
handcrafted and hand-finished in solid
cherry or mahogany and is described in
detail, with its history and price.
Interestingly, each piece comes as a kit
at about half the price of the assembled
and finished product; so if you enjoy
hand-finishing, you can use the
finishing kit, and the assembly is easy
enough. Prices of kits and completely
assembled pieces range from about $65
for a mirror shelf/wall bracket to about
$450 for the handsome Queen Anne
drop-leaf table from the Henry Ford
Museum collection. Separate order
forms with shipping charges for the
individual items included.
MO

CHAPMAN
Dept. CHC
481 West Main
Avon, MA 02322

"Lamps and Accessories," folder, 50
cents, published annually, black and
white, illustrated.

In addition to lamps, Chapman offers
furniture with a one-of-a-kind look,
such as a three-drawer stripped pine
bombé chest, a copy of an original
Dutch one, a bonnet-top secretary in
antique walnut and chestnut burl with
an English ancestor, and a narrow
polished steel-and-brass 18" by 76"
étagère recalling the Napoleonic era.
These are just a small part of the
furniture collection of chairs, chests,
cabinets, étagères, and desks.
Dimensions and style numbers are
included, but prices are supplied only
on request.
RS/ID

CRAFT HOUSE
Dept. CHC
Colonial Williamsburg Foundation
Williamsburg, VA 23185

"Williamsburg Reproductions—Interior
Designs for Today's Living," $2.95, 232
pages, color and black and white,
completely illustrated.

A giant, beautifully produced catalogue
of all the furnishings reproduced for
the Colonial Williamsburg program,
many of which are displayed and sold
at fine stores throughout the United
States and all of which can be ordered
by mail or purchased at the
Williamsburg Craft House. Furniture
reproductions and adaptations by the
Kittinger Company of 18th-century and
Federal antiques comprise the largest
section of the catalogue and the widest
price range. A Queen Anne mahogany
kettle stand is around $275; a small oval

Federal worktable, inlaid and veneered,
around $505; a Hepplewhite sideboard
$920; and a stunning Chippendale
breakfront bookcase, matched in every
detail to its antique prototype in the
Governor's Palace, over $7,000. The
reproductions and adaptations are
available in a variety of finishes and, in
the case of upholstered chairs and
sofas, many different fabrics. The price
list gives information about fabric
yardage, down cushions, leather
upholstery, and so on. All prices
include shipping charges within the
continental United States and are
subject to change without notice.

There's much more to this catalogue
than merchandise—a history of
Williamsburg, color photographs of
artisans at work and many of the
restored houses, close-ups of
architectural details and hardware, a
description of the reproductions
program, a section on furniture periods
and styles, a glossary of furniture terms,
and a decorating portfolio that
illustrates how the traditional furniture
fits into modern settings. It is worth
buying just to read and refer to.
MO/RS

38

Cameo II collection, *Drexel-Heritage*

French Provincial bedroom, *Davis Cabinet*

LAURA COPENHAVER INDUSTRIES, INC.
Dept. CHC
Box 149
Marion, VA 24354

"Rosemont," 50 cents, 31 pages, published annually, black and white, illustrated.

These mountain craftsmen duplicate handmade and hand-rubbed pieces from the collection of antiques at Rosemont or those loaned for reproduction. An unusual "Bird Cage" table of walnut or cherry (only solid woods are used) with rotating top, 25" high and 20" diameter, costs under $60. A bedside table, 28¼" high by 18" wide, with two drawers and leaves on both sides, ideal for sewing or TV table, is about $110. They also make, in several sizes, four-poster canopy beds of solid mahogany, with or without canopy frames, chests and coffee tables, and pieces made to your dimensions.
MO

DAVIS CABINET CO.
Dept. CHC
P.O. Box 60444
Nashville, TN 37206

"Story of Solid Wood Furniture," $1.00, 28 pages, some color, illustrated.

As the title implies, the catalogue provides a step-by-step, illustrated explanation of the making of a fine piece of solid wood furniture, from the raw wood to the finished work. Also included are examples, in full color, of Davis designs in various style categories: Italian, English, Oriental, French, and Victorian. A final section has recommendations for furniture care.
RS

DREXEL-HERITAGE FURNISHINGS
Attention Mrs. Erma Burns
Dept. CHC
Drexel, NC 28619

Five catalogues in Heritage line, plus planning kit, $1.00, some color, illustrated; six catalogues in Drexel line, plus planning kit, $1.00, some color, illustrated.

The five Heritage catalogues comprise the "Cameo II" line of classic styles inspired by the courts of 18th-century Europe, with polished fruitwood and painted accent pieces; "Maracay" (derived from 17th- and 18th-century Mediterranean styles), "Windward" (contemporary Oriental styling with squared-off bamboo detail), "American Tour" (a potpourri of American period pieces in interesting woods and finishes, some with handscreened decorations), and the "Upholstery" line of Heritage sofas and chairs. The Drexel lines are "Cabernet," French Provincial in feeling in solid and veneers of pecan and brushed painted accent pieces; "Bishopsgate," inspired by the oak country pieces of 16th-century England; "Talavera," reflecting Spanish-Mediterranean life-styles; "Crosswinds," with wicker/rattan look in white or natural finish (particularly interesting is the brass gilt finish queen-size tester bed); "Accolade," clean-lined and contemporary; and "Et Cetera," an interesting collection of accent pieces, from an amusing "lily" accessory table with gilt-aluminum base to a chinoiserie black lacquer breakfront bookcase. The planning kit, included with each set, has furniture cutouts based on pieces from the lines and a grid for planning your furniture arrangements.
RS

CARL FORSLUND, INC.
Dept. CHC
122 East Fulton Street
Grand Rapids, MI 49502

"Timeless Furniture Made by Carl Forslund," $2.00, revised every 2 to 3 years, 97 pages, color, illustrated.

Reproductions of all kinds of American furniture from the 18th, 19th, and 20th centuries, fully described, including the source of the original. Among the more interesting items are a Midwestern 19th-century food safe converted to a china cabinet, a carved wood frame Victorian sofa, a tufted-leather upholstered "Sleepy Hollow" chair and ottoman, and a charming bedspread rack. The furniture, which has been made by the Forslund family for 89 years, is all solid cherry in various finishes from light to dark, and the prices are in line with comparable furniture. For instance, the bedspread rack is $74.95, the chair and ottoman $599, and the sofa from $650.25 to $822.85, depending on fabric.
MO

Bedspread rack, *Carl Forslund*

Traditional living-room furniture, *Harden*

Oriental chests, *Henredon Folio 11 Collection*

GREEN BOUGHS CABINETMAKER'S SHOP, INC.
Dept. CHC
2021 Valentine Drive, N.E.
Grand Rapids, MI 49505

Fold-out leaflet, no charge, black and white, illustrated.

A limited inventory of small pieces of furniture in 18th-century styles, handcrafted in sold cherry with a choice of dark, medium, or light finishes. Some furniture is made to order. Included are such traditional pieces as candle stands, book stands, display stands, footstools and benches, tray tables, corner tables, needlepoint tables. Prices range up to $400.
MO

HARDEN FURNITURE CO.
Dept. CHC
McConnellsville, NY 13401

"Harden Furniture," $3.00, published every 18 months, 160 pages, some color, illustrated.

Each piece of Harden's traditional, handcrafted, solid cherry furniture is pictured and its dimensions given. The catalogue index lists all the pieces by number and groups them into categories: upholstered, sofa beds, occasional, dining room, bedroom. The catalogue includes a table of contents that groups the furniture into different collections (i.e., English, American, etc.). Also offered are decorating aids, care of fabrics, skirt treatments, and Harden Furniture's construction features. No prices.
RS

HENREDON FURNITURE INDUSTRIES, INC.
Dept. CHC
Morganton, NC 28655

"Henredon Upholstered Furniture," $1.00, revised annually, 72 pages, color, illustrated.

Sofas, love seats, chairs, ottomans, and benches are shown and specifications given. The 5600 Group enables you to style your own upholstered furniture and have it custom-made in the form and size that suit your home. Various upholstery forms and back and arm styles are illustrated, as well as a selection of flounces. A table of contents and an index are provided.

"Henredon's Four Centuries Collection," $1.00, updated periodically, 49 pages, color, illustrated.

Interpretations of original French country furniture from the 17th century in a variety of complementary designs, some heavy in scale, some light, with a diversity of wood finishes. The last six pages of the catalogue contain a visual index of line drawings with specifications (grouped under room headings) and page number.

"Folio 10," $1.00, updated periodically, 32 pages, some color, illustrated.

An assemblage of special pieces from many styles and periods in a variety of solid woods and veneers accented with wrought iron and glass. Each piece is shown and described, and specifications are given. A visual index concludes the catalogue.

"Henredon Folio 11," $1.00, updated periodically, 40 pages, some color, illustrated.

This loose-leaf catalogue pictures reproductions of 17th- and 18th-century Chinese household furniture and French 18th-century designs that combine well. The Oriental designs are interpreted in mahogany, brightened with veneers of walnut, mahogany, and olive ash burl; the French styles combine solid ash with knotty oak veneer. A choice of finishes is offered. A visual index is provided.

"Henredon's 18th Century Portfolio," $1.00, updated periodically, 46 pages, some color, illustrated.

Reproductions or adaptations of 18th-century English furniture, including Queen Anne, Georgian, Chippendale, Hepplewhite, and Sheraton, in a variety of veneers and solid woods. The different style periods are described and accompanied by selected examples from the collection. Each piece is pictured and described, and specifications are given. A visual index is included.
RS

Hand-decorated breakfront, *Jasper Cabinet*

French display cabinet, *Karges Furniture*

HICKORY CHAIR CO.
Dept. CHC
Hickory, NC 28601

"Furniture Reproductions Inspired by Heirlooms from Historical James River Plantations," $2.00, 100 pages, some color, illustrated.

The catalogue illustrates over 150 fine 18th-century furniture reproductions, including the James River Collection. A map of James River Plantations, the history of the James River furniture, and the characteristics of various 18th-century cabinet makers are given, along with full-color room settings and pages of illustrations of individual pieces with their specifications.
RS/ID

HUNT GALLERIES
Dept. CHC
P.O. Box 2324
Hickory, NC 28601

Catalogue, $2.00, published annually, 40 pages, color, illustrated.

By far the majority of pieces in this catalogue are upholstered chairs and sofas from a small family manufacturing concern that prides itself on personal supervision of all the products. In addition to the larger pieces, there are stools, dressing-table chairs, and upholstered card-table chairs on casters. Prices range from $29 for a small stool to $385 for an 84" Chippendale-style sofa. Prices quoted are for furniture covered in material supplied by the customer, but Hunt will supply samples of their own fabrics on request.
MO

JASPER CABINET CO.
Dept. CHC
P.O. Box 69
Jasper, IN 47546

Catalogue, $5.00, published annually, 98 pages, color, illustrated.

This handsome catalogue in a heavy vinyl loose-leaf binder shows a wide variety of wood cabinets and desks. Secretaries, kneehole and rolltop desks, chairs, breakfronts, cellarettes, trophy, curio, and gun cabinets, and commodes with mirrors in Early American, 18th-century, Italian, French Provincial, and Mediterranean styles are priced from $60 to $1,000. Many are hand-painted and decorated with wood-burning techniques. In the back of the catalogue are samples of colors available in both wood and painted finishes, as well as a price list.
RS

THE KARGES FURNITURE CO., INC.
Dept. CHC
1501 West Maryland Street
Evansville, IN 47707

"Sampler of Fine Furniture," $2.00, published annually, 26 pages, full color, illustrated.

Top-quality period furniture for living rooms, dining rooms, and bedrooms in French, Italian, and Provincial styles. Rare woods like Circassian walnut are used, as well as American walnut, butternut, myrtle, olive ash, and Carpathian elm. Some of the furniture is handcarved in Italy, and the brass ornamentations—pulls, escutcheons, table feet—are also made there to original designs. Expensive. Available only through decorators and showrooms.
ID

Furniture with Oriental overtones, *Kroehler*

Wing chairs and revolving tilt-top table, *Kittinger*

KITTINGER CO.
Dept. CHC
1893 Elmwood Avenue
Buffalo, NY 14207

"Kittinger Library," $4.00 (refundable with purchase), updated periodically, 180 pages, black and white, illustrated; "Williamsburg Furniture," 12 pages, color, illustrated.

Kittinger's appointment as exclusive maker of Williamsburg Furniture Reproductions and Historic Newport Furniture Reproductions attests to the high quality of craftsmanship employed in its furniture manufacture. The weighty catalogue includes tables, chairs, sideboards, desks, beds, sofas, mostly fashioned after 18th-century English and American designs. There are, however, a number of modern sofas and upholstered chairs and even one good-looking reclining chair. In addition to the furniture, the catalogue has some photographs of Williamsburg and Newport restorations, a design dictionary, and a listing of showrooms and sales representatives throughout the country.
RS/ID

KROEHLER MFG. CO.
Dept. CHC
222 East Fifth Street
Naperville, IL 60540

"Lively Living," $2.00, updated periodically, 24 pages, color, illustrated.

This well-known manufacturer produces a full line of upholstered chairs, recliners, sofas in varied styles and fabrics, including leather, tables spanning the design spectrum from Early American to contemporary glass and chrome, plus commodes, étagères, cocktail and lamp tables. Two lines are shown: the Classic, which represents traditional styling with a contemporary feeling, and Avant, purely contemporary. The catalogue includes decorating hints. Prices are moderate.
RS

EPHRAIM MARSH CO.
Dept. CHC
Box 266
Concord, NC 28025

"Catalogue 19," $1.00, published annually, updated with supplement semiannually ("Catalogue 20"), 195 pages, plus 63-page supplement, color and black and white, illustrated.

Traditional furniture for home and office in American Colonial and Georgian styles. There is everything here from a George Washington desk to a wide variety of tables, sofas, bedroom suites. Price lists, order form, and descriptions are included. Expensive.
MO

MGM SHOWROOMS
Dept. CHC
511 East 72nd Street
New York, NY 10021

"Meyer. Gunther. Martini.," $5.00, 91 pages, black and white, illustrated.

This catalogue offers a tremendous collection of Italian and French Provincial chairs, canapés, sofas, Récamiers, and from the Kemm division, tables, commodes, secretaries, étagères, breakfronts, servers, and headboards in painted and wood finishes. There are several unusual items, such as hooded hall-porter chairs, chaise longues (one with adjustable recline), a painted bar-cellaret column, and a petit commode-cum-telephone table. When writing, ask for the nearest furniture dealer, or purchase through an interior designer or architect.
RS/ID

PHYLLIS MORRIS ORIGINALS
Dept. CHC
8772 West Beverly Boulevard
Los Angeles, CA 90048

"Premiere Collection," $5.00, refundable with purchase, updated as necessary, 18 pages, color, illustrated.

Full-color photographs of furniture designed, manufactured, and signed by Phyllis Morris. The furniture runs the gamut of elaborate finishes and trims, styles, and traditions and is available in custom sizes. A glossy toldout illustrates and identifies about 80 different finishes and also lists leaf and antique finishes and colors. Furniture is available only through showrooms. Expensive; prices supplied on request.
RS/ID

Bicentennial chest with drawers, *Ephraim Marsh*

Chippendale library chair, *Bryan Robeson*

Rolltop oak desk, *Riverside Furniture*

MY HOUSE WROUGHT IRON
Dept. CHC
417 North Robertson Boulevard
Los Angeles, CA 90048

"My House Wrought Iron," $4.00, published annually, 40 pages, black and white, illustrated.

Handmade wrought-iron traditional French baker's racks, butcher's tables, day beds, wine racks, and kitchen racks in black or custom colors (price additional), with solid brass finials and trim and a wide variety of sizes and designs. Prices are around $800 for a three-shelf baker's rack, 84" high, 18" wide, 14" deep, about $550 for a butcher's wrought-iron base table with chopping-block top. Dimensions and prices included.
MO

PAINE FURNITURE CO.
Dept. CHC
81 Arlington Street
Boston, MA 02116

"Paine Furniture Company, Catalogue," $3.50, 23 pages, some color, illustrated.

Distinctive, elegant furniture for every room in the house in styles from Queen Anne, Georgian and American Colonial to Contemporary. This 140-year-old New England company has many things for the home in addition to its furniture lines—bedding, rugs, antiques, pianos, TV, and stereos. Prices and order forms on request.
MO/RS

RIVERSIDE FURNITURE CORPORATION
Dept. CHC
P.O. Box 1427
Fort Smith, AR 72901

"Bringing Beauty to the Home," no charge, 14 pages, black and white, illustrated.

A booklet on "eclectic" decorating (the word is defined on the first page), with combinations of the various pieces in the Riverside line, broken up into sections on tables, bedrooms, dining, upholstery, and accent furniture. Among the more interesting pieces are a rolltop maple desk, oak gun cabinet, and a pine bean-box-cum-end table. At the back of the booklet are hints on care and protection of furniture.
RS

BRYAN ROBESON, INC.
Dept. CHC
Route 10, Box 793
Hickory, NC 28601

"Bryan Robeson," 50 cents, published annually, 39 pages, black and white, illustrated.

Traditional chairs, sofas, tables, chests, and desks in all manner of wood finishes, styles, and fabrics. All chairs are handcrafted, fabrics are treated with a protective finish, and only imported cane is used. Your own fabric can be used on most of the upholstered pieces, and a request form for swatches is provided with the order form. Prices are moderate to high.
MO

ROMWEBER FURNITURE CO.
Dept. CHC
4 South Park Avenue
Batesville, IN 47006

"Viking Oak" and "Dorchester House," $2.00, published annually. Viking Oak catalogue, 36 pages; Dorchester House catalogue, 31 pages, color, illustrated.

Viking Oak, as the name implies, is sturdy solid oak furniture in provincial Scandinavian designs and motifs made by Romweber since 1934. The pieces are large in scale and work best in big rooms. A seven-chip-compartment poker table with leather top sells for about $1,200. Other interesting pieces are a 48" square cocktail table with grape carving around the apron and wood parquetry top for about $600 and a tuxedo-style loose-cushion sofa with exposed carved frame for around $1,800.

The Dorchester House group combines designs based on English and French 18th-century pieces. There are many unusual pieces with interesting details, such as an open sideboard, 80" long, 14" deep, 42" high, with lighted interior, glass shelves, cherry top, and painted base in Provincial motif of blue on antique white (around $1,400), or a handsome armoire in wood or painted finish that can be a bar, a man's wardrobe, a secretary, or a stereo-TV cabinet, depending on fittings, from about $2,200 to $2,900. Other notable items include a sculpture or plant pedestal of walnut with black trim, about $600, and a walnut escritoire with fold-down writing surface covered in hand-embossed leather for about $1,300. All pieces are handcrafted with hand-applied finishes and hand-painted patterns. Dimensions, variety of woods and finishes, and prices are included.
RS/ID

Wrought-iron throne chair, *Spanish Villa*

Small-scale dining group, *Stanley Furniture*

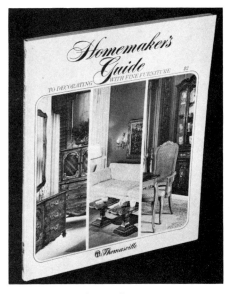

Catalogue cover, *Thomasville Furniture*

SPANISH VILLA
Dept. CHC
Building 1101, L.A.F.B.
Laredo, TX 78040

"Spanish Villa," $1.00 (refundable with purchase), published annually, 34 pages, black and white, illustrated.

A marvelous curly wrought-iron throne chair measuring 48" high x 33" across at $125 is part of the imported furniture collection. There are elaborately hand-carved wooden cocktail tables, commodes, and credenzas from $75 to $136; a tall, graceful slim-line hand-turned and rubbed chair with velvet seat and back, choice of colors, for $50; and provincial Mexican rush seat and back turned-wood side chairs with charcoal stain for only $58.50 a pair or $54.50 unfinished. All dimensions and prices are included along with an order blank.
MO

STANLEY FURNITURE
Dept. CHC
Stanleytown, VA 24168

"Home Decorating Portfolio," $1.00, some color, illustrated.

The Portfolio (a collection of booklets and pamphlets) contains folders of the many and various furniture fashions that Stanley makes, floor-plan graph paper, and templates—scaled furniture shapes that you can cut out and move around to achieve balanced arrangements. Also included is a 35-page booklet, "Everything You Should Know Before You Buy Another Piece of Furniture," which gives an introduction to decorating (design, color, finishes, room planning, etc.), plus glossaries of furniture terms and styles. Additional booklets provide tips on what to consider before you buy, how to care for the furniture you do buy, and how to decorate with color.
RS

STUCKEY BROTHERS HEIRLOOMS
Dept. CHC
Box 99
Sumter, SC 29150

"Stuckey Brothers Heirlooms," 50 cents, 30 pages, black and white, illustrated.

Furniture for every room in the house, including many occasional pieces in Queen Anne, Chippendale, and Sheraton styling. Wood finish and fabric samples will be loaned on request. Most pieces are in solid mahogany or cherry. A four-poster bed with canopy, in double size, is under $200.
MO

THOMASVILLE FURNITURE INDUSTRIES, INC.
Dept. CHC
P.O. Box 339
Thomasville, NC 27360

"Homemaker's Guide," $2.00, 100 pages, color, illustrated.

Built around the Thomasville furniture collection, the "Homemaker's Guide" is a consumer handbook on decorating, color coordinating, space planning, and buying and caring for furniture, with a glossary of terms for every room in the house. Most of the furnishings shown are reproductions or adaptations of earlier design eras, but the section of "Founders" furniture at the end of the book is devoted to the contemporary style. This is not a mail-order catalogue, and dealers are not listed, but the company will furnish names on request.
RS

Sideboard from the Dorchester House Group, *Romweber Furniture*

44

Handcrafted chest on stand, *Ake Tugel*

Traditional living-room furniture, *Tomlinson*

Portable TV cabinet, *Yield House*

TOMLINSON FURNITURE
Attention Beth Richards
Dept. CHC
High Point, NC 27261

"Tomlinson," $1.00, 18 pages, color, illustrated.

This handsome color catalogue of the unusual and beautiful pieces of traditional furniture in the Tomlinson collection, in both wood and colorful painted finishes, shows clearly the infinite detail and craftsmanship that goes into the making of each piece. Tomlinson will even label your upholstered furniture with your own name. When writing, ask Mrs. Richards for the name of the dealer nearest you.
RS/ID

AKE TUGEL
Dept. CHC
266 Sea Cliff Avenue
Sea Cliff, NY 11579

Folio of color photographs, 50 cents, revised at random.

Swedish cabinetmaker-artist Ake Tugel, assisted by his son Mikael and another cabinetmaker, produces fine handcrafted furniture in styles from Queen Anne to Shaker to modern but more particularly native Swedish designs that he finishes or paints in the traditional way. Other handsome wooden objects include mirror frames, clock cases, boxes, an amusing hobby horse, and unusual dulcimers. Mr. Tugel will also undertake the restoration of fine antiques. A separate price list for the above-mentioned pieces is included with dimensions. A 48" bench with a hand-painted panel in the top is $110, and a handcrafted wood chair with cane seat and back is $140.
MO

UNION-NATIONAL, INC.
Dept. CHC
226 Crescent Street
Jamestown, NY 14701

"Furniture Designed for Gracious Living," $1.50, updated every 18 months, 44 pages, color, illustrated.

This catalogue shows tables, chairs, china cabinets , secretaries, settees, tea carts, desks, vitrines, armoires, and beds made from beech, cherry, and maple in the tradition of the fine Scandinavian craftsmen who emigrated to this area. An outstanding feature of the furniture is the hand painting and decoration in chinoiserie and floral designs.
RS

WHITE FURNITURE
Dept. CHC
Mebane, NC 27302

"Tiara II Collection," 50 cents, 48 pages, color, illustrated.

Dining-room and bedroom groups in painted and wood finishes and classic styling that mix with every decorating scheme. The pieces, scaled for apartments and smaller homes, are in a moderate price range and are shown in room settings with many decorating ideas.
RS

YIELD HOUSE
Dept. CHC
North Conway, NH 03860

"Yield House Country Pine Furniture and Furniture Kits," 25 cents, 50 pages, some color, illustrated.

Yield House is most famous for its furniture kits that come ready-to-assemble and finish. There are many interesting desks in kit form, such as a rolltop, a trestle, or a home-office desk, from about $90 up. There are also bookcases, file cabinets, a dictionary stand, all kinds of tables and chairs and storage pieces. Many pieces (including those sold in kits) are available completely finished. A beautiful chinoiserie lady's desk, 39" high x 27" wide, 17" deep, is under $400. Bentwood chairs that come kd (knockdown) are sold in pairs, the side chairs for under $110 the pair. However, you save considerably if you buy the kits.
MO

Victorian love seat, *Martha M. House*

Bentwood and cane chair, *Bon Marché*

VICTORIAN

CONTEMPORARY

MARTHA M. HOUSE
Dept. CHC
1022 South Decatur Street
Montgomery, AL 36104

*"Southern Heirlooms," $1.00
(refundable with purchase), published
annually, 44 pages, black and white,
illustrated.*

Reproductions of Victorian furniture
originally made for Southern mansions,
with illustrations and detailed
specifications. Fabric samples will be
sent on receipt of the order form
included in the catalogue, which also
has a map for finding the showroom.
Prices on request.
MO/RS

MAGNOLIA HALL
Dept. CHC
726 Andover
Atlanta, GA 30327

*"World's Largest Collection of Victorian
Furniture," $1.00, published quarterly,
62 pages, black and white, illustrated.*

If you like Victoriana, you will revel in
the selection of pieces found in this
catalogue. A charming mirror-back
hand-carved mahogany love seat is
under $400. Five side chairs with solid
mahogany frames, four with tufted
seats and backs in amusing Victorian
styles such as heart and balloon, are
$119 each. You can buy complete
parlor sets or lady's and gentleman's
horseshoe-back armchairs, a beautiful
hand-carved mahogany four-poster
bed, or authentic Victorian-styled brass
beds, gilt pier mirrors, and handsome
hall trees. Dimensions of each piece are
given, with price. Write for fabric
samples.
MO

AMERICAN CONTEMPORARY
Dept. CHC
P.O. Box 634
Simsbury, CT 06070

*"American Contemporary," 25 cents,
two 6-page brochures, black and white,
illustrated.*

Clean-lined contemporary furniture of
solid, beautifully grained wood in easy-
to-assemble kits. Each piece is precut,
drilled, sanded smooth, ready to
assemble in minutes. Finishes are your
choice of stain, paint or natural
(finishing tips included with
instructions). Pieces include cocktail
and end tables in several sizes, some
with glass-insert tops which you
provide to save shipping costs, stacking
wall units with adjustable shelves and a
cabinet for stereo or, on ball casters, as
a bar. Prices range from about $35 for a
30" x 30" x 10" modular shelf-unit to
$130 for a four-door cabinet.
MO

BON MARCHÉ
Dept. CHC
74 Fifth Avenue
New York, NY 10011
or
3221 M Street, N.W.
Washington, DC 20007

Leaflets, no charge.

A good source for inexpensive
contemporary furniture, imported and
domestic. Although Bon Marché has no
catalogue, they will send you pages of
reproductions of their ads. The latest
ones received showed the 1926 Breuer
side and arm chairs with chrome-steel
frame and seat and back of black
lacquer or beech with cane for under
$55. A butcher-block 18"-square end
table was under $40. A comfortable
swivel-back chrome-steel frame chair
with seat, back, and arms of black or
white vinyl, reinforced and double-
stitched, was under $60. Items can be
shipped collect anywhere for an
additional $2.50 charge.
MO/RS

Leather chair and ottoman, *Brazil Contempo*

Contemporary upholstered furniture, *Creative Comfort*

BRAZIL CONTEMPO
Dept. CHC
4 East 34th Street
New York, NY 10016

"Fine Leather Furniture—Imported Direct to You," 50 cents, color folder.

This is not a mail-order catalogue, as the company sells directly through its own stores, thus eliminating distributors and keeping prices low. Several handsome furniture groupings are available in beautiful buttery leather colors. Especially attractive are the modular seating units you arrange yourself—and then rearrange to form new groupings.
RS

BREWSTER CORPORATION
Dept. CHC
River Street
Old Saybrook, CT 06475

"Expression," no charge, 12 pages, black and white, illustrated.

New plastics and fibers for seating, storage-space organization, and work surfaces. There are free-floating tabletops to combine with hassocks or toss on the carpet; panels to use on walls, floors; brightly colored foam blocks and chair shapes; stacking fiberglass shelves for upright worktables. Prices moderate.
MO

CHROMCRAFT CORP.
Dept. CHC
P.O. Box 126
Senatobia, MS 38668

"Dining Fashions by Chromcraft," 25 cents, published annually, color, illustrated.

Glass, chrome, and plastic are appearing as a decorative feature of more and more houses now that living has become more casual. This leaflet shows all three in the dining room along with amber, smoke onyx, smoke mirror, marble, cork, cane, exotic woods, velvet, and nylon. One model is a bumper pool-cum-poker-cum-dining table, all with the flip of a top.
RS

CREATIVE COMFORT COMPANY
Dept. CHC
472 Massachusetts Avenue
Central Square
Cambridge, MA 02139

"Creative Comfort," no charge, published annually, 12 pages, black and white, illustrated.

Contemporary upholstered furniture (including convertible sofas) with hardwood frames, seats in three different depths, and backs in two heights in a choice of fabrics, woods, and finishes. There are also butcher-block tables and custom shelf arrangements. The furniture is designed to disassemble easily. Prices, on a separate sheet, vary because different options are offered. Reasonable prices.
MO

Bronze disk bar, *Directional Furniture*

Loft bed, *D.O. Unto Others*

Knockdown storage piece, *Genada Imports*

DIRECTIONAL FURNITURE
Dept. CHC
979 Third Avenue
New York, NY 10022

Three catalogues, 50 cents the set: "Cityscape," "Sculptured Metal," and "The Directional Collection"; some color, illustrated.

Sold only through decorators, the furniture produced by Directional is an exciting amalgam of art and practicality. The featured designer, Paul Evans, is a sculptor who turned his talents to furniture, and his designs, like the cabinet called "Cityscape," allow art to function as furniture. Two of the catalogues offered show Evans' work (one particularly interesting design is an Aztec-inspired wall bar) in metals and woods. The third catalogue is a handsome collection of contemporary tables, chairs, sofas, and cabinets.
RS/ID

DOOR STORE
Dept. CHC
3140 M Street, N.W.
Washington, DC 20008

Catalogue, $1.00, published annually, 48 pages, black and white, illustrated.

The Door Store catalogue presents an overwhelming array of chairs, Parsons tables, expanding tables, butcher-block tables, legs, pedestals, wall systems, storage cabinets, sofas and sofa beds, platform and trundle beds, chests, desks, and a few children's chairs in a wide range of prices. Some of their best chairs are line-for-line reproductions of the great classic designs. A new element is the Stuns Collection of chairs and sofas with bright canvas-colored cushions and matching lacquered steel frames imported from Sweden.
MO/RS

D.O. UNTO OTHERS, INC.
Dept. CHC
392 Amsterdam Avenue
New York, NY 10024

"Ideas in Space," no charge, published periodically, 10 pages, black and white, illustrated.

Loft beds designed to liberate space, to utilize waste space, and to provide comfort and privacy: bunk type, singles, doubles, king size, L-shape, or U-shape. Built-in units (for records, tapes, etc., or for study areas) are pictured for use under the beds. Also available: a banquet table that stores, a "country closet," and an elevated platform bed. Specifications and prices given. Prices range from about $100 to $360.
MO

GENADA IMPORTS
Dept. CHC
P.O. Box 204, Dept. H-5
Teaneck, NJ 07666

"Import'ant Shopper," 50 cents, published annually, 48 pages, black and white, illustrated.

The catalogue shows all types of modern furniture, much of it with a Scandinavian design influence. The pieces are imported from Europe and made in America, and some are shipped knockdown for lower costs. Genada offers a comprehensive selection of furniture, especially in chairs, that ranges from copies of the Barcelona chair, Saarinen fiberglass shell chair, and Eames chair and ottoman to folding rope chairs, the wood-and-canvas British officer's chair, bentwood chairs, and inflatable plastic chairs. Replacements are available for chair and sofa covers and cushions, and an extra 25 cents brings a fabric selection card. Prices moderate.
MO

48

Dining group, *Henredon Artefacts Collection*

Environmental furnishings, *H.U.D.D.L.E.*

HENREDON FURNITURE INDUSTRIES, INC.
Dept. CHC
Morganton, NC 28655

"Henredon Artefacts," $1.00, updated periodically, 49 pages, some color, illustrated.

An original collection, inspired by ancient themes and architectural in line, that is designed to blend with any style or period and displays a warm, informal contemporary quality. Two special groups are made to bunch and stack. The woods include solid ash, knotty oak, and olive-ash burl veneers and in some pieces are complemented by glass and wrought metal. With a visual index but no prices.

"Henredon Circa 76," $1.00, updated periodically, 28 pages, some color, illustrated.

This collection, which "celebrates the present with the best of the past," has a contemporary informality. Ash wood is used throughout, both for solid parts and veneers, and is complemented with pewter-finish hardware. All surfaces are random matched, and the finish is a warm gray tone. A visual index is included.
RS

H.U.D.D.L.E. INC.
Dept. CHC
3416 Wesley Street
Culver City, CA 90230

Catalogue in preparation, $1.00.
The catalogue shows a system of rounded "environmental furnishings" that uses as the basic element fiberply cylinders made from recycled materials and reinforced with a special laminate. Designed and built by Jim and Penny Hull, founders of Hull Urban Design Development Laboratory, Etcetera (hence, H.U.D.D.L.E.), the pieces have an engaging simplicity and come in a wide range of colors, fabrics, and forms. There is also a line of semi-finished furnishings for those who like to do some of the creative work themselves, as well as a children's series. Prices moderate.
MO/RS

LEATHERCRAFTER
Dept. CHC
303 East 51st Street
New York, NY 10022

Catalogue, 50 cents, published annually, 32 pages, black and white, illustrated.
With the neat little catalogue comes an envelope filled with samples of colors for the heavy saddle leather used on the chairs shown. They will also send, on request, color samples of bucksuede, soft cowhide, and glove leather. The chairs are in a variety of modern designs, and the techniques used are the same as those that made early American saddlers and leather craftsmen famous for fine workmanship. Leathercrafter offers versions of some of the most famous chair designs of this century and seems to have a chair or stool to suit every taste at prices ranging from around $40 to $650. They also have a collection of chairs, pillows, and rugs in genuine steerhide. Price list and order form are included in the package.
MO

Catalogue cover, *Leathercrafter*

Plant stand, *Pipe Dream*

Seating multiples, *Roche-Bobois*

Danish beach chair, rope seat, *Scan*

NORSK
Dept. CHC
114 East 57th Street
New York, NY 10022

"Norsk Scandinavian Furniture," no charge, 10 pages, black and white, illustrated.

Norsk offers a variety of well-priced Scandinavian furniture—cabinets, tables, chairs, desks, serving carts and the like in teak, rosewood, or walnut—as well as contemporary designs in upholstered furniture, including a colorful foam-filled chair that unfolds into a bed.
MO/RS

PIPE DREAM
Dept. CHC
1121 East Commercial Blvd.
Ft. Lauderdale, FL 33308

"Pipe Dream," $2.20 (refundable with purchase), published annually, 8 pages, swatches, black and white, illustrated.

Fun contemporary furniture of white P.V.C. tubing that will not chip or peel, with cushions covered in P.V.C.-coated polyester cord, comes as a kit, easy to assemble with complete do-it-yourself instructions. You have a choice of blue, green, or yellow covers. A club chair with seat and back cushions is under $40, a desk and two-cushion side chair just $92 for the two pieces. The furniture can be used both outdoors and indoors.
MO

ROCHE-BOBOIS USA, LTD.
Dept. CHC
200 Madison Avenue
New York, NY 10016

"Roche-Bobois," $5.00, published annually, 132 pages, color, illustrated, with 52-page illustrated price list.

Handsome international designs in contemporary furniture from the latest in low-level seating multiples to wall-to-wall storage systems to the new "twenty tube" series designed by France's Marc Berthier (beds, bookcases that stem from three basic elements combined in many different ways) to see-through glass and acrylics from Italy. Prices range from about $450 for a low-level two-seater sofa and about $135 for the "twenty tube" desk unit to $54 for the chrome-plated steel-frame see-through folding chair. The price list has full information on each piece. The firm also has a complete decorating service.
MO/RS

ROYAL SYSTEM, INC.
Dept. CHC
57-08 39th Avenue
Woodside, NY 11377

"Cado Collection," $3.00, 64 pages, full color, illustrated.

A beautifully illustrated catalogue of handsome Danish contemporary furniture for conference rooms, offices, and homes, including wall systems that can be used as partitions, as well as occasional tables, canvas desk chairs, chairs that stack. Specifications for each piece are provided in five languages. Six pages of Cado fabrics are described.
RS/ID

SCAN
Dept. CHC
11310 Fredrick Avenue
Beltsville, MD 20705

Portfolio of 12 folders, $2.00, black and white, illustrated.

This portfolio is the collection of the largest direct importer of Scandinavian furniture and accessories in the United States. The furniture is upholstered in denim, modern-weave wools, vinyl, and leather. There are lounge chairs, Danish rockers, lighting and office furniture, children's beds and chairs, wall systems—all with the stylized look we have come to expect from Scandinavia.
MO

Molded plastic chairs and table, *Royal System*

Luscious leather sofa, *Selig*

Lifestyle ABC plastic furniture, *Syroco*

SCHOOLFIELD FURNITURE INDUSTRIES
Dept. CHC
P.O. Box 111
Mullins, SC 29574

Four brochures, no charge, published periodically, color, illustrated.

Each brochure shows a different furniture collection: the Swingers, 3400 Series for bedrooms, 3400 Series for dining rooms, and Bamboo and Wicker Motif, with all the pieces illustrated and the dimensions and specifications given. Swingers Line comes in 48 *House & Garden* colors to mix or match. The Bamboo and Wicker collection also comes in a range of *House & Garden* colors, with brushed white plastic tops. Moderately priced.
RS

SELIG MANUFACTURING CO.
Dept. CHC
Leominster, MA 01453

"Design Folio," $1.00, 28 pages, some color.

The Selig catalogue shows two categories of furniture—the Monroe Collection, in the medium price range, and the more expensive custom Imperial Collection. The furniture is contemporary, for the most part upholstered, with a choice of about 500 materials, including tweed, leather, corduroy, and suede cloth. "The Playpen" in the Monroe Collection is an interesting grouping composed of sofas, ottomans, and corner units that combine to give an almost completely closed-in look. Some of the sofas convert to beds.
RS/ID

STOREHOUSE, INC.
Dept. CHC
3106 Early Street, N.W.
Atlanta, GA 30305

"Palaset Cubes," 25 cents, 6 pages, some color, illustrated; "Full Line," $1.00 (includes Palaset and Storehouse).

Palaset is the versatile and flexible Finnish system whose basic element is a cube 13½" square. Separate sheets show some of the combinations possible with the four types of open cubes and two cubes with drawers and suggest uses to which Palaset can be put in home or office. Dimensions and prices are given. The Storehouse Full Line also includes the original Innovator Collection, the "museum chair," bentwood, butcher-block, Parsons tables, and wall units. Prices are moderate.
MO

Palaset cubes, *Storehouse*

SYROCO
Dept. CHC
Syracuse, NY 13201

"Life Style Catalogue," $1.00, 10 pages, color, illustrated.

Syroco has translated plastics technology into innovative contemporary home furnishings. Their catalogue offers a full line of inexpensive casual indoor/outdoor furniture, including Parsons tables, sofas, chairs, game and coffee tables, dining tables, and even bar supplies and ice buckets.
RS

THOMASVILLE FURNITURE INDUSTRIES, INC.
Dept. CHC
P.O. Box 339
Thomasville, NC 27360

"Founders Guide to Modern Decorating," $2.00, 96 pages, some color.

A breezily written, basic and informative little paperback book by three home-furnishings experts. It has sketched floor plans and photographs of room settings with Thomasville's "Founders" contemporary furniture.
RS

CHARLES WEBB
Dept. CHC
28 Church Street   Harvard Square
Cambridge, MA 02138

"Catalogue of Designs," $1.00, 24 pages, black and white, illustrated.

High-style, clean-lined handsome contemporary furniture, some of which looks as if it were handmade. The pieces range from beds to tables to sofas to chairs to desks and a shelf system, in white oak and natural matte vinyl finish. Price list gives dimensions and descriptions. Moderate to expensive.
MO

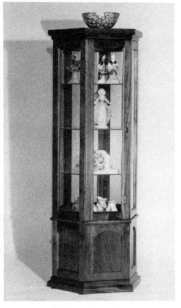

Curio cabinet, *Baroness*

Victorian footstool, *Fiesta Arts*

"Everything" folding table, *Cosco*

OCCASIONAL

WORKBENCH, INC.
Dept. CHC
470 Park Avenue South
New York, NY 10016

Annual catalogue, $1.00, 64 pages, black and white, illustrated.

Design and workmanship at a good price are the prime concerns of The Workbench. Contemporary styles, many of them imported, are reflected in wall systems, chairs, dining tables, drawing tables, desks, sofas, even wastebaskets. Materials are walnut, teak, birch, oak, chrome, butcher-block, plastic, and bentwood. The Workbench carries the Stuns Collection of canvas-and-chrome chairs and sofas from Sweden. The Children's Workbench section provides simple, flexible furniture designed to grow up with the child.
MO

BARONESS CURIO CABINETS
Dept. CHC
P.O. Box 9122
Mobile, AL 36609

Single color sheet with assembly instructions, no charge.

You can purchase the three-sided collectors' cabinet completely finished for under $260, if you are not inclined to buy the kit. The cabinet is solid mahogany with three sides of glass across the front and mirror-backed interior, and it measures 68" high by 12" deep by 27" wide (back), 13½" each front panel. An interior light is also available for under $10. Two more models will be available shortly.
MO

COSCO, INC.
Dept. CHC
2525 State Street
Columbus, IN 47201

"Cosco Home Products," "Cosco Contemporaries," no charge, 11 pages each, color, illustrated.

"Cosco Home Products" is a collection of inexpensive kitchen stools, bar stools, step stools, light desk chairs, serving and utility carts, and folding chairs and tables, fashioned for the most part from chrome and vinyl, with occasional touches of butcher-block, enamel, or brass finish. Most of the designs are unpretentious and functional. Particularly outstanding is a folding octagonal poker table with pockets for chips, glasses, etc. around the rim and a separate hard cover that converts the top to a plain surface.

"Cosco Contemporaries" is a small leaflet with a variety of chairs, tables, serving carts, and ottomans in bent chrome. The chairs and ottomans are variously upholstered in heavy cloth in yellow, purple, red, or clear, white, or brown vinyl. Tabletops are butcher-block or smoked glass.
RS

FIESTA ARTS, INC.
Dept. CHC
Greenvale, NY 11548

Brochure, no charge, published semiannually.

Primarily a poster house, Fiesta Arts also has Victorian footstools with removable tops in mahogany, walnut, and fruitwood finishes, priced from $17 to $25.
MO

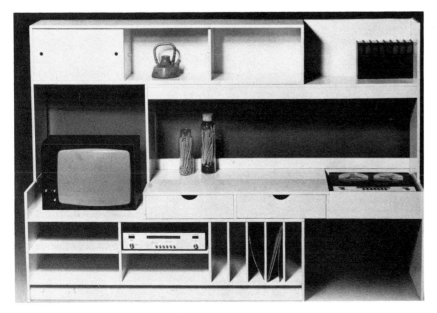

Contemporary storage piece, *Workbench*

British officer's chair, *Gold Medal*

Hand-decorated tea cart, *Hekman Furniture*

Sheaf-of-wheat design table, *LaBarge*

FINISHING TOUCH
Gravely Furniture Co., Inc.
Dept. CHC
Ridgeway, VA 24148

Furniture brochures, no charge, updated as new lines are introduced, some color, illustrated.

Finishing Touch is a collection of pieces of occasional furniture from three groups: "Old Salt" oak chests, tables, and desks trimmed in brass or with marine motif—ship's-wheel tops for tables, ship's blocks as table bases complete with line, or compass table with simulated slate top. "Charter," a more sophisticated group of design styles from France and England, boasts no less than six different curio cabinets or commodes of interest to the collector and several secretary or desk units. "Burnt Chimneys" is a pine group that draws its inspiration from Colonial American times. A dough box, schoolmaster's desk with open hutch top, a tote chair, and bean-box end table are among the more interesting pieces. Sizes are given along with finishes but no prices.
RS

GARGOYLES, LTD.
Dept. CHC
512 South 3rd Street
Philadelphia, PA 19174

"Gargoyles, Ltd.," $4.00 (refundable with purchase), updated monthly, 32 pages, some color, illustrated.

If massive sideboards are your bag, Gargoyles has them—from medieval "serving tables" to a Victorian waitress station; also old round oak tables, cast-iron and wood benches, bars and bar fittings. Dimensions and materials are given. Prices on request.
MO

GOLD MEDAL, INC.
Dept. CHC
1700 Packard Avenue
Racine, WI 53403

"Gold Medal Casual Furniture Collection," no charge, published annually, 19 pages, some color, illustrated.

The director's chair has obviously been the inspiration for the various chairs, folding tables, folding bars and bar stools, screens, and the like in this collection. Chair covers are made from canvas, nylon, Naugahyde, linen, vinyl, and leather. The price range is from $16 to $126.
RS

P. E. GUERIN
Dept. CHC
23 Jane Street
New York, NY 10014

"Artistic Hardware," $2.00, 54 pages, revised as required, black and white, illustrated.

At the back of this fabulous catalogue are seven pages of superb reproductions of 18th- and 19th-century French bronze doré or steel tables and two by Robsjohn-Gibbings. The designs have been adapted to coffee-table heights. A Directoire stainless-steel and polished brass coffee table, 20" x 42" x 18" high, is $625. The Robsjohn-Gibbings bronze doré scroll table, 24" x 48" x 15½" high, is $1,200. There is a Directoire x-bench of steel with bronze doré trim for $375. You may also send in your drawings for custom models.
MO/ID

HEKMAN FURNITURE CO.
Dept. CHC
1400 Buchanan S.W.
Grand Rapids, MI 49502

"Hekman Tables and Chairs," $1.00, published annually, 80 pages, black and white, illustrated.

This "idea book" pictures the vast collection of unusual furniture made by the well-known Grand Rapids firm. Among the latest interesting additions are the Federal-style tambour curio desk in cherry, mahogany, or yew wood veneers for around $900; an 84" tall replica of a Victorian hall tree with mirror, umbrella holder, and eight porcelain knobs for hats for $290; and a beautiful hand-decorated Oriental-style lacquer three-drawer chest on legs for about $500. Prices are not out of line for such one-of-a-kind furniture that covers the traditional style field.
RS

LaBARGE CO.
Dept. CHC
875 Brooks Avenue
Holland, MI 49423

"Tables," booklet, no charge, color.

LaBarge tables are mainly brass, wrought iron, and glass, with a few wooden and stainless-steel pieces as well. In addition to tables imported from Spain and Italy the catalogue offers tea carts, one handsome wood, leather, and brass folding director's chair, a chess table, and a tufted stool.
RS

Brass-clad chest, *Sarreid*

Magnum Rattan Group, *California-Asia and Hermosa Rattan*

WICKER AND RATTAN

LARBI'S, INC.
Dept. CHC
726 East Elm Street
Conshohoken, PA 19085

"Backgammon Tables," no charge, published annually, fold-out, black and white, illustrated.

The leaflet illustrates three different types of backgammon tables: cocktail, bridge-size, and trestle-foot (folding) and gives dimensions. The tables are available in Chippendale, Hepplewhite, or Sheraton styles, handmade of Honduras mahogany or cherry with polished English leather. Prices on request.
MO

Backgammon table, *Larbi's*

SARREID, LTD.
Dept. CHC
P.O. Box 3545
Wilson, NC 27893

"Sarreid, Ltd.," color folder, no charge.

Sarreid makes what they call "fine accent furniture," unusual pieces to complement different styles and periods, and the sampling in the brochure indicates that their description is right. A brass-clad two-drawer chest, about $450, can be used on the floor as a cocktail table or mounted on a red-lacquered riser base to serve as a console. The hand-painted Viennese carousel horse, turned into a cigarette table by the addition of a glass top, about $350, would add an amusing accent to any room. Then there's a glorious dark-green lacquer chinoiserie Queen Anne-style secretary with beautiful animal decoration in gold/black/red for around $1,800. A list of showrooms is included on the price list.
RS/ID

THE WEIMAN CO.
Dept. CHC
P.O. Box 217
Ramseur, NC 27316

Two fold-out brochures, no charge, some color, illustrated.

One brochure illustrates the Regency collection of furniture in updated Regency designs. The second brochure presents a collection of individual tables, commodes, and cabinets in Mediterranean, Italian, and French styles. Occasional furniture of every size and proportion intended as accents for any room.
RS

CALIFORNIA-ASIA AND HERMOSA
** RATTAN**
Dept. CHC
9860 Gidley Street
El Monte, CA 91734

"Calif-Asia/Hermosa Rattan," $2.00, published every two years, 84 pages, color, illustrated; also a free brochure, 18 pages, black and white, illustrated.

Rattan furniture handcrafted in a wide range of styles: Chinese, Indian, Chinese Chippendale, Williamsburg. Chairs, beds, sofas, tables, bar sets in a variety of colors and designs shown in full-color room settings. Accessories include headboards, étagères, shelves, racks, frames, corner tables. A list of representatives and showrooms is provided, as well as an index, but no prices.
RS

54

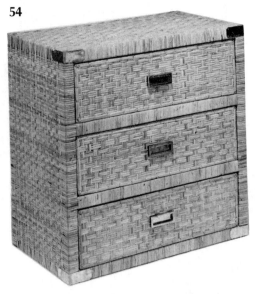

Rattan chest, *Deutsch*

Willow and rattan furniture, *Fran's Basket House*

DEUTSCH, INC.
Dept. CHC
196 Lexington Avenue
New York, NY 10016

Catalogue, $1.00, published annually, 64 pages, black and white, illustrated.

Deutsch imports what is described as America's largest selection of rattan furniture, and the prices are just as varied. There are beds, trundle-bed sofas, rockers, screens, swing chairs, cabinets, tables of all sorts in rattan and wicker styles from Victorian to Italian Modern and the squared-off Parsons look. Because of a big warehouse inventory, almost immediate delivery is promised, and cushions and custom finishing are available on request.
MO/RS/ID

FRAN'S BASKET HOUSE
Dept. CHC
Route 10
Succasunna, NJ 07876

"Fran's Basket House," 25 cents, 46 pages, black and white, illustrated.

A vast collection of willow and rattan imported furniture from around the world for every room and every need at every price. There are lacy and classic Victorian pieces, simple contemporary shapes, combinations of rattan and solid frames, traditional Oriental designs, and bentwood pieces.
MO

MAGNOLIA HALL
Dept. CHC
726 Andover
Atlanta, GA 30327

"World's Largest Collection of Victorian Furniture," $1.00, published quarterly, 63 pages, black and white, illustrated.

Simple Victorian wicker pieces, five in all, from this house of Victoriana are finished in white with choice of cushions in red, yellow, or avocado green. Any of the pieces could fit with ease into a living room, sunroom, or bedroom. The 47"-long settee is $139.95 and its matching armchair $79.95. A charming 21"-long table with shelf that could serve as telephone stand or night table costs just $49.95.
MO

Rattan furniture with mother-of-pearl inlay, *McGuire*

Ready-to-finish chest, *Country Workshop*

UNFINISHED AND UNPAINTED

THE McGUIRE COMPANY
Dept. CHC
1201 Bryant Street
San Francisco, CA 94103

Brochure, 50 cents, 22 pages, some color, illustrated.

An intriguing sampling of the stunning, superbly crafted furniture of rattan and rawhide, willow, cane, black bamboo, bamboo-turned redwood, and round oak for which this company has long been noted. The 18 different design series encompass style influences from Oriental and Regency to English Gothic and American Southwest. There are over 80 McGuire chairs, 30 sofas, 100 tables, as well as buffets, bar stools, benches, serving carts, and bedroom furniture, of which the brochure shows just enough to whet your interest. The furniture, available only through dealers and decorators, can be seen at the McGuire showrooms in San Francisco, Los Angeles, New York, Chicago, Cleveland, Grand Rapids, Boston, Atlanta, Miami, Dallas, Seattle, Toronto, and Vancouver. Expensive.
RS/ID

COUNTRY WORKSHOP
Dept. CHC
95 Rome Street
Newark, NJ 07105

Catalogue, 25 cents, 16 pages, black and white, illustrated.

Modern, ready-to-finish hardwood furniture made since 1949. The family-operated business sells by mail or through retail showrooms in Newark, Princeton, New Jersey, and Cambridge, Massachusetts. The furniture is modular, made of solid white maple or solid walnut, and comes sanded and ready to oil, stain, varnish, enamel, or what you will. The pieces, which range from chests, bookcases, cabinets, and file cabinets to Parsons tables, butcher-block tables, bunk and storage beds, and storage systems, are available in a vast number of sizes and range of prices. Country Workshop also offers the familiar bentwood chairs, fiberglass chairs, and stacking stools.
MO/RS

FURNITURE-IN-THE-RAW
Dept. CHC
8 Rewe Street
Brooklyn, NY 11211

"Decorating with Unpainted Furniture," $3.00, *published semiannually, 56 pages, some color, illustrated.*

A handy and informative booklet on the uses of unpainted furniture, with room settings, in full color, that illustrate how to achieve the eclectic look, or mix, through combinations of color, fabrics, wallcoverings, and furniture of different types. There are decorating hints and ideas, advice on the use of color and transparent finishes, and instructions for making floor plans. The furniture available is described in complete detail, and custom variations that can be performed during the manufacturing process are also listed. Prices are in the medium range, and a price list is included.
MO/RS

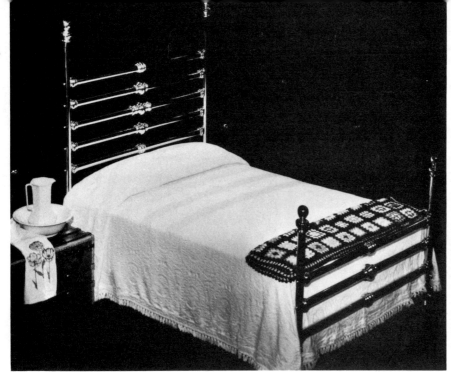

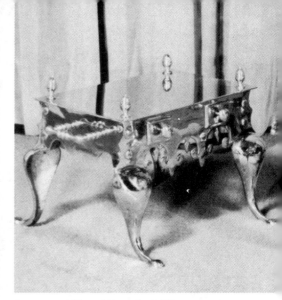

Brass trivet, *Old World Foundry Guild*

Queen-size brass bed, *João Isabel*

BRASS

BEDLAM BRASS BEDS
Dept. CHC
19–21 Fairlawn Avenue
Fair Lawn, NJ 07401

Color catalogue, $2.00, black and white catalogue, $1.00 (refundable with purchase); 24 pages, illustrated.

These catalogues promise "the largest selection of brass beds in the United States." There are 35 styles illustrated in which the design ornaments are reproductions of antique parts. An infinite number of variations can be obtained by simply interchanging tubing diameters, and the manufacturers will also work with individual customers to vary basic designs to create a custom look. Prices range from $535 for a single bed to $1,430 for the most elaborate king-size bed. In addition to the beds, the catalogue offers end tables, a coffee table, and a coat rack made from brass rods.
MO

JOÃO ISABEL, INC.
Dept. CHC
120 East 32nd Street
New York, NY 10016

"The Isabel Selection," $2.00, published annually, 16 pages, color, illustrated.

Fine handcrafted brass headboards, exquisitely styled in original and traditional designs, dipped and baked for protection, and covered with a lifelong warranty. Free delivery and installation in New York City; anywhere in the world at normal shipping prices. Price list included. You can combine or vary styles or have your original idea created. Also available are combinations of brass and porcelain enamel, stainless steel with brass castings and curlicues. Expensive.
MO

OLD WORLD FOUNDRY GUILD, INC.
Dept. CHC
1612 Decatur Street
Ridgewood, NY 11227

"Metal (Brass) Reproductions," no charge, 30 pages, black and white, illustrated.

An unusual collection of brass and other metal pieces from elegant brass headboards starting around $435 for a single size, a variety of brass trivets, steel and brass tables, and a French provincial brass magazine rack, circa 1890, about $114. Sizes, weights, and prices are given on a separate sheet.
MO

A PARABLE'S TAIL
Dept. CHC
172 Ninth Avenue
New York, NY 10011

"A Parable's Tail's World of Fine Brass Designs," $1.00, 15 pages, black and white, illustrated.

A range of handsome brass headboards, beds, and tables. Beds with such giddy names as "Tout Doux Tout Simple" sell for under $300 for twin-size headboard. A full canopy king-size bed called "Napoleon's Seduction" is about $1,150. The tables are cocktail or end height and start around $275. Dimensions are given for the tables. The headboards and beds come in twin, full, queen, and king. All prices are included on the order form.
MO

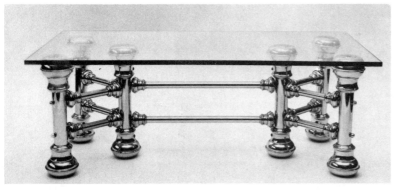

Brass and glass cocktail table, *A Parable's Tail*

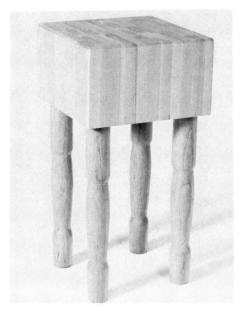

Butcher-block table, *J & D Brauner*

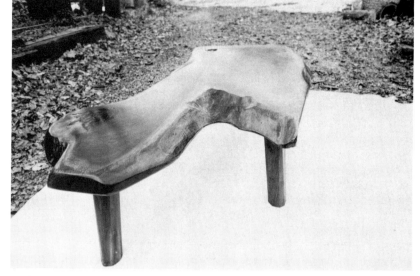

Wood sculpture table, *Tables by Davis*

BUTCHER BLOCK AND NATURAL WOODS

J&D BRAUNER
Dept. CHC
298 Bowery
New York, NY 10012

"The Butcher Block," $1.00, published annually, 49 pages, black and white, illustrated.

Butcher block is sweeping America. Its natural good looks blend with almost any decorating scheme, and today you can find butcher-block furniture almost anywhere in the house. It is easy to care for. Nicks and scratches just add character, or they may be sandpapered away. This catalogue from an old-established supplier shows kitchen counters, shelves, cutting boards, lazy Susans, tables, chairs, carts, and sofas in a variety of prices.
MO

FAIRMONT WOODCRAFT
Dept. CHC
Box 10
Waterville, VT 05492

"Fairmont Woodcraft," no charge, 4 pages, black and white, illustrated.

Fairmont makes "treeform tables" constructed from rough planks bearing the original marks and shape of the tree from which they were cut, built to your specifications. Ideal for end tables, cocktail tables, fireside benches. Also lazy Susans and electric clocks, irregular in shape and designed to accentuate the beauty of the wood, knots and all. Moderate prices.
MO

THE SCHOENHEIT COMPANY
Dept. CHC
1600 S. Clinton Street
Chicago, IL 60616

"Butcher Block & More," 50 cents, 44 pages, black and white, illustrated.

Everything in butcher-block furniture in stock or custom sizes. For instance, a two-inch-thick maple butcher-block top with bench-construction frame becomes a worktable at 34" height or for dining at 30". It comes in three sizes: 24" x 36", $124; 24" x 48", $140; or 30" x 60", $175; with locking Shepherd casters, add $25.
MO

TABLES BY DAVIS
Dept. CHC
84 Forest Road
Milford, CT 06460

"Tables by Davis," no charge, published annually, 6 pages, black and white, illustrated.

One-of-a-kind tables handcrafted from solid American black walnut are the specialty of the house. The story of the making of the tables from the old trees through milling and drying is very interesting. Depending on size and height, tables seem to range in price from around $250 to $300. A visit to the showroom would be well worthwhile.
MO

THOMPSON MANUFACTURING CO.
Dept. CHC
Lancaster, NH 03548

"Butcher Block Furniture by Thompson," free folder, black and white, illustrated.

Butcher-block tables, sofas, lounge chairs, a two-drawer bed, and a carpeted bench, all made of maple, are part of the collection. Simple, straightforward pieces in prices ranging from around $225 for a nest of three Parsons tables, 23", 19", and 15" square, to under $1,000 for a king-size sofa bed. The tables come in many different widths and lengths. Pieces can be specially ordered to your specifications.
MO/ID

Tamiami group aluminum furniture, *Brown Jordan*

Teak garden bench, *Hawker Siddeley*

LEISURE AND GARDEN

SAWMILL PRODUCTS
Dept. CHC
North Leverett Road
Montague, MA 01351

Annual brochure, no charge.

The brochure offers a small selection of roughhewn, primitive wood products such as woodboxes, planters, chunky benches and tables, and bookcases made at a sawmill and sold from a shop on the site. Some even have the bark left on them. The wood used is mostly pine, but some other hardwoods are available. The Sawmill also alerts its customers to twice-yearly tag-end sales at the mill that offer, in addition to their products, a number of antiques and memorabilia.
MO

THE WOODSHED
Dept. CHC
315 Sunrise Highway
Lynbrook, NY 11563

"The Woodshed Butcher Block," $1.00 (refundable with purchase), black and white, illustrated.

A handsome catalogue with all kinds of butcher-block furniture: dining, cocktail, kitchen tables with wood, cast iron, chrome, wrought iron, or aluminum bases, serving carts, sofas, chairs, and modular seating, as well as some thirty-odd side and armchairs in a variety of styles and types from about $38 to $110. Separate price list gives order information, sizes, finishes, and custom-work information.
MO

BROWN JORDAN
Dept. CHC
9860 Gidley Street
El Monte, CA 91734

"Brown Jordan," $2.00, published every two years, 62 pages, color, illustrated. A 30-page brochure condenses the big catalogue.

Contemporary aluminum leisure furniture custom-designed by skilled industrial designers. Many pieces are shown in color, but a line-drawing section shows every item, in every design group, produced by Brown Jordan. Product number and principal specifications are included. Additional information, such as tabletop materials, can be found in the current price list. An index and a list of representatives and showrooms are provided.
Expensive.
RS/ID

Catalogue cover, *The Woodshed*

HAWKER SIDDELEY, INC.
Lister Furniture Division
Dept. CHC
7 Delaware Drive
Lake Success, NY 11040

"Lister Teak Garden Furniture," no charge, published annually, 8 pages, color, illustrated.

The brochure illustrates teak garden furniture—chairs, tables, benches, and seats—two plant boxes, and litter baskets. Complete specifications are given on a separate page, and advice on care of teak is included. Prices on request.
MO/RS

MEADOWCRAFT CASUAL FURNITURE
Dept. CHC
P.O. Box 1357
Birmingham, AL 35201

"Meadowcraft," no charge, 16 pages, color, illustrated.

A colorful brochure showing the several lines of indoor-outdoor aluminum and wrought-iron casual furniture made by this company. There are café tables and chairs, a Continental-height dining table with swivel or regular cane-back party chairs, magazine and plant stands, baker's racks, and the "All-Weather" contoured mesh group. The name of the nearest dealer will be sent when you write for the brochure.
RS/ID

58

Butterfly chairs, *The Patio*

Wrought-iron gourmet stand, *Woodard*

THE PATIO
Dept. CHC
550 Powell Street
San Francisco, CA 94108

*"Spring/Summer Sunny Thoughts,"
$1.00, 30 pages, black and white;
"Fall/Winter San Francisco Gift Book,"
$1.00, 30 pages, black and white,
illustrated.*

The first catalogue shows a wide variety
of outdoor furniture under such group
names as "Rattan," "Malibu" (plastic
with upholstered nylon cushions), "Rid-
jid" (tubular steel mesh with a
wrought-iron look), "Spring Things"
(tubular steel frames and vinyl
strapping), and "Oak Group" (cast-iron
Victorian reproductions). Perhaps the
most unusual is the medium-priced
Malibu group of sofas, chairs, and a
selection of tables (pedestal for the
most part) designed by a young
California architect, comfortable and
modern in style, with covers that resist
mildew, rot, and deterioration. Also
included in the summer catalogue are
more familiar pieces, such as director's
chairs and butterfly chairs.
   The Fall/Winter catalogue includes
less furniture and many more
accessories. There are bamboo stacking
tables, chess tables, and what is
described as "our famous Barwa chair,"
a contoured lounge chair of tubular
aluminum with duck covers.
MO

SYROCO
Dept. CHC
Syracuse, NY 13201

*"Life Style Catalogue," $1.00, 10 pages,
color, illustrated.*

This catalogue presents a full line of
inexpensive indoor-outdoor furniture in
the casual mood of contemporary
living, translating plastics technology
into innovative home furnishings. There
are Parsons tables, sofas, chairs, coffee
tables, game tables, dining tables, and
even bar supplies and ice buckets.
RS

THINLINE
Dept. CHC
9860 Gidley Street
El Monte, CA 91734

*"Thinline," $2.00, published every two
years, 62 pages, color, illustrated. Free
brochure, 6 pages, color, illustrated.*

The catalogue features Thinline metal
furnishings with all-welded frames,
baked enamel finishes, vinyl-laced
seating on outdoor groups, and tables
with clear or smooth rough-tempered
glass tops; dining and seating groups in
solid cast aluminum and in wrought
iron. All are in a variety of designs and
a wide choice of colors. About 12 pages
of accessories: decorative tables, stools,
benches, racks, and miscellaneous. In
addition to the residential furnishings,
the catalogue shows commercial
furnishings: executive and secretary
seating, lobby and foyer seating and
tables, occasional pieces, tables and
chairs for cafeterias. The line-drawing
section gives specifications but no
prices.
RS/ID

WALL TUBE AND METAL PRODUCTS
COMPANY
Dept. CHC
P.O. Box 330
Newport, TN 37821

*"The Sun Set" and "The Entertainers,"
50 cents each, 6 pages, color, illustrated.*

These two lines of casual outdoor
furniture are shown in a variety of
striking settings. "The Sun Set" line has
lounge and dining chairs, sun cots,
ottomans and chaise longues, and end,
coffee, café, and umbrella tables (the
latter with color-coordinated umbrellas)
with a choice of frame colors and style-
strap wrappings. "The Entertainers,"
with frames of square steel tubing,
comes in ten color combinations.
RS

WOODARD
Dept. CHC
Owosso, MI 48867

*"Woodard," color leaflets, no charge,
illustrated.*

Woodard presents a handsome
collection of hand-forged iron indoor-
outdoor furniture in a dozen complete
groups and many finishes. Some of the
more unusual pieces are the "Eighteen
Ninety" brass-plated and tufted rocker;
Gourmet stand, 72" high x 33" wide x
19" deep, in black iron with brass trim,
two glass shelves and a butcher-block
cutting-board shelf. Designs range from
simple contemporary to elaborate lacy
Spanish in a wide range of pieces.
RS/ID

Contemporary children's furniture, *Brewster*

"Toob" furniture and bunk beds, *H.U.D.D.L.E.*

CHILDREN'S

BREWSTER CORPORATION
Dept. CHC
River Street
Old Saybrook, CT 06475

"Expression," folder, no charge, some color, illustrated.

To make two spaces for a couple of children out of one room, "Sho Wall," free-standing burlap- or chalkboard-covered partitions, is ideal. To furnish the areas there are "bitty" bean-bag chairs, furry-mushroom stools and hassocks, low foam or fiberglass chairs, tables made by adding a plastic top to a hassock. All great fun, in brilliant colors, at low prices.
MO

BROYHILL FURNITURE INDUSTRIES
Dept. CHC
Lenoir, NC 28633

"Americana Decorating Guide," $1.00, 80 pages, black and white and color, illustrated.

Broyhill offers several suggestions for decorating girls' and boys' rooms with their pine, maple, and painted bedroom groups.
RS

HEYWOOD-WAKEFIELD COMPANY
Dept. CHC
Gardner, MA 01440

"The Registered Collections of Heywood-Wakefield Furniture," $2.50, 187 pages, some color, illustrated.

It's easy to plan a child's room with Heywood-Wakefield's "Old Colony" or "Publick House" groups of stacking storage units, corner desks, captain's trundle or bunk beds for boys, canopies or four-posters for girls, all in maple or pine or painted finishes.
RS

H.U.D.D.L.E.
Dept. CHC
3416 Wesley Street
Culver City, CA 90230

Catalogue in production, $1.00.

Part of the "environmental furnishings" system developed by Jim and Penny Hull, founders of Hull Urban Design Development Laboratory, Etcetera (H.U.D.D.L.E.), is the children's "toobs series," an extension of the fiberply cylinders made from recycled materials and reinforced with a special laminate. There are beds (bunk and single), a study toob, vertical and horizontal bookcases, tables, and stools, all at moderate prices in a wide choice of colors.
MO

ROCHE-BOBOIS USA, LTD.
Dept. CHC
200 Madison Avenue
New York, NY 10016

"Roche-Bobois," $5.00, published annually, 132 pages, color, illustrated, with 52-page illustrated price list.

Roche-Bobois has several imported lines designed especially for children, including the Marc Berthier molded fiberglass flower cradle for around $160 and mini-desk for under $135. From the "twenty tube" system a pair of bunk beds costs around $270, a complete child's desk unit with built-on pivoting "tractor" seat about $126. In the Pop Art class is the "Apple," a combined desk and board of multi-ply panels in red and white, about $132, and a child's chair to be used with the "Apple" for about $25. Dimensions and prices are included.
MO/RS

Finnish grow-with-the-children beds, *Scan*

Swinger's collection, *Schoolfield Furniture*

SCAN
Dept. CHC
11310 Frederick Avenue
Beltsville, MD 20705

Catalogue of folders, $2.00.

One of the 12 folders in the Scan catalogue is devoted to moderately priced, versatile, well-constructed, and functional Scandinavian furnishings to meet the needs of children from infancy to young adulthood. Pictured are bunk beds, chests that can be stacked or bunched, desks, a worktable with adjustable trestle height, chairs and lamps in wood or lacquer finishes. All dimensions are given.
MO

**SCHOOLFIELD FURNITURE
 INDUSTRIES**
Dept. CHC
P.O. Box 111
Mullins, SC 29574

"The Swingers Collection," folder, no charge, 8 pages, color, illustrated.

For teenage (and older) boys and girls, the "Swingers" collection of furniture is the perfect answer. A group of furniture in 48 *House & Garden* colors from hot to pastel for mix-or-match, with bunk beds for boys, poster beds for girls, all kinds of modular storage and desk units with campaign-chest brass trim. The folder offers four possible furniture arrangements for basic room sizes 8' x 10' to 12' x 16' for one or two children.
RS

STANLEY FURNITURE
Dept. CHC
Stanleytown, VA 24168

"Home Decorating Portfolio," $1.00, some color, illustrated.

Stanley has three groups designed for the younger members of the family. "Toujours Moi" in French Provincial styling and a choice of celadon green, lemon-chiffon yellow, or the Berries blue, for the young lady, has three bed selections—a four-poster with or without tester, a day bed, and a spindle headboard, all kinds of storage pieces, and even a cheval glass. For boys or girls, "Olé," another painted group with South-of-the-Border overtones, comes in hot colors or white with color-contrasting highlights and has corner beds with table, a hutch desk and vanity, and storage units. "Sea Island," a variation on the campaign-chest look in a weathered-oak finish of woods and laminates, has bunk beds, a captain's trundle bed, sea chest, and brass porthole mirror—a delight for any young boy.
RS

WORKBENCH, INC.
Dept. CHC
470 Park Avenue South
New York, N.Y. 10016

"Workbench," $1.00, 64 pages, published annually, black and white, illustrated.

The Workbench has a large selection of modern, well-designed sturdy furniture for children at good prices. Clean-lined bunk and trundle beds from Sweden, Finland, and Canada, natural lacquered birch chests from Sweden, or colorful mix-and-match components from Denmark are not just "temporary" pieces but will grow up with the child. Look for the complete selection in the Children's Workbench section at the back of the catalogue.
MO/RS

Sea Island group, *Stanley Furniture*

Elevator chair, *Burke*

Catalogue cover, *R.V. Cole*

BEDS, SOFA BEDS, HAMMOCKS, AND RECLINERS

Rope hammock, *House of Hammocks*

BEDS AND THINGS, R. V. COLE, LTD.
Dept. CHC
16 East 30th Street
New York, NY 10016

Free folder, color.

The "things" seem to outnumber the beds. They consist of wall systems—bookshelves, storage cabinets, built-in bars, desks, stereo cabinets, which you select separately and assemble in whatever way suits your space and needs. A price list is tucked into the folder along with a flyer showing three beds. One is a floating-platform double bed (around $300 complete), the second a single mate's bed with a storage drawer beneath, under $200, and the third a double bed with four large storage drawers underneath, around $360. All cabinets and beds come in either teak finish or white.
MO

AVERY BOARDMAN
Dept. CHC
979 Third Avenue
New York, NY 10022

"Sleep Sofas," $1.00, 48 pages, black and white, illustrated.

Custom-made sofas and sofa beds in customer's own fabric and a range of styles, sizes, heights, widths, depths, mattress sizes, and prices—from $750 to about $1,500. All sleep sofas are available without the bed feature, and there are many possible variations.
RS/ID

BURKE, INC.
Dept. CHC
P.O. Box 1064
Mission, KA 66222

"Burke Offers Complete Elevator Patient-aid Systems," no charge, published annually, color, illustrated.

For people who have difficulty getting in or out of chairs, Burke has the answer—recliners, swivel rockers, and a contemporary elevator chair with a choice of two fabrics. There is also a portable elevating device for wheelchairs and toilets. The solution is a simple push-button device that raises you and the seat to standing position or gracefully seats you. Touch another switch on the recliner and you can take any position, while the footrest automatically rises to elevate the feet. Seats can be elevated in the reclining position to relieve back pressure. Prices on request.
MO/RS

HOUSE OF HAMMOCKS
Dept. CHC
65 Peterson Road
Falmouth, MA 02540

"Brazilian Sleeping Hammocks," leaflet, 25 cents.

Roomy (8' long x 5' wide), sturdy, and extremely decorative cotton-yarn hammocks, handwoven in Brazil, that would look great indoors or out. They are available in white, solid colors, and plaid, are embellished with ball fringe, and range in price from $19.95 to $36.95.
MO

LA-Z-BOY CHAIR COMPANY
Dept. CHC
Monroe, MI 48161

"La-Z-Boy Brochure," no charge, color, illustrated foldout.

These chairs have been around for about 40 years, and most Americans are familiar with the style that resembles a reclining airplane seat. There are 24 styles of rockers in a wide variety of colors, fabrics, and vinyls, featuring a three-way adjustable footrest. The Lounger, a stationary model, has the same footrest and can be chosen in a number of varying styles as well. One model has an electric reclining mechanism for total ease.
RS

Wall cabinet bed, *Murphy Door Bed*

Hide-a-bed sofa, *Simmons*

MURPHY DOOR BED COMPANY, INC.
Dept. CHC
Raynes/Gilbard Corp.
40 East 34th Street
New York, NY 10016

"Murphy In-a-Door Bed," leaflets and brochures, 25 cents.

The leaflets and brochures show seven different styles of wall cabinets, from modern to traditional to Oriental, with the familiar tucked-away Murphy bed, in single, double, and queen sizes. The beds are also sold without cabinets. Price sheets list the different styles and finishes.
MO

LOFTCRAFT
Dept. CHC
120 West 20th Street
New York, NY 10011

"Loftcraft," no charge, 10 pages, black and white, illustrated.

Space-saving and space-gaining ideas for the apartment dweller are given in this interesting booklet of contemporary platform beds that provide a complete environment. The functional loft bed can be made to order in any height and standard bed size. The Sleep Box, a one-of-a-kind design, comes in a variety of finishes. Among Loftcraft's other ingenious ideas are a cantilevered desk the length and width of any bed that fits under or over it and an under-the-bed dining set that converts to a spare bed. Closets, shelves (basically book boxes), and couches with storage space can all be incorporated into the basic bed units. Send the size and finish of the bed you want, and Loftcraft will give you the price. Each item comes knocked down and is easy to assemble and completely free-standing.
MO

REID CLASSICS
Dept. CHC
P.O. Box 8383
3600 Old Shell Road
Mobile, AL 36608

Brochure, $1.00, black and white, illustrated.

If you are looking for handsome, solid-mahogany hand-carved or turned poster or tester beds, authentic reproductions of early Southern and Colonial designs, Reid Classics is for you. Every bed is made to order in your choice of over 30 styles of posts and headboards, available in all sizes from twin to king, from $300 to $3,500.
MO

SIMMONS COMPANY
Dept. CHC
2 Park Avenue
New York, NY 10016

"Simmons Guide to the Great Indoors," $1.00, 15 pages, color, illustrated.

Based on the vast array of Simmons Hide-A-Bed sofas, this booklet offers inexpensive solutions to common decorating problems in five general classifications: 1) decorating basics for you to follow; 2) young ideas for your city apartment; 3) grassroots decorating for your country home; 4) decorating your vacation house; and 5) budget decorating for your first home. At the back is information about and pictures of the Hide-A-Beds and a map of the 67 Simmons Service Centers.
RS/ID

Sleep box, *Loftcraft*

Slumber seat lounge, *Victor Stanley*

"Custom room plans" storage system, *Ethan Allen*

STORAGE SYSTEMS

VICTOR STANLEY, INC.
Dept. CHC
P.O. Box 93
Dunkirk, MD 20754

"Slumber/Seat," brochure, no charge, black and white, illustrated.

"Slumber/Seat" shows a number of club chairs that convert at one pull into chaises and at another into full-length beds. Also shown are some love-seat-size sofas, a fold-up ottoman that unfolds to a flat mat, and rotary style record holders and tape holders.
RS

ETHAN ALLEN, INC.
Dept. CHC
Ethan Allen Drive
Danbury, CT 06810

"The Treasury of Ethan Allen American Traditional Interiors," $7.50 (no charge at showrooms), published every two years, 408 pages, color, illustrated.

To solve all your storage problems, Ethan Allen offers "Custom Room Plan" which lets you custom-design storage to fit your room. The free-standing modular units, inspired by Shaker designs, are characterized by paneled or shuttered doors, armoire-shaped upper cabinet units in decorative Provincial styling, wrought-iron hinges, and apothecary-style drawers.
RS

NAOMI GALE/SHELVES UNLIMITED
Dept. CHC
2400 Ryer Avenue
Bronx, NY 10458

"Custom Wall-Systems," Catalogue 15A and price book, $1.00, 24 pages, black and white; "Inventory Groups," Book 2E, no charge; "The Acrylics and . . . ," Catalogue 30, no charge; all illustrated.

Each wall unit in Catalogue 15A can be redesigned to fit a customer's wall area exactly, and the various styles are hand-carved from fine hardwoods and finished to individual specifications. One system is lucite. Prices start at $375 and, in one case, reach $6,290.

"Inventory Groups" shows the wall units of Shelves Unlimited kept in stock at all times. They can be ordered only in the sizes shown but in a choice of several different finishes.

"The Acrylics and . . . " has clear acrylic systems, acrylic teamed with tulipwood, butcher-block, black lacquer, and one quite spectacular cabinet housing record player, bar, records, a deep drawer, adjustable shelves, and concealed lighting.
MO/ID

Acrylic wall system, *Naomi Gale/Shelves Unlimited*

Wall-together storage units, *Lustro-ware*

Cado Collection storage system, *Royal System*

GREATWOOD
Dept. CHC
101 S. Robertson Blvd.
Los Angeles, CA 90048
or
290 Madison Avenue
New York, NY 10017

"The Organizer," leaflet, no charge, color.

The Norwegian-designed "Organizer" is an intriguing product of Scandinavian ingenuity, a cabinet that unlocks and opens into an enormously roomy desk with, seemingly, a place for everything. Available in three different woods, at prices ranging from $450 to $500, it comes with a 60-day money-back guarantee.
MO

HEYWOOD-WAKEFIELD COMPANY
Dept. CHC
Gardner, MA 01440

"The Registered Collections of Heywood-Wakefield Furniture," $2.50, 187 pages, some color, illustrated.

Both "Publick House" and "Old Colony" offer stacking storage systems in maple, pine, and painted finishes with the Early American look.
RS

LUSTRO-WARE DIVISION
Borden Chemical Co.
Dept. CHC
Columbus, OH 43223

"Ideas with Lustro-ware Wall-togethers," no charge, 11 pages, color, illustrated.

Fifteen ways to gain storage in every room with easy-to-install Lustro-ware Wall-together storage units. There are eight different units, ranging from 12" x 12" pegboard panels to three sizes of shelves, two clocks and a mirror, two sets of storage and spice jars, or individual shelves. All are wall-hung.
RS

ROCHE-BOBOIS USA, LTD.
Dept. CHC
200 Madison Avenue
New York, NY 10016

"Roche-Bobois," $5.00, published annually, 132 pages, color, illustrated, with 52-page illustrated price list.

Contemporary storage units to fill every need from a simple wall-mounted ABC plastic hold-all, 20" x 26", for under $65, to a complete wall-to-wall storage system for $3,000 or more. Some are center-of-the-room cabinets to create a room-within-a-room, others store folding beds or surround a platform bed; all are multi-unit systems for every conceivable type of storage.
MO/RS

ROYAL SYSTEM, INC.
Dept. CHC
57-08 39th Avenue
Woodside, NY 11377

"Cado Collection," $3.00, 64 pages, color, illustrated.

As part of the "Cado Collection," Finn Juhl has designed a variable system of bookcases, called Cresco, consisting of cabinets with shelves, doors, drawers, bureau, bar cabinet, and loose shelves arranged on bases. Adjustable screws under the base ensure level standing on uneven floors. The system can be made to fit any wall length and, as the backs are finished, can act as a room divider. Write for a price list and brochure showing the many combinations.
RS/ID

Commode-cum-dining table, *Saginaw Furniture*

SAGINAW FURNITURE SHOPS
Dept. CHC
7300 North Lehigh
Chicago, IL 60648

"Expandaway by Saginaw," folder, no charge, 6 pages, black and white, illustrated.

Open the drawer in the top of one of the commodes shown in this catalogue and out comes the framework for a dining-room table. The leaves for the table are stored in the commode. The tables, which range from 35" to 110" long, are housed in cabinets in Early American, French Provincial, Spanish, and contemporary styles. The company also offers folding chairs and a cabinet that flips open to become a buffet or drinks server.
RS

SCAN
Dept. CHC
11310 Frederick Avenue
Beltsville, MD 20705

Catalogue of folders, $2.00.

Contemporary free-standing or wall-hung storage systems for living rooms, bedrooms, dining rooms, and home offices are shown in several of the folders. In addition to the usual component systems there are individual storage pieces such as handsome file cabinets with tambour doors, long sleek buffets with fitted drawers and adjustable shelves, several rolling bar or tea carts, all with the stylized look of Scandinavian design.
MO

THOMASVILLE FURNITURE
   INDUSTRIES, INC.
Dept. CHC
P.O. Box 339
Thomasville, NC 27360

"Homemaker's Guide," $2.00, 100 pages, color, illustrated.

The contemporary Founders line is famous for its space-saving storage systems for today's minimum-space rooms. The trim, handsome architectural "Stoaways" offers four modular cabinet sizes in 11 styles to fit almost every storage need and space. The multifunctional "Keepers' Two" is a system that stacks, bunches, and organizes storage, lets you create on one wall a home office, sewing, or study/work area, or entertainment center, with a self-storing table that flips down when needed. "Patterns 30" and "31" offer storage units of different heights with little bulk, great versatility, and lots of storage. Write for name of the nearest dealer for system you want.
RS

Practicolor Formica studio piano, *Everett Piano*

PIANOS

EVERETT PIANO COMPANY
Dept. CHC
South Haven, MI 49090

"Everett Pianos," no charge, 20 pages, color, illustrated.

Console and studio pianos, including the Practicolor Formica studio piano in a choice of six colors. The distinguishing differences in console pianos are explained in the booklet. Two other free booklets, available on request, are "The Craftsman's Story of Making a Piano," designed to help you evaluate a piano, and "Pianos, People and Places," which helps you to select a piano that matches your life-style.
RS

SOHMER & CO.
Dept. CHC
31 West 57th Street
New York, NY 10019

"The Story Behind the Sohmer Piano,"
$1.00 (refundable with purchase), 17 pages, color, illustrated.

The Sohmer Piano Company began in 1872 at 14th Street and Third Avenue in New York, and in 1884 Hugo Sohmer developed the first five-foot grand piano, small enough to fit into a living room without sacrificing depth of tone. The catalogue-cum-history shows both grand pianos and console models in walnut, mahogany, cherry, oak, distressed pecan, ebony finish, and antiqued white and gold. Price list on request.
RS

STEINWAY & SONS
Dept. CHC
Steinway Place
Long Island City, NY 11105

Brochures, no charge, color.

The brochures have color photographs of the famous Steinway grand and vertical pianos, with details of length and height, finish, and style number but no prices.
RS

Walnut grand piano, *Steinway*

FLOOR AND WALL COVERINGS

wood paneled living room, *U.S. Plywood*

Patterned hooked rug, *Ethan Allen*

CARPETS AND RUGS

Catalogue cover, *Armstrong Cork*

ETHAN ALLEN, INC.
Dept. CHC
Ethan Allen Drive
Danbury, CT 06810

"The Treasury of Ethan Allen American Traditional Interiors," $7.50 (no charge at showrooms), published every two years, 408 pages, color, illustrated.

A few pages in this huge catalogue from a major home-furnishings manufacturer are devoted to broadloom carpet in a wide range of colors, fibers, and surface finishes, and rugs, some of Oriental inspiration and design and others in both traditional and contemporary styles—American Indian, American Primitive, plaids, stripes, braids, all intended to harmonize and coordinate with Ethan Allen furniture.
RS

ARMSTRONG CORK COMPANY
Dept. CHC
Lancaster, PA 17604

"Carpeting Your Indoor World," no charge, 16 pages, color, illustrated.

A handy guide to man-made carpet fibers and their uses in different areas, with advice on selecting the right carpet color, buying carpet, caring for carpet, and lay-it-yourself carpeting.
RS

E. T. BARWICK INDUSTRIES
Attention Mort Kahn
Dept. CHC
5025 New Peachtree Road
Chamblee, GA 30341

"What You Should Know About Carpet," $1.25, 208 pages, paperback, black and white, illustrated.

Written by Annette Stramesi, the book is a guide to getting value, quality, and fashion in rugs and carpets. There's a brief history of carpets, a glossary of terms, advice on choosing carpet for beauty and practicality and what to use where, and sections on carpet care and cleaning.

BERKSHIRE UNLIMITED
Dept. CHC
472 West Street
Pittsfield, MA 01201

"Handcrafted Rug Catalogue," brochure, no charge, published annually.

Berkshire Unlimited, a private, non-profit workshop, makes two styles of rugs—a loom-woven rag rug made entirely of new cotton cloth and a latch-hooked Rya rug made from 75 percent rayon and 25 percent cotton rug yarn. The Rya rugs come in a rust or gold floral design, measure 20" x 36", cost about $22, and can also be special-ordered. The rag rugs are also available in 34" strips, any length, at $1.65 a square foot.
MO

CAROL BROWN
Dept. CHC
Putney, VT 05346

Leaflet, no charge.

A family-run mail-order business that specializes in interesting fabrics from around the world. They offer a line of linen pile rugs from Belgium in a variety of sizes at modest prices. A 4' x 6' is around $45.
MO

Numdah rugs, *Gurian Fabrics*

Oriental rugs, *Charles W. Jacobsen*

CHAPULIN
Dept. CHC
Route 1, Box 187
Santa Fe, NM 87501

*"Southwestern Primitive Crafts," $1.00,
published every 18 months, 14 pages,
black and white, illustrated.*

Individually handwoven Navajo rugs of
hand-carded and dyed wools in
geometrics, storm patterns from the
Grand Canyon area, or figures of
Navajo dancers (Yeis) in classic colors,
no two exactly alike. The geometrics
start at $100 for a 2' x 3'. Also included
are a group of small wall hangings—a
single Yei figure, 16" x 18", is about $45.
You may order directly or write for
photos of rugs in your size and price
range.
MO

**LAURA COPENHAVER INDUSTRIES,
   INC.**
Dept. CHC
Box 149
Marion, VA 24354

*"Rosemont," 50 cents, published
annually, 31 pages, black and white,
illustrated.*

Every loop in Rosemont hooked rugs is
firmly and closely hooked by hand, not
punched, with no loose ends on the
right side. Some of the rug designs are
taken from those in the Metropolitan
Museum of Art in New York, such as
the charming 27" x 55" "Ring Around
the Rosy," about $65, and the 32" x 60"
"Shulamite Maid," about $83, both in
soft colorings. You can also buy
stamped rug designs ready for hooking,
$15, and handwoven rug hall and stair
carpet to order.
MO

FRAN'S BASKET HOUSE
Dept. CHC
Route 10
Succasunna, NJ 07876

*"Fran's Basket House," 25 cents, 46
pages, black and white, illustrated.*

This vast collection of wicker and rattan
items includes a group of lacy sea grass
rugs in three sizes and three styles. A
six-foot butterfly round is under $25, a
3' x 5' intricately patterned oblong
under $16. They can be reversed for
even wear, left natural, or painted in
brilliant colors with water-base paint.
MO

GURIAN FABRICS, INC.
Dept. CHC
276 Fifth Avenue
New York, NY 10001

*"Exclusive Collection of Hand
Embroidered Crewel and Numdah
Rugs," 50 cents, published biannually,
12 pages, color.*

Gurian offers a small collection of
beautifully embroidered floral Numdah
rugs from India in 3' and 5' rounds and
three sizes of rectangles, ranging in
price from about $5 to $20. As each rug
is hand-decorated with brilliant colors
on a natural wool-and-cotton ground,
no two are exactly alike.
MO

HERCULES INCORPORATED
Dept. CHC
910 Market Street
Wilmington, DE 19899

*"How to Be a Color Schemer," no
charge, updated as needed, 23 pages,
color, illustrated.*

In this brochure carpets are shown
"working their color magic in every
room of your home"—not only on
floors but also to provide a wainscot
effect, to "paper" a bedroom alcove, to
display family photos.

CHARLES W. JACOBSEN, INC.
Dept. CHC
401 South Salina Street
Syracuse, NY 13201

*Folder, no charge, updated weekly,
color, illustrated.*

Detailed information about Oriental
rugs, including new and antique rugs
from Iran, Turkey, India, China, and
elsewhere, and advice on what to look
for when buying. The company will
send rugs on speculation with no
obligation to buy, and a questionnaire
is included to help them select the
right rug for you. The price range is
wide, and price lists and order forms
are included.
MO

Carpet ideas, *Magee Carpet*

Handwoven Indian carpet, *Pande, Cameron*

KARASTAN RUG MILLS
Dept. CHC
919 Third Avenue
New York, NY 10022

"Oriental Design Rug Handbook," 50 cents, 30 pages, published regularly, color, illustrated.

A handbook designed to give consumers basic information that will make them more knowledgeable about Karastan rugs, 15 of which are shown and described. There is information on the background of Oriental rugs and an explanation of their types and names, symbolism and colors.
RS

MAGEE CARPET COMPANY
Dept. CHC
919 Third Avenue
New York, NY 10022

"Decorating Color Ideas That Make Your House a Home," 25 cents, 12 pages, color, illustrated.

Starting with six color families—green, blue, orange, yellow and gold, brown, beige and earth tones, and reds—you are given four choices in each color category based on different carpet and wall-paint colors. One scheme in each group is shown in a completed room. Helpful up to a point, but a lot of necessary information that could be useful to the room planner is missing.

PANDE, CAMERON AND COMPANY OF N.Y., INC.
Dept. CHC
295 Fifth Avenue
New York, NY 10016

Booklet, $1, published every 2 years, 22 pages, color, illustrated.

Shown and described are 17 outstanding designs, recreated by master weavers, of handwoven Indian carpets. Other colors and designs are available, or you may custom-order. Two pages are devoted to the making of the carpets, with black and white photographs.
RS

OMALON ROOM PLANNER
Dept. CHC
P.O. Box 456
Mount Vernon, NY 10551

"Omalon Room Planner," 25 cents, 8 pages, some color, illustrated.

A booklet by a company that makes carpet underlay designed to help you decorate from the floor up. A check list to analyze your family life-style comes first, followed by a brief description, with sketches, of types of furniture, upholstery fabrics, then room planning, starting with carpet color, construction (woven, tufted, knitted), and cushion. A room-planner grid with scaled cutouts of furniture and a guideline check list help you arrange your room. A very useful and compact decorating guide.

Foam carpet underlay, *Omalon*

Contemporary Oriental rug, *Karastan Rug Mills*

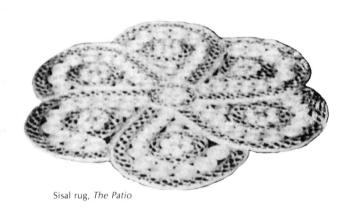

Sisal rug, *The Patio*

Catalogue cover, *Peerless Imported Rugs*

THE PATIO
Dept. CHC
550 Powell Street
San Francisco, CA 94108

"Spring/Summer Sunny Thoughts,"
$1.00, some color, illustrated;
"Fall/Winter San Francisco Gift Book,"
$1.00, some color, illustrated.

The Spring/Summer catalogue has a
nice selection of sisal and straw rugs,
usable year round. The tone-on-tone
natural Tientsin straw 12" squares run
$1.10 a foot, and you can order any
size, even irregular shapes, as squares
can be cut and sewn together. There is
woven sisal carpeting from Taiwan in
several sizes and color choices and
tough, durable handwoven 12" rice-
straw squares from mainland China at
50 cents per square foot. These can also
be ordered in any desired size.
MO

PEERLESS IMPORTED RUGS, INC.
Dept. CHC
3028 North Lincoln Avenue
Chicago, IL 60657

"Peerless Imported Rugs," $1.00,
published biannually, 19 pages, color,
illustrated.

A collection of beautiful modern
Oriental and Indian rugs imported from
England and Europe, made of the finest
wools and cottons in classic colors and
designs—Kerman, Bokhara, Sarouk,
Heriz, Eberstan, to name a few. An
interesting group of boldly patterned,
all-cotton Navajo designs is also
included. All rugs are available in many
sizes. Prices on request.
MO

ROCHE-BOBOIS USA, LTD.
Dept. CHC
200 Madison Avenue
New York, NY 10016

"Roche-Bobois," $5.00, published
annually, 132 pages, color, illustrated,
with 52-page illustrated price list.

An exclusive collection of wool carpets
by painter Kozo are part of the group
of carpets, plain and patterned, narrow
and wide widths. Write for free
estimates, design plans, and additional
samples or, better still, work through
their interior designers.
MO/RS

SOUTHWESTERN CRAFTS, INC.
Dept. CHC
Box 10525
Albuquerque, NM 87114

"Navajo Design Rugs . . . The Newest
Decorator Idea," $1.00, 16 pages, color,
illustrated.

These handsome rugs are handwoven
on the ancient vertical loom from
hand-spun, hand-dyed raw wool. About
30 rugs are shown and described in the
catalogue, with information about the
background of the pattern. Sizes range
from about 30" x 60" to 54" x 77" and
prices from $50 to $400.
MO

Navajo Indian rugs, *Southwestern Crafts*

Hexagonal ceramic tile, *American Olean Tile*

Selection of ceramic tiles, *Country Floors*

CERAMIC TILE

STURBRIDGE YANKEE WORKSHOP
Dept. CHC
Sturbridge, MA 01566

"Sturbridge Yankee Workshop Handbook and Catalogue," 50 cents, 64 pages, some color, illustrated.

If you are looking for handmade braid rugs in beautiful color combinations at sensible prices, look no further than this catalogue. They come in half a dozen sizes, from 21" x 38" (about $25) up to 114" x 162" (about $500), and they are 90 percent wool, reversible, and wear like iron. There are also a few Numdah and Kashmir rugs. A 4' x 3' Kashmir alphabet rug is just $20.
MO

ERNEST TREGANOWAN, INC.
Dept. CHC
306 East 61st Street
New York, NY 10021

"Treganowan Moroccan Rugs," 25 cents, two-page color brochure.

Just a few of the 90 patterns in hand-knotted wool Moroccan rugs that come in a choice of 103 stock colors and many sizes are shown in the brochure. Individual color cards, samples of wool colors, and prices are sent on request for a specific design.
MO/ID

AGENCY TILE, INC.
Dept. CHC
979 Third Avenue
New York, NY 10022

"This is Our World," 50 cents, revised when new designs are made, 15 pages, color, illustrated.

Ceramic floor and wall tiles from all over the world in a wide range of choices, from the brilliant contemporary designs of Franco Pecchioli (circles or squares in hot red on white 8"-square tiles, $3.75 each) to quiet hand-painted traditional designs from the "Jollj" series, which start at about $4.29 per square foot. The tiles illustrated are but a few of the vast collection of ceramic, quarry, and marble tiles in the company's regional showrooms.
MO/RS/ID

Contemporary ceramic tiles, *Agency Tile*

AMERICAN OLEAN TILE COMPANY
Dept. CHC
1000 Cannon Avenue
Lansdale, PA 19446

"Product Catalog Decorating Ideas Booklet," no charge, published annually, 16 pages, color, illustrated.

A rundown on the use of ceramic tile in bathrooms, foyers, living rooms, dining rooms, and kitchens. New products shown are Redi-Set silicone-grouted ceramic tile systems, Caribbean tile in eight hot colors, and new shapes in crystalline-glaze tile. Thirty-six color combinations that coordinate with plumbing-fixture colors are suggested.
RS

ARIUS TILE COMPANY
Dept. CHC
116 Don Gaspar
Santa Fe, NM 87501

"Decorative Tile and Murals," $1.00, (refundable with purchase), 8 pages, color, illustrated.

Mr. and Mrs. Len Goodman have gathered together an interesting collection of tiles for walls, counter, and tabletops. Some designed by Mrs. Goodman, such as the Kachina figures, are framed panels, 22" x 34", ready to hang, about $175. Colorful backgammon boards, 20" square, which can be used alone as a tabletop, cost about $65, with the two dice cups an additional $15. All the tiles are colorful and have some unique designs, such as the Pre-Columbian series. A descriptive price list is enclosed, and designs can be made to your order.
MO

Contemporary ceramic tile floor, *Pomona Tile*

Carillo handmade Mexican ceramic tile, *Elon*

COUNTRY FLOORS, INC.
Dept. CHC
1158 Second Avenue
New York, NY 10021

"Country Floors," 50 cents, published every three years, 20 pages, color, illustrated.

A handsome and varied collection of American-made and imported wall and floor tiles. Especially noteworthy are the handmade or hand-molded terra-cotta floor tiles from Mexico and France, decorative Mediterranean patterns in floor tiles from Italy, brilliant glazed floor tiles from America. While mail-order is hardly the ideal way to buy heavy items like tiles, it is the only answer in most parts of the United States if you wish some range of choice. The price list includes dimensions and weight of each tile.
MO/RS/ID

ELON INCORPORATED
Dept. CHC
964 Third Avenue
New York, NY 10022

"Carrillo Tile Handmade in Mexico," no charge, 15 pages, published annually, color, illustrated.

Rustic handmade or hand-molded plain or decorated terra-cotta tiles for floors, walls, and countertops. Unglazed terra-cotta or chocolate tiles in 4", 6", 8", 10", or 12" squares sell for $3.35 a square foot, precast decorated floor tiles, 4" square, for about $6.75 a square foot. The decorated tiles have charming provincial motifs such as fruit, flowers, or sunbursts. Standard or custom trim to coordinate with all tiles is available too.
MO/ID

POMONA TILE
Dept. CHC
P.O. Box 2249
Pomona, CA 91766

"Step into the All-Tile House," no charge, color folders, illustrated.

How ceramic tile can be used throughout the house to accent a wall, create a dramatic foyer, a worry-proof kitchen, and a work-proof bathroom. The brochure shows the choice of colors, shapes, and designs, including textured and sculptured tiles. In Redi-Set systems, each sheet contains about 16 factory-grouted glazed tiles.
RS/ID

TILE COUNCIL OF AMERICA, INC.
Dept. CHC
P.O. Box 2222
Princeton, NJ 08540

"Ceramic Tile Makes a Lot of Sense in a Lot of Rooms Besides the Bath," no charge, 12 pages, color, illustrated.

Many suggestions for places and ways ceramic tile can be used—on walls; on floors; in recesses; to frame windows and doors; as tabletops, baseboards, and ceiling borders. The versatility and durability of ceramic tile is cleverly illustrated.
RS

Counter tops and backsplash, Americana collection of ceramic
Tile Council of America

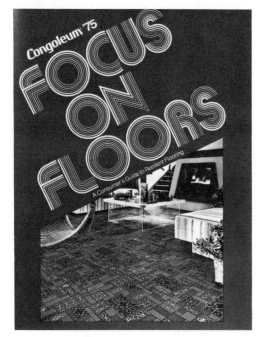

Catalogue cover, *Congoleum Industries*

VINYL

Patterned vinyl flooring, *National Floor Products*

ARMSTRONG CORK COMPANY
Dept. CHC
Lancaster, PA 17604

"Step Out in Style," no charge, color,
illustrated.

A guide to resilient flooring, sheet
materials, and tile, which comes in
hundreds of designs and colors, with a
chart for those you can install yourself.
RS

CONGOLEUM INDUSTRIES, INC.
Dept. CHC
195 Belgrove Drive
Kearny, NJ 07032

*"Focus on Floors: A Consumer's Guide
to Resilient Flooring,"* 50 cents,
published annually, 15 pages, color,
illustrated.

The focus of the booklet is
Congoleum's shiny vinyl no-wax
flooring that brings durable color and
practicality to kitchens, dining rooms,
family rooms, and so on. Other
furnishings are discussed and
decorating ideas given. The last four
pages are devoted to facts about
flooring, value, cost, care, prevention of
problems, with a quick pricing table.
RS

THE FLINTKOTE COMPANY
Dept. CHC
480 Central Avenue
East Rutherford, NJ 07073

"Floors, All Styles," no charge,
published annually, 28 pages, color,
illustrated.

The latest patterns, styles, and colors in
Peel-and-Stick or regular non-adhesive-
backed vinyl floor tiles are shown,
some in room settings that suggest uses
other than floors. Some patterns have a
Mediterranean feeling; others resemble
parquet, slate, brick, or travertine.
Information on ordering, installation,
maintenance, and warranty is included,
as well as some of the maintenance
products.
RS

MANNINGTON MILLS, INC.
Dept. CHC
Mannington Road
Salem, NJ 08079

*"The Most Colorful Floor Shows in
Town,"* no charge, published annually,
color, illustrated.

Patterned sheet vinyl floor coverings are
shown in room settings with color
insets of each pattern to provide a
quick guide to the various styles and
most popular color combinations. This
flooring never needs waxing or special
care. The sheets come in 6' or 12'
widths.
RS

**NATIONAL FLOOR PRODUCTS
COMPANY, INC.**
Dept. CHC
P.O. Box 354
Florence, AL 35630

"Supreme Vinyl Flooring," 50 cents, 33
pages, color, illustrated.

The catalogue shows the wide range of
styles and prices in sheet vinyl, solid
vinyl tile, vinyl asbestos tile, and other
resilient floor coverings. Various styles
and designs are shown in room
settings, with insets of color choices.
Detailed specifications and a list of
distributors are given.
RS

Catalogue cover, *Mannington Mills*

Prefinished parquet flooring, *Bruce Floors*

Catalogue cover, *Hoboken Wood Floors*

WOOD

METAL

BRUCE FLOORS
Dept. CHC
Box 397
Memphis, TN 38101

"Bruce Hardwood Floors," 25 cents, 16 pages, color, illustrated.

A handsome catalogue showing the complete line of Bruce hardwood floors in room settings. There are prefinished parquet designs in many shades of oak and pecan, herringbone blocks, teak in mosaic pattern, random and alternate-width planking, and strip oak with beveled ends and sides. Of interest to apartment dwellers are the low-noise laminated oak blocks with sound-absorbing polyethylene foam padding on the back. For prices consult list of dealers supplied by Bruce.
RS

DESIGNED WOOD FLOORING CENTER
Dept. CHC
940 Third Avenue
New York, NY 10022

"Custom Designed Wood Floors in Unlimited Patterns," 50 cents (refundable with purchase), published annually, 10 pages, color, illustrated.

Exotic woods from Thailand—teak and karpawood—are combined in interesting and unusual designs such as finger mosaic or basket weave, swirl or foursquare, diamond or double herringbone, to create exciting floors. There are also preassembled designs such as the miniature herringbone, 9" x 9" paper-faced sections in combinations of teak, karpawood, oak, and walnut that must be sanded and finished. Preassembled ornamental borders are also available. Prices on request.
MO/ID

HOBOKEN WOOD FLOORS
Dept. CHC
100 Willow Street
East Rutherford, NJ 07073

"Custom Design Wood Floors," $1.00, 12 pages, color, illustrated.

Color illustrations of ideas for every room in the house, using all types of wood flooring. Ten different rooms are shown, with a surrounding wheel of eight different choices of suitable wood flooring, parquet, herringbone, domino, block, plank among them. Wood-tone finishes and designer colors are also suggested.
RS

BARNEY BRAINUM-SHANKER STEEL COMPANY
Dept. CHC
70-32 83rd Street
Glendale, NY 11227

"Artistic Decorations in Sheet Steel," no charge, black and white, illustrated.

"Tin ceilings" were all the rage in the 19th century, and they have now been copied in decorative repoussé plates of sheet steel for walls as well as ceilings. The plates come in sizes from 3" to 24" in 18 different patterns. Prices on request.
MO/ID

Repoussé sheet steel plates on walls, *Barney Brainum-Shanker Steel* (courtesy *Celanese*)

Paint-by-the-numbers mural, *Double M Marketing*

Woodland supergraphic, *Environmental Graphics*

MIRROR   MURALS

PPG INDUSTRIES, INC.
Dept. CHC
One Gateway Center
Pittsburgh, PA 15222

"All American Homes," no charge, published every three years, 39 pages, color, illustrated.

Mirrored walls are one of the best and most traditional ways to expand space visually. This booklet is loaded with ideas for ways to use mirrors on walls, doors, as dividers, shields, and reflectors.
RS

DOUBLE M MARKETING COMPANY, INC.
Dept. CHC
P.O. Box 8500
Fountain Valley, CA 92708

"Magic Mural," 35 cents, 32 pages, updated as needed, color, illustrated.

You become the artist and decorator with magic mural paint-by-the-number kits. There are mural designs to fit any wall space and decorating scheme, from mini-murals a mere 8" wide to giant panoramic murals nearly 12' wide, in more than 100 different color combinations. All the murals are illustrated and specifications given, and the prices of the kits, which include a numbered pattern, paints in numbered containers, and brushes, range from $2.95 to $49.95.
MO

ENVIRONMENTAL GRAPHICS, INC.
Dept. CHC
1117 Vicksburg Lane North
Wayzata, MN 55391

"Environmental Graphics," $1.00, published annually, 32 pages, color, illustrated.

For the utmost in supergraphics, this catalogue can fill any bill from a tropical garden to a cloud-filled blue sky to an outsized Art Deco design. Each supergraphic is shown in a room setting, and overall dimensions, colors, and prices are given. For instance, the Art Deco comes in black/silver/burgundy, is 8' 9" high x 20' 6" wide, and costs about $125. A list of cross-country dealers is provided. You can hang it yourself, as each graphic comes with complete instructions.
MO/RS

THE GALLERY
Dept. CHC
Amsterdam, NY 12010

"The Gallery," no charge, 32 pages, some color, illustrated.

Two photo-murals—one a woodland scene, the other a landscape of fields and mountains—come in eight giant sections to fit walls up to 12' 9" x 9'. They are easily installed, have washable lacquered surfaces, and glue and step-by-step instructions are included, all for $49.95.
MO

Textured striped grasscloth, *Shibui Wallcoverings*

Brochure cover, *Celanese Coatings*

NATURAL MATERIALS

PAINT

SHIBUI WALLCOVERINGS
Dept. CHC
P.O. Box 1268
Santa Rosa, CA 95403

Samples, 50 cents.

Exotic grasscloths and cork in colors and textures for traditional and contemporary decorating schemes are the samples sent to you for selection. These beautiful wallcoverings have the added bonus of acting as sound softeners, an advantage for apartment dwellers. Complete do-it-yourself instructions are furnished with your order.
MO

CELANESE COATINGS COMPANY
Dept. CHC
Box 1863
Louisville, KY 40201

"Historic Charleston," folder, no charge, black and white, color chart, illustrated.

If you want historically accurate wall colors for your traditional house, this folder by Devoe, the official paint for Historic Charleston restorations, includes a color chart of all the interior and exterior paint colors, some shown in settings, along with a brief history of the city. There are also lists of the types of paint available and a cross-country dealer list.
RS

COTTER & COMPANY
Dept. CHC
Chicago, IL 60614

"Let's Live Color," 50 cents, 32 pages, color, illustrated.

The booklet is loaded with ideas to help you color-plan your rooms and liven up your life, using the brilliant colors of Tru-Test paints. By bringing color into your rooms with paint you can dramatize your walls with red, beautify them with blue, or calm both colors with green.
RS

CRAFT HOUSE
Dept. CHC
Colonial Williamsburg Foundation
Williamsburg, VA 23185

"Williamsburg Reproductions—Interior Designs for Today's Living," $2.95, 232 pages, black and white and color, illustrated.

At the back of this huge catalogue of the furnishings reproduced for the Colonial Williamsburg restoration is an insert with color chart showing the authentic Colonial interior and exterior paint colors reproduced by the Martin-Senour company and sold by its dealers throughout the country. These are the only paints matched to the specimens in Williamsburg and approved by the Williamsburg Restoration. For mail-order sales there is a price list with shipping charges per gallon and quart.
MO/RS

Brochure cover, Williamsburg paint colors, *Craft House*

Flags of Early America wallcovering, *Jack Denst Designs*

PAPER AND VINYL

ETHAN ALLEN, INC.
Dept. CHC
Ethan Allen Drive
Danbury, CT 06810

"The Treasury of Ethan Allen American Traditional Interiors," $7.50 (no charge at showrooms), published every two years, 408 pages, color, illustrated.

In this huge furniture catalogue-cum-decorating idea book is one page of wallcoverings by J. Josephson, sold through the Ethan Allen Home Fashion Centers, in traditional and contemporary patterns color-compatible with the drapery and upholstery fabrics and rugs that are part of this vast home-furnishings collection.
RS

CLOPAY CORPORATION
Housewares Division
Dept. CHC
Clopay Square
Cincinnati, OH 45214

"Decorative Coverings Idea Book," $1.00, 29 pages, color, illustrated.

Unusual ways to decorate indoors and out with Clopay self-adhesive decorative coverings that come in patterns from wet-look vinyls to suedelike, flocked designs in a wide range of colors. Ideas include supersized graphics for walls, ways to revitalize old rooms and furniture, games, crafts, and special occasions, with pages of illustrated how-to's and decorator tips.
RS

CRAFT HOUSE
Dept. CHC
Colonial Williamsburg Foundation
Williamsburg, VA 23185

"Williamsburg Reproductions—Interior Designs for Today's Living," $2.95, 232 pages, black and white and color, illustrated.

Copies of Colonial Williamsburg's rare documentary prints in wallpapers, reproduced by Katzenbach and Warren, are shown in color and black and white in a ten-page section of the catalogue. Many of them derive from 18th-century wallpaper fragments discovered on the walls of the old buildings; others are based on antique textiles from the Williamsburg collection. They range from a simple tavern check and multistripe to a delightful aviary print and a stunningly beautiful adaptation of the hand-painted antique Chinese wallpaper in the Governor's Palace supper room. Prices listed per roll include shipping charges within the continental United States. Price range is from about $6 a roll up, and a large wallpaper catalogue will be sent on loan for a $6 deposit (refundable if returned within 30 days) plus mailing charge.
MO/RS/ID

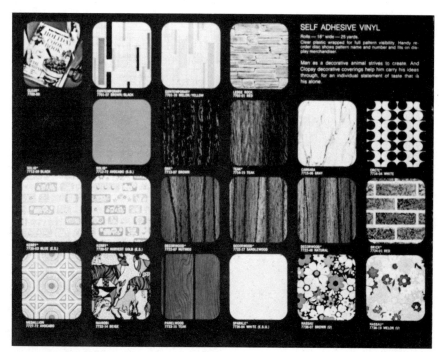

Vinyl wallcoverings, *Clopay*

Prepasted, scrubbable, strippable vinyls, *Imperial Wallcoverings*

Patterned vinyl wallcoverings, *General Tire and Rubber*

THE JACK DENST DESIGNS, INC.
Dept. CHC
7355 South Exchange Avenue
Chicago, IL 60649

"The Great American Happy Birthday Book," 50 cents, limited edition, 16 pages, color, illustrated.

A fascinating collection of Americana designs for walls and ceilings in vinyl and paper, sold as murals, panels, and by the roll. To celebrate the Bicentennial there's a large-scale mural of "The Star-Spangled Banner," with black or red notes on a white ground and a star-spangled flag kit in two designs—white stars on blue ground, red and white stripes, or both on shiny Mylar—and some simpler traditional American motifs with a more formal look. Prices are on request or through your interior designer.
RS/ID

THE GENERAL TIRE AND RUBBER COMPANY
Dept. CHC
P.O. Box 951
Akron, OH 44329

"Decorator Six Pack," $1.00, six booklets, color, illustrated.

The booklets describe and show ways to use vinyl wallcoverings all over the house. Three of the booklets deal with bathrooms, kitchens, and bedrooms. Of the remaining three, "Other Places, Other Rooms" covers various rooms in apartment or house. "Color It You" concentrates on the use of color, and "The Hang of It" is a guide to measuring, preparing walls, and hanging the wallcoverings.
RS

IMPERIAL WALLCOVERINGS
Dept. CHC
23645 Mercantile Road
Cleveland, OH 44122

"Secrets That Decorators Don't Always Tell You About Wallcoverings," 75 cents, 35 pages, color, illustrated.

Among the "secrets," the best-kept one is how to hang wallcoverings yourself, using the prepasted and pretrimmed Imperial papers, and save money. Another secret—how to liberate yourself from "landlord-white" walls with strippable papers from Imperial—is of special value to renters. The booklet is crammed with home decorating ideas that involve the many patterns in wallcoverings from this famous company. Also included are complete instructions on hanging prepasted wallcoverings, with an alternate method for the unpasted type, how to line problem walls before papering, decorating do's and don'ts, and a wallcovering estimate chart for walls, ceiling, and borders.
RS

THOMAS STRAHAN COMPANY
Dept. CHC
150 Heard Street
Chelsea, MA 02150

"Wallcovering Information Kit," 50 cents, three booklets, some color.

"Wallcoverings: It All Started Here" is a 12-page booklet intended to enhance your pleasure in selecting wallcoverings and clear up some of the misconceptions about them. It tells you what you can do at home before going out to shop for wallcoverings, how your dealer can help you, and what you should look for when making a selection. A glossary of the various types of wallcoverings is included, a chart of categories the Strahan wallcoverings come in—screen-printed, vinyl acrylic, vinyl-coated, scrubbable, strippable, etc.—and whether there is a correlated fabric. The second booklet, "The Strahan Spirit of 1776," is a Bicentennial brochure with background and color illustrations of historic wallcovering reproductions. The third booklet, "Think Wallcoverings," is put out by the Wallcovering Industry Bureau and covers color schemes, patterns, and styles in wallcoverings.
RS/ID

"But it looks so different on the wall."
How to take the "surprises" out of selecting a wallcovering.

New ideas in wallcoverings — what to use where and how to approach color scheming and pattern selection as well as an explanation of the different types, textures and uses of wallcoverings.

Three booklet covers, *Thomas Strahan*

Simulated fieldstone, *Z-Brick*

SIMULATED BRICK AND STONE

WOOD AND PANELING

Paneled room, *Architectural Paneling*

CRAFT HOUSE
Dept. CHC
Colonial Williamsburg Foundation
Williamsburg, VA 23185

"Williamsburg Reproductions—Interior Designs for Today's Living," $2.95, 232 pages, color and black and white, illustrated.

Delft tiles with typical designs in cobalt blue on white, copied from those used as a facing for the fireplace in the northeast bedroom of the Governor's Palace at Colonial Williamsburg, might be used to tile kitchen, bathroom, or patio walls, or as tabletops. They cost $6.70 each, or $34.50 for a set of six. The tiles are 5¼" square and come in 12 different designs.
MO

Z-BRICK COMPANY, DIVISION VMC
CORPORATION
Dept. CHC
2834 N.W. Market Street
Seattle, WA 98107

"Decorative Brick and Stone Wall Covering," folder, no charge.

A brochure of simulated antique brick, country-rustic brick, and fieldstone wallcoverings, all imitation but of good quality, with pictorial installation instructions. Available only through dealers, a list of whom in the buyer's area will be furnished on request.
RS

ARCHITECTURAL PANELING
Dept. CHC
969 Third Avenue
New York, NY 10022

"Architectural Paneling," no charge, black and white, illustrated.

The folder illustrates typical Louis XIV, Louis XV, Louis XVI, and Régence paneling with hand-rubbed finishes. The walls are specifically designed for your room and can be installed anywhere in the U.S. Prices on request.
MO/ID

BRUCE FLOORS
Dept. CHC
Box 397
Memphis, TN 38101

"Bruce Hardwood Floors," 25 cents, 16 pages, color, illustrated.

In addition to the hardwood floors (the plank and block styles also make excellent walls), the catalogue has a page on handsome solid wood prefinished wall planking, 3/4" thick, offered in pecan, elm, or oak and widths from 2" to 6". All are prefinished, waxed, and ready to install.
RS

CALIFORNIA REDWOOD
ASSOCIATION
Dept. CHC
617 Montgomery Street
San Francisco, CA 94111

"Redwood Interiors" and *"Redwood Interior Guide,"* no charge, published periodically, color, illustrated.

Redwood's adaptability to formal or informal, traditional or contemporary living is emphasized in "Redwood Interiors," which shows a variety of possible effects and gives ideas and suggestions for the use of various tones, textures, patterns, and grains. There are several pages covering and illustrating surfaces, grains, finishes, and special color effects, with rules for interior finishing. "The Redwood Interior Guide" has more technical information on grades, moisture content, installation, and so on.
RS

Catalogue cover, *California Redwood Association*

Printed plywood paneling, *Evans Products*

Ranchero plywood paneling, *U.S. Plywood*

EVANS PRODUCTS COMPANY
Dept. CHC
1121 Southwest Salmon Street
Portland, OR 97205

"Evans Remodeling Paneling Decorating Ideas," 25 cents, 35 pages, black and white, illustrated.

A booklet designed to point out how you can personalize your home with color through the use of Bright-Ons (plywood panels, ready-cut and colored, to nail or glue on existing walls). Six pages show decorative uses of Evans Bright-Ons in *House & Garden* colors for every room in the house. A special directory lists the many manufacturers who match their merchandise to the 36 *House & Garden* colors.
RS

GARGOYLES, LTD.
Dept. CHC
512 South 3rd Street
Philadelphia, PA 19174

"Gargoyles, Ltd," $4.00 (refundable with purchase), updated monthly, 32 pages, some color, illustrated.

Paneling and carved appointments in mahogany, oak, walnut, and pine, salvaged from grand mansions, range from whole rooms to single panels and wainscoting. You are invited to send measurements of your room and the style you are looking for (Georgian, Louis XVI, etc.), and if they have something suitable they'll send you a description, photos (charge refundable with purchase), and price.
MO

GEORGIA-PACIFIC CORPORATION
Dept. CHC
900 S.W. Fifth Avenue
Portland, OR 97204

"The Great American Look in Paneling," 25 cents, 29 pages, color, illustrated.

Six colorful folders featuring prefinished plywood wall paneling in every room in the house give a glimpse of American ways of life in various sections of the country. The different paneling styles are named for areas such as the Oregon Trail, Valley Forge, Portsmouth, and the like. A how-to-install section is part of the package.
RS

MARLITE
Division of Masonite Corp.
Dept. CHC
Dover, OH 44622

"Marlite Guide to Beautiful Interiors," no charge, 11 pages, color.

This is an illustrated brochure of Marlite, the trade name for decorative interior wall panels and planks in over 70 colors and wood tones, designs, and surfaces. New on the scene are two kits, "A Complete Bath-in-a-Box" tub recess kit and "A Complete Package for Tub-Area Remodeling," designed for do-it-yourself installation. There is a regional listing of sales offices and warehouses for further information and prices.
RS

U. S. PLYWOOD
Dept. CHC
Box 61
New York, NY 10046

"All About Wall Paneling," 50 cents, 27 pages, color, illustrated.

The catalogue shows 26 ways to decorate with wood paneling, has 50 illustrations, a handy color guide, a paneling planning chart, instructions and diagrams for installing paneling, different types of moldings available, and a selection index that gives name, type, description, and colors of U. S. Plywood's paneling.
RS

Catalogue cover, *Marlite*

Ready-made bedroom ensemble, *Nettle Creek*

BEDDING, CURTAINS, FABRICS, AND WINDOW TREATMENTS

Handmade quilt, hand-tied fishnet canopy, *Laura Copenhaver*

Custom-made sheet ensemble, *Chrisalem*

BEDDING AND QUILTS

ETHAN ALLEN, INC.
Dept. CHC
Ethan Allen Drive
Danbury, CT 06810

"The Treasury of Ethan Allen American Traditional Interiors," $7.50 (no charge at showrooms), published every two years, 408 pages, color, illustrated.

The catalogue has an array of bedspreads, all with matching drapery fabrics, valances, some with matching wallcoverings. There are floral designs, stripes with overprints, tone on tone damasks, some fully quilted, in natural and manmade fabrics.
RS

BETTER SLEEP, INC.
Dept. CHC
New Providence, NJ 07974

"Better Sleep Catalogue," no charge, published semiannually, 24 pages, black and white, illustrated.

The catalogue is filled with suggestions and gadgets for greater comfort in bed and for better sleep, among them sleep hints, special pillows and back rests, blanket supports, and masks (anti-snore and anti-light).
MO

CAROLINA STUDIOS
Dept. CHC
P.O. Box 191
Southern Pines, NC 28387

"Carolina Studios," $1.00, 10 pages, color, illustrated, samples included.

Carolina Studios will quilt your fabric from a design of your choice. They also can supply hundreds of fabrics of different kinds in almost any color you might desire and will make draperies, tie backs, and valances. Each custom-made spread has an attached signature label.
MO

CHRISALEM
Dept. CHC
2159 Charlton Road
Village of Sunfish Lake, MN 55118

Samples sent on request, $1.00 (refundable with order).

Design your own set of sheets, pillowcases, and blanket covers from over three dozen swatches in ten colors of nylon crepeset trimmed in embroidered sheer or lace. A price list suggests various styles and combinations. Custom designing enables Chrisalem to fit any size bed.
MO

CHURCHILL WEAVERS, INC.
Dept. CHC
Box 30
Berea, KY 40403

"Churchill Weavers Handwoven Throws," 50 cents, 6 pages, color.

Handwoven, all-wool throws in many colors and designs—plaid, overplaid, houndstooth, solids—all 50" x 70" except the new Bicentennial "Rebecca Boone Carriage Throw," adapted from a Colonial design, which is 34" x 48". Prices on request.
MO

Rebecca Boone carriage throw, *Churchill Weavers*

Hand-loomed honeycomb bedspread, hand-tied fishnet canopy, *Virginia Goodwin*

LAURA COPENHAVER INDUSTRIES, INC.
Dept. CHC
Box 149
Marion, VA 24354

"Rosemont," 50 cents, 31 pages, published annually, black and white, illustrated.

The Rosemont craftsmen are best known for beautiful handmade quilts, coverlets, and hand-tied fishnet canopies. The quilts can be made in any size or combination of colors to blend with your decorating scheme. The "Virginia Beauty" quilt, primitive and gay, usually with turkey-red, yellow, and green on white, costs about $250 for twin and double sizes. The coverlets are made almost exactly like the old ones with handmade hems and fringes, in one or two colors, depending on design, in cotton or wool and cotton. The most unusual one, the "Lovers Knot" with pine-tree border, 90" x 108", sells for about $85 and comes in indigo or Delft blue or in combinations with red or rose. The fishnet canopies are made to order in four designs for straight or curved testers. Rosemont craftsmen also make to order bed petticoats of hand-hemmed muslin with or without fringe, 18" deep, starting at about $3.25 per yard; curtains of panels of coverlet fabric or of natural or white muslin or natural basket weave (samples are enclosed with catalogue); blanket covers and hand-tied fringes.
MO

CRAFT HOUSE
Dept. CHC
Colonial Williamsburg Foundation
Williamsburg, VA 23185

"Williamsburg Reproductions—Interior Designs for Today's Living," $2.95, 232 pages, color and black and white, completely illustrated.

Three beautiful bedspreads in different fabrics and a wide selection of contemporary colors have been reproduced for Craft House by Bates Fabrics Inc. There's the Lafayette Resist with a design of stylized pomegranates and acanthus leaves; the white 100 percent cotton William and Mary spread, a copy of a late 17th-century quilted coverlet that combines mythological birds and animals with leaf and plant motifs; and the Wythe House bedspread, which suggests the overshot patterns popular in the 18th and 19th centuries. Prices range from under $40 for the twin-size Lafayette Resist to over $100 for the double-size William and Mary. Color samples of the bedspreads are available on request, with a 50-cent deposit requested for each pattern, refunded when samples are returned.
MO/RS

VIRGINIA GOODWIN
Dept. CHC
Box 3603
Charlotte, NC 28203

Brochure of leaflets, 25 cents, black and white, illustrated.

Weavers since 1812, the Goodwin family continues the tradition of craftsmanship using antique patterns and handmade antique looms to create elaborate fishnet canopies, woven bedspreads, afghans, and tablecloths to your order. In addition to this brochure, which includes measuring and laundering instructions, the weavers will supply customers with swatches (to be returned, of course) and other pertinent information on request.
MO

GREEK ISLAND LTD.
Dept. CHC
215 East 49th Street
New York, NY 10017

"Greek Island Ltd.," no charge, published annually, 39 pages, black and white, illustrated.

Although Greek Island Ltd. is primarily a showcase for handmade Greek fashions, it does offer unusual wool bedspreads from Mykonos, full size, 80" x 112", for $85, and a beige-and-white seersuckery stripe spread with hand-knotted edging on all sides, 65" x 120", for $45.
MO

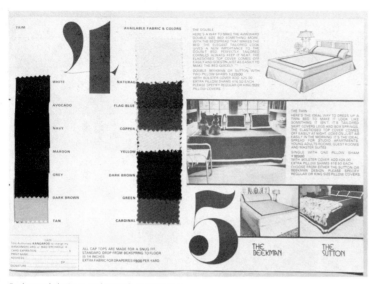

Bedspread designs and swatches, *Kangaroo*

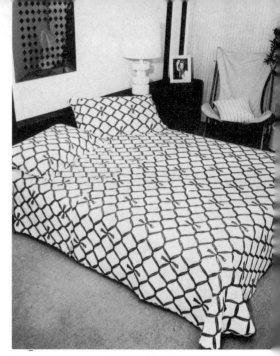

Unusual printed percale sheets, *Pratesi*

GURIAN FABRICS, INC.
Dept. CHC
276 Fifth Avenue
New York, NY 10001

"Exclusive Collection of Hand Embroidered Crewel and Numdah Rugs," 50 cents, published biannually, 12 pages, color.

In addition to their Numdah rugs, Gurian has four sizes of multicolored ready-made crewel bedspreads, priced from $70 to $100, two crewel pillow covers, 12½" round or square (multicolor on natural ground), for $7 and one crewel chair seat cover, 24" square, $10.
MO

KANGAROO
Dept. CHC
269 Green Street
San Francisco, CA 94133

"Introducing the Bedspread That Makes the Bed," $3.00 (refundable with purchase), updated periodically as new designs are developed, 5 pages with fabric swatches, black and white, illustrated.

Kangaroo, a new company, has five designs in tailored bedspreads with kick-pleated skirts and separate tops with elasticized corners to slip on and off easily. The spreads are made for king, queen, double, or twin beds. Matching pillow shams and bolster covers are available. The catalogue includes all designs, swatches of available fabrics in a choice of seven colors and trims.
MO

NETTLE CREEK INDUSTRIES
Dept. CHC
95 Madison Avenue
New York, NY 10016

"Beautiful Rooms," $1.00, 65 pages, color, illustrated.

Decorating the Nettle Creek way starts with a large collection of fashion fabrics—silks, velvets, damasks, tweeds, prints—all color-coordinated to harmonize with each other. There is a Nettle Creek fabric for almost every decorating style and period, and the catalogue pictures rooms in which the fabric sets the mood. Prints and solids and accent colors are combined in bedspreads, furniture, draperies, studio couches, wallcoverings. Included are decorating tips, tips about quilting, and accessories.
RS/ID

PRATESI
Dept. CHC
829 Madison Avenue
New York, NY 10021

"Pratesi," $3.00, 24 pages, color, illustrated.

A catalogue of stunning designs for bed and bath from this famous Milanese house. Beautiful printed percale sheets in unusual colors and patterns and printed or embroidered deluxe-quality terry towels are among the expensive, luxurious items offered. There are also seamless cotton brocade tablecloths and napkins in an array of colors. A price list with sizes available is included.
MO

Ready-made crewel bedspread, *Gurian Fabrics*

Hand-stitched quilt, *The Quiltery*

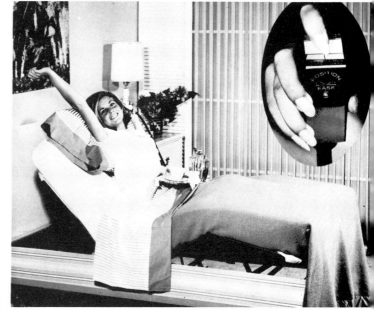

Electrically adjustable bed, *Wuensch*

THE QUILTERY
Dept. CHC
Box 280, RD 1
Barto, PA 19504

Color illustrations of heirloom quilts, 50 cents.

The cards are photographs of heirloom quilts delicately hand-stitched by Mennonite craftswomen—patched, embroidered, or appliquéd in all colors, patterns, and sizes. The Quiltery will match your wallpaper samples or color swatches or make special things such as chair seats or cornice covers to match your quilt. Order form with quilt patterns and prices included. Wide price range.
MO

SCANDO DUO, INC.
Dept. CHC
518–181 Avenue N.
Seattle, WA 98121

"Worldwide Bedding Shop," $1.00 (refundable with purchase), published annually, 64 pages, color, illustrated.

A collection of bedding from Europe and around the world: comforters, handmade (appliqué) spreads, quilts, pillows, comfort covers. Send Scando Duo your sheets and they'll custom-sew a Scandia Down sheetcase for you.
MO

VERMONT FAIR
Dept. CHC
P.O. Box 338
Brattleboro, VT 05301

"Vermont Fair," no charge, 30 pages, color, illustrated.

The catalogue of this 90-year-old Vermont store shows locally made items—furniture, foods, quilts, and pillows for the home. The quilts are handmade by Whitney Mason Germon, the great-granddaughter of one of the founders of the store. Two styles of quilt are offered, one called Indian Summer in varied shades of red, brown, beige, and pumpkin squares, 65" x 102" for $195, or 88" x 102" for $235, and the reversible Plantation Calico in red, blue, or gray with matching solid-color back and binding, $180 for the 65" x 100", $220 for the 80" x 100". Crib quilts in charming "Carnival" or "Balloon Tender" patterns are $100. Quilted pillows in four patterns are $14.95 to $32.50, depending on size and design.
MO

PATRICIA WING, LTD.
Dept. CHC
Birdwood
Mathews, VA 23109

Brochure, $1.00 (refundable with purchase), published periodically.

In addition to original, reversible, hand-quilted, velvet-trimmed quilts, made with shams and pillows to match, Patricia Wing, designer of the first velvet-framed, linen-backed pillow, also has pillows for every room and interest—with designs of birds, hunting prints, botanical prints, and so on. Prices range from $25 for an 18" x 18" pillow to $150 for a 26" x 32" floor cushion.
MO

WUENSCH
Dept. CHC
33 Halsted Street on the Plaza
East Orange, NJ 07018

"Relief from Pain and Insomnia Without Drugs," no charge, 16 pages, black and white, illustrated.

1,001 tested devices to relieve pains, aches, tension, and discomfort. The items are shown, described, and priced. Bath aids, headwarmers, bedboards, pillows of all kinds, also BarcaLoungers in various designs. Order form included. Average prices.
MO

Catalogue cover, *Scando Duo*

CURTAINS AND FABRICS

ETHAN ALLEN, INC.
Dept. CHC
Ethan Allen Drive
Danbury, CT 06810

"The Treasury of Ethan Allen American Traditional Interiors," $7.50 (no charge at showrooms), published every two years, 408 pages, color, illustrated.

Ethan Allen offers a vast selection of curtain fabrics, colors, and textures, all correlated with their floor coverings and upholstery fabrics, and their Home Planners will suggest curtains to suit any size and shape of window.
RS

CAROL BROWN
Dept. CHC
Putney, VT 05346

Leaflet, no charge.

Aunt and nephew run this family mail-order business that offers Irish tweeds from the Avoca handweavers in Wicklow and The Weavers' Shed in Dublin. In addition to many types of clothes, there are richly colored blankets, heavy unbleached yarn for upholstery, and cottons from India, Hawaii, Finland, Malaysia in yard goods or bedspreads at moderate prices. Carol Brown is a small business, so any delay in reply to inquiries may indicate a rush of mail, a broken arm, or even a family vacation. Be patient. It's worth it.
MO

CENTRAL/SHIPPEE, INC.
Dept. CHC
24 West 25th Street
New York, NY 10010

"Felt Colors and Textures," three different swatchbooks, no charge.

"The Felt People" claim to have the biggest color assortment in America. Prices are according to fiber, grade, and weight. Minimum order is three yards.
MO

LAURA COPENHAVER INDUSTRIES, INC.
Dept. CHC
Box 149
Marion, VA 24354

"Rosemont," 50 cents, published annually, 31 pages, black and white, illustrated.

Traditional mountain crafts are encouraged and directed from the Rosemont home. The curtains come in a choice of four fabrics (samples are enclosed): heavy solid weave, basket weave, natural color, or white muslin. You can design your own curtains, combining any of the fabrics and hand-tied fringe. By the yard, material is wool and cotton or cotton only, in one or two colors on the white warp, and in old English or Early American designs, 19" widths. Price list and samples are enclosed.
MO

COUNTRY CURTAINS
Dept. CHC
Stockbridge, MA 01262

"Country Curtains," no charge, 39 pages, black and white, illustrated.

The catalogue emphasizes country charm with unbleached or white muslin shams, dust ruffles, and canopy covers in the crisp, fresh tradition of Colonial New England. The country curtains come with all kinds of fringes: ball, tassel, short-knotted, old-fashioned, or bedspread. Also available are crochet-type edging, pompom trim, Irish lace ruffles. The curtains may be ordered in cotton muslin, perma-press, lawn, dotted swiss, organdy, and gingham—in tiers or tie backs. Some floral prints are also illustrated. Order blank, specifications, and prices are included.
MO

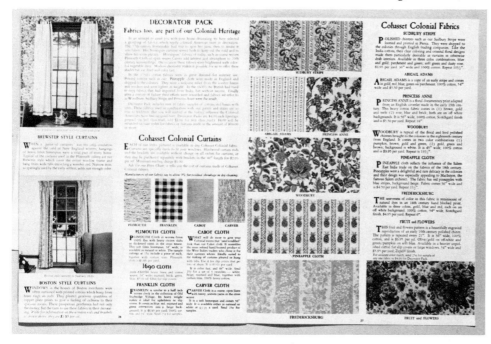

Chintzes, other fabrics, and
window treatments, *Hagerty*

CRAFT HOUSE
Dept. CHC
Colonial Williamsburg Foundation
Williamsburg, VA 23185

*"Williamsburg Reproductions—Interior
Designs for Today's Living," $2.95, 232
pages, color and black and white,
completely illustrated.*

More than 45 different patterns in some
250 color variations make up the
collection of Williamsburg Fabrics
produced exclusively for Craft House
by F. Schumacher and Company. The
majority are reproductions of antique
textiles used in Colonial Williamsburg;
some are commemorative patterns. The
range is wide, from simple floral
printed cottons, liner stripes and checks
to lush silk damasks and a delightful
toile de Jouy copy. Many of the fabrics
have coordinated wallpapers by
Katzenbach and Warren. Samples are
available on request for a small deposit,
refundable when the samples are
returned. Prices for the fabrics range
from $8 to $116 per yard. In the fabrics,
bedspreads, and wallcoverings section
of the catalogue are sketches of
Williamsburg window treatments, with
a window-measuring chart, typical
valance designs, and bed treatments.
MO/RS/ID

EXOTIC THAI SILKS
Dept. CHC
393 Main Street
Los Altos, CA 94022

*Price lists and swatches, 20 cents to 80
cents according to swatch.*

The price lists indicate the different
weights and kinds of fabrics. Besides
the brilliantly colored, handwoven Thai
silks, fabrics such as pongee, voile, and
batik are available from India, China,
Indonesia, Malaysia, Japan, Philippines,
Hawaii, and Italy, and the importer
claims he saves you from 30 percent to
50 percent by buying directly. Prices
start at about $3.50 for 36" Thai cotton
and tetoron fiber to about $14 per yard
for 40"-width upholstery-weight
Siamese silk.
MO

GURIAN FABRICS, INC.
Dept. CHC
276 Fifth Avenue
New York, NY 10001

*"Exclusive Collection of Hand
Embroidered Crewel and Numdah
Rugs," 50 cents, published every two
years, 12 pages, color, illustrated.*

Gurian's traditional hand-embroidered
crewel fabrics in 50" width are
excellent for upholstery, draperies,
bedspreads, and all decorative
purposes. New colorations away from
the traditional are shown in various
designs. Prices range from $14 to $24
per yard.
MO

HAGERTY COMPANY
Dept. CHC
38 Parker Avenue
Cohasset, MA 02025

*"Cohasset Colonials by Hagerty," 50
cents, published annually, 32 pages,
some color, illustrated.*

A group of polished chintz fabrics, all
copies of 18th- or 19th-century designs,
ranging in price from about $4 to $6 a
yard, are part of the Cohasset Colonial
collection. For an accurate color match,
send 25 cents for a sample of any one
fabric or $4 for the complete set. They
also offer two Colonial window
treatments—Brewster- or Boston-style
curtains—in a variety of cloths with
wooden rods and brackets, especially
made to fit your windows. Price chart
and samples on request.
MO

HOMESPUN FABRICS
Dept. CHC
10115 Washington Boulevard
Culver City, CA 90230

*"Homespun Fabrics," $1.00 for
brochure and swatches.*

If you want to make your own floor-to-
ceiling draperies without seams, you
can order fabric, starting at $1.50 a yard,
in widths of 96" to 120", directly from
Homespun Fabrics. Most of the fabrics
are preshrunk, machine-washable, and
no-iron. Homespun will also custom-
make curtains to your measurements.
MO

Crewel swatches, *Gurian Fabrics*

92

Ready-made Kodel bedroom ensemble, *Old Colony Curtains*

Custom-made window treatment, *Ronnie Sales*

DECORATING IDEAS WITH FABRIC

NIZHONIE, INC.
Dept. CHC
P.O. Box 729
Cortez, CO 81321

"Bahah-Zhonie Fabrics," leaflet, no charge.

This Indian-owned enterprise produces hand-printed, silk-screened textiles adapted from Indian designs by Bahah-Zhonie, a noted artist. Patterns come from such varied inspirations as storm-pattern rugs (Navajo), sand paintings, pictographs from cliff dwellings, and Pueblo pottery. Priced by the yard from $3 to $10, the materials available are homespun, cotton broadcloth, batiste, linen, and velveteen. There are also towels, place mats, calendars, and handwoven fabric from Guatemalan Indians.
MO

OLD COLONY CURTAINS
Dept. CHC
Box 787
Westfield, NJ 07090

"Old Colony Curtains," brochure, no charge.

For traditional or modern homes, Old Colony has ready-made curtains of bleached or unbleached muslin, trimmed with 2" knotted fringe, in lengths from 24" to 72", that cost from about $4.50 to $8 the pair, tie backs included. They also have bedroom ensembles in Kodel permanent-press fabric, natural or white, complete with bedspread, canopy, dust ruffle, pillow sham, and ruffled curtains, for a modest price. Except for a few items, everything is in stock for immediate delivery. Special orders can also be handled.
MO

RONNIE SALES, INC.
Dept. CHC
145 Broad Avenue
Fairview, NJ 07022

"Ronnie Fiberglass Draperies," 25 cents, published semiannually, 31 pages, color, illustrated; *"Ronnie Draperies,"* 25 cents, 22 pages, color, illustrated.

Ready-made draperies, hemmed to exact length specified, lined or unlined, or custom-made draperies. The materials include sheers and heavier weights, modern and traditional designs, and a range of textures. All Ronnie fabrics are available by the yard. Price lists enclosed.
MO

TRIBLEND MILLS, INC.
Dept. CHC
Tarboro, NC 27886

"Window Magic Style Suggestions," no charge, two-color, illustrated; *"How to Sew Draperies of Triblend Fabric,"* no charge, 11 pages, black and white, illustrated.

These two booklets, plus a swatch book of easy-care, drip-dry Triblend curtain fabric, a blend of cotton/rayon/acetate/polyester, comprise the drape-it-yourself information kit. The color brochure shows 14 different window treatments. The drapery booklet gives information on selection of the right style for your windows, how to measure, cut, and sew draperies, and a guide to selecting the proper hardware. The fabrics are mill ends, available in plain or fancy patterns, and sell for just $1.98 a yard with a money-back guarantee.
MO

CELANESE CORPORATION
Dept. CHC—HF5
1211 Avenue of Americas
New York, NY 10036

"Room Service," $1.00, 41 pages, illustrated, some color.

Using a beautiful, historic house (Celanese House) as a base, the brochure takes you through room by room showing just what can be done with fabrics and how to do it.

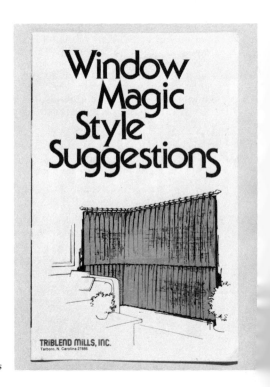

Brochure cover, *Triblend Mills*

Wood window grilles, *Grillon*

Custom-made screen panels, *Panel Creations*

PILE FABRIC PRIMER

CROMPTON-RICHMOND CO.
Dept. CHC
1071 Avenue of the Americas
New York, NY 10018

"A Pile Fabric Primer," $3.00, 54 pages,
some color, illustrated.

The primer is intended to widen your
acquaintance with pile fabrics—
corduroys, velveteens, and velvets—to
tell something of their history, diversity,
and types; how they are made, used,
and cared for. A glossary of terms is
provided. Illustrations include reprints
of woodcuts, engravings, paintings.
Actual samples of six types of pile
fabric are attached.

GRILLES AND PANELS

GRILLON CORP.
Dept. CHC
189–193 First Street
Brooklyn, NY 11215

"Ply-Grilles," $1.00, published annually,
12 pages, black and white, illustrated.

The decorative wood grilles shown in
this catalogue can be used to create
screens, room dividers, headboards, and
dropped ceilings. Adding a translucent,
frosted backing to the grilles allows
lighting to be set up behind or within
the grille for a luminous wall or screen.
You can order the grilles custom-
painted to match your color chip and
sized to your specifications.
MO/ID

PANEL CREATIONS
Dept. CHC
979 Third Avenue
New York, NY 10022

"Panel Creations," no charge, 6 pages,
black and white, illustrated.

Custom-made screen panels in a variety
of styles, on sliding tracks, for windows
and closets, are shown in this brochure.
Each panel is made to measure, finished
to your specifications, and can be
backed with plastic, glass, or fabric you
supply. You can order through your
decorator, or if you send in drawing
and measurements you'll get a free
estimate. You or your carpenter can
easily install the tracks.
MO/ID

IDEAS FOR WINDOW TREATMENTS

GRABER COMPANY
Dept. CHC
Graber Plaza
Middleton, WI 53562

*"How to Create Your Own Beautiful
Window Fashions,"* $1.00, published
seasonally, 35 pages, color, illustrated.

This catalogue covers curtains, shades,
decorative rods, valances; discusses
color, fabrics, accessories, problem
windows and what to do about them,
light and sun control, and the framing
or screening out of views attractive and
unattractive. There's also a dictionary of
window and drapery hardware terms.
RS

Window ideas, *Graber*

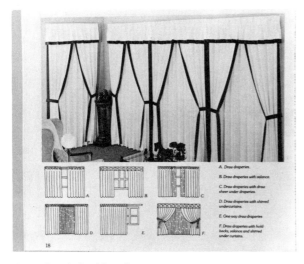

Decorative window ideas, *Kenney*

Wood and yarn Roman shade, *Del Mar Woven Wood*

STAINED GLASS

WINDOW SHADES AND BLINDS

KENNEY MANUFACTURING CO.
Dept. CHC
1000 Jefferson Boulevard West
Warwick, RI 02887

"Creative Windows," $1.25, published annually, 72 pages, color, illustrated.

"A guide to making your windows a beautiful part of your home" is the subtitle of this handsome and helpful catalogue, which shows window treatments designed by interior designers and gives practical guidelines for choosing the right treatment and style. How-to sections, complete with instructions and sketches, tell you how to make curtains, select hardware, use color, and handle problem windows.
RS

PPG INDUSTRIES, INC.
Dept. CHC
One Gateway Center
Pittsburgh, PA 15222

"All American Homes," no charge, published every three years, 39 pages, color, illustrated.

Two pages of this catalogue offer 14 illustrated suggestions for decorating windows of various types, from gable to slanted to narrow, small, or bay.

GARGOYLES, LTD.
Dept. CHC
512 South 3rd Street
Philadelphia, PA 19174

"Gargoyles, Ltd.," $4.00 (refundable with purchase), updated monthly, 32 pages, some color, illustrated.

A selection of 19th- and early 20th-century American and European stained-glass windows and panels, restored and reframed where necessary, ready for immediate installation. If you have a special requirement, Gargoyles can provide a custom-made modern window to your specifications. Prices on request.
MO

CLOPAY
Dept. CHC
Clopay Square
Cincinnati, OH 45214

"Clopay Window Shades," no charge, 20 pages, color, illustrated.

A wide choice of window shades—plain, fancy, room-darkening, light-filtering, fluted, scalloped, fringed, embossed—is illustrated in room settings. Striped, patterned, white, or colored, all are washable and some have valances to match. "The Matchmaker," a do-it-yourself self-adhesive fabric shade, enables you to coordinate shade and curtains or bedspread by applying a matching fabric.
RS

DEL MAR WOVEN WOOD
Dept. CHC
7411 Lorge Circle
Huntington Beach, CA 92646

"Idea Windows 2," $1.00, updated periodically, 20 pages, color, illustrated.

This company's window specialty is decorative combinations of colorful yarn and painted or stained wood woven into distinctive shades and curtains. The catalogue gives details and uses of the product, pages of pattern samples, and color illustrations of rooms decorated with Woven Wood. Not only windows are shown but also room dividers. How-to-measure information is included but no prices.
RS/ID

Booklet, *Window Shade Manufacturers' Association*

Riviera window blind, *Levolor Lorentzen*

FRAN'S BASKET HOUSE
Dept. CHC
Route 10
Succasunna, NJ 07876

"Fran's Basket House," 25 cents, 46 pages, black and white, illustrated.

Among the assortment of willow, rattan, and wicker items are matchstick and bamboo roller shades to add a touch of tropical decor to any window. They come in seven sizes, starting in price from $6 for a 24" x 72" matchstick shade up to $25.50 for a 72" x 72" bamboo slatted one.
MO

LEVOLOR LORENTZEN, INC.
Dept. CHC
720 Monroe Street
Hoboken, NJ 07030

"Window Magic," 50 cents, 40 pages, color, illustrated.

A decorating idea catalogue featuring Levolor standard and slat blinds and woven aluminum blinds, which are available in a wide range of decorator colors. Instructions are given for laminating materials to and painting designs on the blinds. Blinds are shown as part of a decorating scheme, for light, sun, and privacy control, for concealing storage, shelving, and unattractive areas. A 16-page insert gives useful information on measuring for blinds, taking a blind apart, installing or removing, and cleaning.
RS/ID

ROCHE-BOBOIS USA, LTD.
Dept. CHC
200 Madison Avenue
New York, NY 10016

"Roche-Bobois," $5.00, published annually, 132 pages, color, illustrated, with 52-page illustrated price list.

All types of shades from Roman to roller; vertical-slat blinds in metal or plastic, plain or printed; sheer fabrics and curtainings of velvet, linen, cotton, and synthetics are part of the "window dressing" collection. Free estimates and design plans are provided by the Roche-Bobois interior designers.
MO/RS

WINDOW SHADE MANUFACTURERS'
ASSOCIATION
Dept. CHC
230 Park Avenue
New York, NY 10017

This association of manufacturers offers a number of booklets and leaflets, some free. Among them are:

"Window Shade Primer," 25 cents, 16 pages, which proves there's a shade for every window and shows a wide variety of installations.

"The Decorative Window Shade," 25 cents, 16 pages, all kinds of window treatments and ideas for using shades to control light or enhance a room.

"Do-It-Yourself Ideas for Window Shades," 25 cents, 16 pages, which gives instructions on decorating plain shades with trimmings, appliqué, stencils, and painted designs.

"How to Make Decorator Window Shades," "Facts about Laminated Window Shades," "The Bottom-up Window Shade," and "Lam-Eze Pressure Sensitive Laminating System" are helpful, factual leaflets available on request with a stamped, self-addressed #10 envelope.

Bamboo roller window shade, *Fran's Basket House*

Lighting ideas, *General Electric*

LAMPS AND LIGHTING FIXTURES

Globe table and floor lamps, *George Kovacs*

Hanging grow-light planter lights, *George Kovacs*

Contemporary table lamps, *Laurel Lamp*

CONTEMPORARY

GEORGE KOVACS, INC.
Dept. CHC
831 Madison Avenue
New York, NY 10021

"George Kovacs Lamp Catalogue,"
$1.00, 40 pages, black and white,
illustrated.

This catalogue shows a really large
selection of the lamps and ceiling
fixtures imported or made by George
Kovacs, a company with showrooms in
New York, Chicago, Dallas, San
Francisco, Seattle, Atlanta, and High
Point, North Carolina. They range from
the simple to the light fantastic—lamps
that look like sections of industrial
tubing, dumbbells, pieces of sculpture.
There are special designs for Kovacs by
Milo Baughman of furniture fame,
some carved from pine, oak, and exotic
veneers in the mountains of Utah, and
by John Mascheroni. Many of the
lamps are ingeniously constructed to
dim when the stem is twisted, to be
turned on and off by a tug at dangling
brass balls, or to latch onto a magnetic
column, in the case of the "Zonking
System." Indoor gardeners will be
especially pleased with the good-
looking designs for planters with grow-
light bulbs. Prices range from around
$50 to $500.
MO/RS/ID

LAMPLAND
Dept. CHC
579 Avenue of the Americas
New York, NY 10011

Catalogue, 35 cents, 16 pages, color,
illustrated.

This 16-page catalogue has an excellent,
wide-ranging selection of the most
popular types of contemporary lamps at
reasonable prices. Here you can find
the simple globular white ceiling
fixture, the mandarin-hat-shaped wicker
wall lamp, as well as stainless-steel arc
floor lamps, clusters of bubblelike lights
on a round steel base, and skinny,
graceful "Studio Eight" swiveling lights
of polished chrome with cylindrical
shades. Lampland also has a few
cylindrical chrome-and-glass coffee
tables and a matching étagère. Prices
for the lamps start at under $20 and rise
to around $450.
MO

LAUREL LAMP CO., INC.
Dept. CHC
230 Fifth Avenue
New York, NY 10001

"Laurel Lamp," 50 cents, updated
annually, 48 pages, color, illustrated.

This all-color catalogue from a
company that has been designing and
manufacturing modern lamps for over
50 years contains a remarkably
comprehensive selection of well-styled
lamps of all types—table, tray, floor,
even illuminated end tables. Many of
the lamps are sculptural in shape; some
actually have original sculptures as
bases. The materials are mainly brass
and polished chrome, wood and clear
or opal case glass. Two of the more
unusual and striking lamps are a tall,
slender Art Deco torchette and a
Tiffany shade reinterpreted in
burnished brass. Laurel Lamp has
showrooms across the country in the
main home-furnishings centers, and
while their products are available only
through stores and interior designers,
the catalogue is well worth studying if
you are looking for a modern lamp that
is well designed and different.
RS/ID

HOWARD MILLER LIGHTING
Dept. CHC
Zeeland, MI 49464

"Howard Miller Lighting," no charge, 5
pages, black and white, illustrated.

The white plastic "Bubbles," designed
by George Nelson, in all shapes, sizes,
singly, as clusters, ceiling- or wall-hung,
or as table lamps are perennial favorites
that have been around so long they
have become a trademark of
contemporary decorating. Prices range
from $25 for a single bubble to $125 for
a cluster of four.
MO/RS

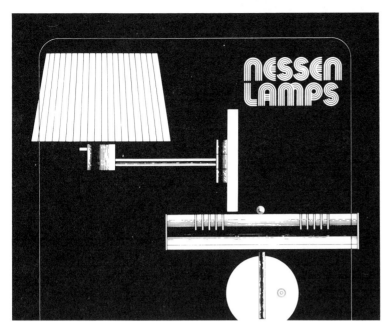

Catalogue cover, *Nessen Lamps*

Brass lighting fixture, *Progress Lighting*

NESSEN LAMPS
Dept. CHC
3200 Jerome Avenue
Bronx, NY 10468

Brochure, no charge, 3 pages, black and white, illustrated.

Simple modern floor, wall, and desk lamps in solid brass or chrome. Some are tubular in shape, others the more conventional swing-arm type with white vinyl pleated shades. All have a very functional aspect. Prices are in the $70 to $200 range.
RS/ID

PROGRESS LIGHTING
Dept. CHC
Box 12701
Philadelphia, PA 19134

"700 Ideas for Decorating with Lighting," $1.00, 160 pages, color, illustrated.

No matter what type of lighting fixture you are looking for, be it traditional Mediterranean, Oriental, Early American, or contemporary, Progress has it. From an elegant seven-arm antique bronze Colonial chandelier to track lights, fixtures for every room in the house, even patios and gardens, are included in this complete lighting catalogue. Each item is fully described, dimensions and finishes given. When writing, ask for nearest dealer so that you can check out the prices.
RS/ID

RAINBOW ART GLASS CORPORATION
Dept. CHC
49 Shark River Road
Neptune, NJ 07753

"Rainbow Art Glass Corporation," folder, 50 cents (refundable with purchase), published annually, color, illustrated.

If you are looking for Tiffany-style hanging shades or table lamps, this firm has a marvelous selection, not only in kit form but completely assembled. An 18"-diameter fruit-pattern dome shade with crown, finished price $297, is only $89.95 in kit form, a considerable saving if you are a do-it-yourselfer. The kits come complete with all the parts, including the electrical ones, and 3' chain. Illustrated instructions.
MO

Tiffany-type domes and shades,
Rainbow Art Glass

ROCHE-BOBOIS USA, LTD.
Dept. CHC
200 Madison Avenue
New York, NY 10016

"Roche-Bobois," $5.00, published annually, 132 pages, color, illustrated, with 52-page illustrated price list.

The stunning collection from Europe of contemporary lamps and lighting fixtures includes the now-classic shiny chrome Arco lamp with soaring 78" stem for $532, a recreation in mother-of-pearl of a Tiffany hanging lamp for $236, and brilliant-color lacquer metal table lamps for $40. A wide variety of styles and prices for the modern-minded.
MO/RS

SCAN
Dept. CHC
11310 Frederick Avenue
Beltsville, MD 20105

Catalogue of folders, $2.00.

A handsome line of contemporary Scandinavian lighting fixtures and lamps is shown throughout the 12 Scan folders. Typical are the hanging billiard lamps in a choice of colors and two sizes at $14.50 or $22.50 and the Femo lamp, the Swedish version of the architect's clamp-on lamp, for $19.75.
MO

100

Dramatic indoor and outdoor lighting, *Wendelighting*

DECORATIVE LIGHTING IDEAS

TRADITIONAL LAMPS AND LIGHTING

ETHAN ALLEN, INC.
Dept. CHC
Ethan Allen Drive
Danbury, CT 06810

"Getting Beauty and Value for Your Decorating Dollars," 50 cents, 96 pages, some color, illustrated.

This comprehensive decorating booklet includes several pages on lighting, explaining its function, different types of lighting, and lamps as accessories. Hints about lamp height and proportion are given.

GENERAL ELECTRIC CO.
Lamp Business Division
Dept. CHC
Nela Park
Cleveland, OH 44112

"The Light Book—how to be at home with lighting," no charge, 39 pages, black and white, illustrated.

Lighting is perhaps the most important and most abused element of decorating today. This booklet attempts to familiarize the consumer with the problems involved in lighting and how to handle them all over the house—both inside and out. G.E.'s considerable experience in the field makes this book really informative, and the book certainly gives a comprehensive view of the problem. For instance, reading lights are handled in five sections—table lamps, wall lamps, floor lamps, suspended lamps, and bed reading lamps.

WENDELIGHTING
Dept. CHC
9068 Culver Boulevard
Culver City, CA 90230

"Wendelighting," $1.50, 28 pages, published annually, color, illustrated.

A handsome brochure with dramatic photographs of the Wendelighting systems in use. A single painting is bathed in bright, even light or several objects are lit with one light, all from concealed sources. The optical inventions of Rudolf Wendel were first applied to illuminating the exteriors of gardens and castles in England and Europe, and through proper distribution of light and shadow the illusion of moonlight can be brought to any garden. Each system is custom-designed, from the manufacture of the equipment to the final installation. At the back of the catalogue is a page of outdoor lighting equipment available by mail. Write for price quotations.
ID/RS

ETHAN ALLEN, INC.
Dept. CHC
Ethan Allen Drive
Danbury, CT 06810

"The Treasury of Ethan Allen American Traditional Interiors," $7.50 (no charge at showrooms), published every two years, 408 pages, color, illustrated.

There are ten pages of floor and table lamps and chandeliers in the Ethan Allen Treasury, among them glass lamps reminiscent of the old "whale oil" lamps and some attractive and simple ceramic lamps in classic ginger jar, temple jar, and urn shapes.
RS

AUTHENTIC DESIGNS
Dept. CHC
139 East 61st Street
New York, NY 10021

"Catalogue of Early American Lighting Fixtures (hand-crafted recreations and adaptations)," $1.00, 64 pages, black and white, illustrated.

This catalogue presents a collection of well-researched designs of antique chandeliers and sconces made from woods often used in 18th- and 19th-century America: maple, birch, or poplar. The metal parts are either brass or pewter-plated brass, and whenever feasible hand-manufacturing processes are used to create a really antique look. The designs lean to the rustic but are varied and quite beautiful in their simplicity. Prices range from around $35 for a simple sconce to $80 to $400 for the chandeliers.
MO/RS

Wood and iron chandelier, *Authentic Designs*

Georgetown collection of brass candelsticks and lamps, *Baldwin Hardware*

Gamboled ship's lantern, *Bluejacket Ship Crafters*

BALDWIN HARDWARE MFG. CORP.
Dept. CHC
841 Wyomissing Boulevard
Reading, PA 19603

Folio of catalogue sheets, no charge, some color, illustrated.

All kinds of beautifully made, well-priced solid-brass candlesticks, wall sconces, and hurricane lamps, part of the James River and Georgetown collections, are based on designs from the Colonial homes along the James and Potomac rivers. A brass candlestick lamp with linen shade, 39" high, is $100; a lovely classic one-arm brass wall sconce with glass hurricane shade is $45.
MO/RS

BALL AND BALL
Dept. CHC
Whitford-Exton, PA 19341

"Fine Quality Reproductions by Ball and Ball," $1.00, 52 pages, black and white, illustrated.

In addition to their line of handsome reproduction hardware, Ball and Ball have several finely crafted solid-brass chandeliers, lanterns, and wall sconces (for candles or electrified), some with glass shades. All are based on 18th-century models. A handsome three-arm chandelier with glass shades, ready to install, is about $250; a pair of simple solid-brass one-arm candle wall sconces with shades are about $85. There are also some inexpensive tin sconces and black-painted copper lanterns that may be ceiling-hung, wall-mounted, or used on tables.
MO/RS

BAXWOOD CRAFTERS
Dept. CHC
1141 Commercial Drive
Lexington, KY 40505

Two brochures, no charge, published semiannually, color, illustrated.

About 20 lamps, completely assembled, wired, and sanded, are ready for you to finish, at reasonable prices. Directions for suggested lamp finishes are part of the first brochure. Lamp shades for all models are available in white or beige textured shantung, oyster or natural burlap fabric. The lamps are also sold completely finished, and eight are pictured in full color (if it's $18.50 unfinished, it's $25 finished). The second brochure describes and shows six needlepoint lamp kits in a wide variety of color combinations and details the contents of each kit.
MO

BLUEJACKET SHIP CRAFTERS
Dept. CHC
145 Water Street
South Norwalk, CT 06854

"BlueJacket Shipcrafters," 75 cents, 64 pages, black and white, illustrated.

If you are looking for authentic ship's lanterns, this catalogue has real gimbaled ones in brass, electrified or oil-burning, for under $60 and a heavy forged brass gimbaled candle wall sconce for about $20. These can be used on the wall or the table. There is also a wired ship's lantern table lamp with shade, about $95, and a pair of forged brass dolphin candlesticks, about $27.
MO

102

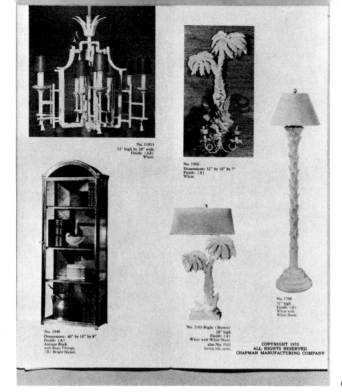

Japanese glazed earthenware jug lamp, *The Coastal Trader*

Collection of lighting fixtures, *Chapman*

THE BRASS LANTERN
Dept. CHC
353 Franklin Street
Duxbury, MA 02332

"The Brass Lantern," 25 cents (refundable with purchase), updated annually, black and white, illustrated.

The folder illustrates about a dozen handcrafted and electrified brass replicas of Colonial lanterns (night watchmen, riverboat, street) that may be ordered for wall, table, swag, sconce, or post lights. A choice of clear or antique glass is available, as is custom work from photos or sketches. Prices range from about $30 to $175.
MO

CHAPMAN
Dept. CHC
481 West Main
Avon, MA 02322

"Lamps and Accessories," folder, 50 cents, published annually, black and white, illustrated.

A very sophisticated selection of lamps and lighting fixtures is offered by Chapman. There are lamps in palm-tree forms; a bamboo-fashioned tole chandelier; a tortoiseshell-finished, overscaled spiral twisted table lamp, as well as a more conventional copy of a 17th-century brass chandelier and a replica of an 18th-century brass bouillotte lamp with black tole shade. If you are looking for the unusual, this is a very good source. Dimensions and style numbers are given, but prices vary across the country, so it is advisable to write.
RS/ID

THE COASTAL TRADER, INC.
Dept. CHC
423 15th Avenue East
Seattle, WA 98112

"Presentations from the Coastal Trader," 25 cents, 16 pages, published annually, black and white, illustrated.

Coastal Trader has unique lamps (with custom linen shades) made from old Japanese glazed earthenware jugs in earth tones with black calligraphy. Each is original and differs slightly in color, shape, size. There is a color choice of tan glaze with beige shade or gray-white glaze with off-white shade, $125.
MO

THE COUNTRY LOFT
Dept. CHC
552 Forest Street
Marshfield, MA 02050

"The Country Loft: Unique Antique Reproductions by Mail," 25 cents, 3 pages, black and white, illustrated.

Authentic reproductions of early lanterns and sconces. "The Doctor's Light" lantern, about $50, is handcrafted in solid antiqued brass, copper, or old pewter-finish terne metal. "The Tavern Sconce," "The Meetinghouse Sconce," and the fluted oval sconce are made in a choice of pewter-finished terne metal, antiqued copper or brass, electrified with 10-watt clear-flame bulb, $30 to $40.
MO

CRAFT HOUSE
Dept. CHC
Colonial Williamsburg Foundation
Williamsburg, VA 23185

"Williamsburg Reproductions—Interior Designs for Today's Living," $2.95, 232 pages, color and black and white, completely illustrated.

Craft House has some very handsome traditional lamps and lighting fixtures, the latter careful copies of chandeliers, sconces, and lanterns used in the restored buildings of Colonial Williamsburg, electrified for today's purposes. Notable among the lamps are the Delft Brick and Delft Vase lamps (around $149 and $178) and the classically simple pewter chamberstick lamp, $115. The one- and two-tiered wood and metal tavern chandeliers ($660 for the two-tier with candles, $755 electrified) would be especially attractive in a traditional family room or a country dining room.
MO/RS

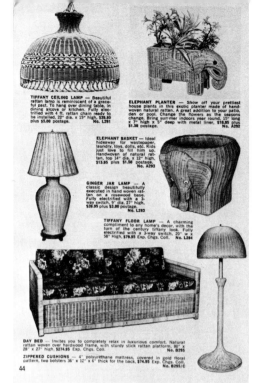

Electrified watchman's candle lantern,
Farmington Craftsmen

Rattan lamps and hanging shade, *Fran's Basket House*

EMPRESS CHANDELIER CO.
Dept. CHC
P.O. Box 2067
Mobile, AL 36601

*"Six Stars from the Empress Galaxy
. . . ,"* no charge, 6 pages, color,
illustrated.

Elegant lead crystal and bronze
chandeliers, designed as direct
descendants of the exquisite
chandeliers of Europe. Comprehensive
descriptions and photographs of
handcrafted details. Prices range from
$99 to $1,495.
MO

FAIRE HARBOUR BOATS
Dept. CHC
44 Captain Pierce Road
Scituate, MA 02066

"The Aladdin," brochure, 25 cents,
illustrated.

Aladdin kerosene-electric mantel lamps,
which convert from or to electricity,
capture the charm of turn-of-the-
century lamps, yet are completely
adapted to 20th-century living. A wide
choice of shelf, table, wall, or hanging
styles with brass or chrome-finished
bases and a selection of glass shades in
the original designs, all at moderate
prices. Price list and order form are
included.
MO

FARMINGTON CRAFTSMEN
Dept. CHC
87 Spring Lane
Farmington, CT 06032

"Wasley Lighting," $1.00, 30 pages,
published annually, supplements as
needed, color, illustrated.

An interesting collection of indoor and
outdoor lanterns, hanging fixtures,
chandeliers, sconces, and a few table
lamps. The most interesting are
watchman's lanterns from the "Firelight
Collection," in brass or pewter finish,
under $50; mirrored wall sconces,
under $60; and from the "Tiffany
Reproductions" an 18"-diameter
hanging shade in hand-leaded stained
glass for less than $150. Except for the
Tiffany types, all of the fixtures have a
traditional feeling and are designed to
go with Colonial rooms.
MO

CARL FORSLUND, INC.
Dept. CHC
122 East Fulton Street
Grand Rapids, MI 49502

*"Timeless Furniture Made by Carl
Forslund,"* $2.00, revised every two to
three years, 97 pages, color, illustrated.

Lamps, too, are part of the Forslund
collection. Perhaps the most beautiful
is the white orchid lamp, an electrified
replica of a two-part Victorian glass-
bowl oil lamp for $125. There are
candlestick lamps in brass, pewter, and
wood, floor lamps—a drop-leaf table-
floor lamp combination—and a tall tole
lamp with matching shade.
MO

FRAN'S BASKET HOUSE
Dept. CHC
Route 10
Succassunna, NJ 07876

"Fran's Basket House," 25 cents, 46
pages, black and white, illustrated.

A wide selection of rattan hanging
shades, table and floor lamps is offered
in this catalogue. A 15"-diameter rattan
shade in diamond pattern with 18' of
chain and hooks for hanging and fully
electrified, with a dimmer switch, costs
under $19. A handwoven rattan lamp
shaped like a ginger jar with rosewood
base and rattan shade, 27" tall, 9"
diameter, with a three-way switch, is
under $40. There are Tiffany-type rattan
shades and lamps and an amusing
elephant table and lamp combination.
MO

GARGOYLES, LTD.
Dept. CHC
512 South 3rd Street
Philadelphia, PA 19174

"Gargoyles, Ltd.," $4.00 (refundable
with purchase), updated monthly, 32
pages, some color, illustrated.

Gargoyles has really unusual lighting
fixtures, most dating from the 19th and
early 20th centuries, one-of-a-kind
chandeliers, from an elaborate French
Art Nouveau three-light ceiling fixture
to a simple hanging ball "Moon,"
reminiscent of the 16th-century Moon
globe fixture, and reproductions of
handcrafted brass carriage lamps. All
prices on request, but you can order
direct.
MO

Painted tole lamp, *Hayfields Studios*

Brass and crystal candlelabra, *Galaxy Promotions*

GALAXY PROMOTIONS
Dept. CHC
P.O. Box 710
Fairhope, AL 36532

Monarch candelabra leaflet, no charge.

Galaxy offers a rather elaborate antiqued brass and crystal electrified candelabra at factory-direct price, well below retail, around $30. They also sell a clock kit.
MO

HAGERTY CO.
Dept. CHC
38 Parker Avenue
Cohasset, MA 02025

"Cohasset Colonials by Hagerty," 50 cents, published annually, 32 pages, some color, illustrated.

Reproductions of antique candlesticks in pewter or brass, made into lamps, are part of the Cohasset Colonial collection. A pewter lamp, attributed to Roswell Gleason, with either black parchment or white linen shade, is under $55. The handsome Newport stick in brass, a copy of the unique 18th-century Robinson candlestick of Newport, Rhode Island, is $130. There are two wood and metal chandeliers, both about $115, and several wall sconces of unusual design.
MO

HAYFIELDS STUDIOS, INC.
Dept. CHC
East Deering Road
Deering, NH 03244

"Things for the House," no charge, color, illustrated.

The "things" have painted or stenciled designs copied from antique originals and include lamps with bases in the shape of sap buckets; candle sconces in metal, painted red, green, mustard, or dark blue with stylized flower designs. Prices are on request.
MO

HERITAGE LANTERNS
Dept. CHC
Sea Meadow Land
Yarmouth, ME 04096

"Heritage Lanterns," $1.00, published periodically, 46 pages, black and white, illustrated.

Handcrafted reproductions and adaptations of Colonial lights from designs of the original craftsmen, among them carriage lights, ship's lanterns, tavern lights, globe lights, Salem lights, sconces, chandeliers, and table lamps in copper, brass, pewter, and wood, all electrified. Prices range from $40 to $100.
MO/RS

Handcrafted wall lantern, *Heritage Lanterns*

Beautiful crystal chandelier, *King's Chandelier*

Hand-forged Mexican wall sconce, *Mexico House*

Victorian, Tiffany, and Art Deco lamps,
Magnolia Hall

MARTHA M. HOUSE
Dept. CHC
1022 South Decatur Street
Montgomery, AL 36104

*"Southern Heirlooms," $1.00,
(refundable with purchase), published
annually, 44 pages, black and white,
illustrated.*

To complement your Victorian
furnishings, Martha House offers a half-
dozen well-priced reproductions of
lighting fixtures and lamps, from a ruby
glass hanging oil-type fixture with
crystal prisms, 15' of brass chain and
canopy, to a gilt-metal repoussé footed
font table lamp with gold decorated
glass dome shade.
MO

IRVIN'S CRAFT SHOP
Dept. CHC
RD 1, Box 58
Mt. Pleasant Mills, PA 17853

*"Handcrafted Tin and Copper
Reproductions," folder, 25 cents, 3
pages, published annually, black and
white, illustrated.*

Country tin and antique copper lamps
in "Americana" designs such as mugs,
milk cans, candle molds, chambersticks,
coffee pots, all electrified, with pierced
tin shades. There is also a selection of
wired lanterns for posts, hanging or
wall mounting, and three S- or U-
shaped chandeliers, also in tin or
copper, that can be ordered wired.
Prices are reasonable.
MO

KING'S CHANDELIER CO.
Dept. CHC
P.O. Box 667
Eden, NC 27288

*Annual catalogue, $1.00, 92 pages, black
and white, illustrated.*

This catalogue has a staggeringly large
selection of beautiful crystal and brass
chandeliers, sconces, and candelabra
made by a family company that has
been in business since 1935. The crystal
parts of the chandeliers are made in
Czechoslovakia and Austria, the metal
parts in the U.S. and Europe, and as
there is always a large stock of parts on
hand, orders can be shipped within
two weeks. As this company does all its
own designing and importing and sells
only through the North Carolina
showroom and by direct mail, it can
offer really good buys as well as top
quality and workmanship. Prices vary
from $65 for a simple circular
chandelier with two tiers of prisms and
$50 for a two-light sconce to over
$1,000 for a really magnificent
chandelier.
MO

LUIGI CRYSTAL
Dept. CHC
7332 Frankford Avenue
Philadelphia, PA 19136

*"Luigi Crystal Creators of Fine Crystal,"
25 cents, 50 pages, black and white,
illustrated.*

Many fine crystal candelabra,
chandeliers, wall sconces, hurricane
lamps, and accessories are designed
and produced by this company. Each
picture is accompanied by a
description of the item shown,
including size. Prices range from
around $30 to $200.
MO

MAGNOLIA HALL
Dept. CHC
726 Andover
Atlanta, GA 30327

*"World's Largest Collection of Victorian
Furniture," $1.00, published quarterly,
63 pages, black and white, illustrated.*

Magnolia Hall's Victorian furniture is
complemented by electrified Victorian
oil lamps with floral painted bowls,
some with prisms, ranging in price from
$59.95 for a copy of the Gone With the
Wind lamp to $99.95 for the prism
lamp. There is also an 18" Tiffany Rose
accent lamp for $39.95 and a 23" table
lamp for $49.95. Two Tiffany hanging
lamps and a most unusual pineapple
glass shade lamp are part of this
rarefied collection.
MO

MEXICO HOUSE
Dept. CHC
Box 970
Del Mar, CA 92014

*"Mexico House," 25 cents, 40 pages,
black and white, illustrated.*

The lanterns, chandeliers, wall sconces,
and candlesticks of hand-forged
ironwork from Mexico are executed
today as in the days of Cortez, in
typical Moorish styles. There are many
sizes and shapes to choose from, and
prices are reasonable.
MO

Metal wall-mounted lantern, *Gates Moore*

Magnificent brass chandelier, *Old World Foundry Guild*

GATES MOORE
Dept. CHC
River Road
Silvermine
Norwalk, CT 06850

"Early American Designs of Lighting Fixtures," $2.00, 26 pages, black and white illustrated.

The Gates Moore lighting-fixture business, begun in 1950, follows the finishes, shapes, and construction methods of early American craftsmen, and the metal and wood chandeliers, sconces, and lanterns in the catalogue, although electrified, have the authentic handcrafted look. The fixtures are available in a choice of finishes—painted, pewter-coated, distressed tin, oxidized copper—or can be matched to a color sample. The price range is from $20 for a metal sconce to $750 for a painted chandelier.
MO

OLD WORLD FOUNDRY GUILD, INC.
Dept. CHC
1612 Decatur Street
Ridgewood, NY 11227

"Metal (Brass) Reproductions," no charge, 30 pages, black and white, illustrated.

Lamps and lighting fixtures are part of this brass collection. A handsome eight-arm chandelier, like the 17th-century Dutch ones, 25" high by 30" across, costs about $500. Two styles of French bouillotte lamps with adjustable painted tole shades are around $185 each. There are pairs of Colonial wall sconces and single candlesticks, a pair of ornate cast double-arm sconces, and a 12-arm scrolled brass chandelier. Dimensions, finishes, weights, and prices are on a separate list.
MO

HOUSE OF ONYX
Dept. CHC
Rowe Building
Greenville, KY 42345

List, no charge.
Among the Mexican onyx pieces are figurine lamps, an owl, an elephant, a rosebud, described as "excellent for night lamps," in a $35 price range.
MO

PRESTON'S
Dept. CHC
116 Main Street Wharf
Greenport, NY 11944

"Of Ships and Sea," 25 cents, published semiannually, 144 pages, black and white, illustrated.

The catalogue contains a number of brass ship's table lamps, hanging brass ship's lights, and wheel chandeliers, as well as a mariner's gallery of floor lamps that double as end tables. Prices range from about $16 for a schooner or lobster-pot lamp to around $195 for the seaman's lamp and table combination.
MO

PRODUCT SPECIALTIES, INC.
Dept. CHC
600 Washington
Eaton, IN 47338

"Product Specialties, Inc.," folder, no charge, published annually, color, illustrated.

A collection called Monterey offers three pendant fixtures, two table lamps, and a pole light with shades or globes of authentic cathedral glass, a type of colored non-leaded glass in brilliant colors, similar to ancient Egyptian glass. A table lamp, like an old Rayo oil lamp, sells for around $80. Panels of this glass, called "Cathedralite," are available for do-it-yourself projects such as door inserts, tabletops, or mirror frames.
MO

SARREID, LTD.
Dept. CHC
P.O. Box 3345
Wilson, NC 27893

"Sarreid, Ltd.," folder, no charge, color.

From the Henry Ford Museum collection, Sarreid makes a 21¼" tall, intricately hand-pierced and hand-painted reproduction tin Empire lantern in an unusual oval shape, about $116. A heavy brass wall sconce with a hand-blown glass egg bowl hurricane, 25" high x 11" wide, about $185, also has that one-of-a-kind look. For retail store information write to the nearest dealer, listed on the price sheet.
RS/ID

Tole lantern from Henry Ford Museum Collection, *Sarreid*

*I*mportant
floor lamp/étagère. The
pedestal of open shelves,
supporting the lighting unit
and shade, is executed in the
classical spirit of the Second
Empire, with base, shelves
and corona formed of lightly
aged cabinet ash and positioned
by brass columns having
solid turned base, capitals
and extraordinary finials. The
étagère is appropriate for the
display of diminutive art
objects. 3210-P.
Height 61¾ inches.

Étagère and lamp combination, *Stiffel*

Sculptured lamp of marlin and tuna, *Sportlamps*

SPANISH VILLA
Dept. CHC
Building 1101, L.A.F.B.
Laredo, TX 78040

*"Spanish Villa," $1.00 (refundable with
purchase), published annually, 34
pages, black and white, illustrated.*

Wrought-iron combined with hand-
blown glass lanterns, chandeliers, and
hanging lamps, imported from Mexico,
are mostly scrolled in traditional
Spanish designs. Prices range from $8.95
for a 6" x 9" lantern and bracket to
$87.50 for a four-light chandelier, 26"
across and 24" high.
MO

62
ELIPTICAL LANTERN
With crown top
Painted tin in very dark blue
Earth red interior
H—21¼" W—9⅝" D—5¾"

WILLIAM SPENCER
Dept. CHC
Rancocas Woods, NJ 08060

*"William Spencer Catalogue," 50 cents,
200 pages, black and white, illustrated.*

This company has been making lighting
fixtures since 1897—lanterns, sconces,
chandeliers of polished or antique
brass, pewter, silver, or tin. A 26"-high
copy of an old coach lantern is under
$90; a brass Colonial chandelier with
glass hurricane shades, 20" across, is
about $80. All are based on, or replicas
of, 18th- and 19th-century lighting
fixtures. Spencer will repair and restore
your old fixtures and supply missing
glass parts. The price list gives all
dimensions and finishes available. The
catalogue also illustrates several
hardware items, including a solid
forged-brass knocker 7½" long, very
handsome, for under $17.
MO

SPORTLAMPS
Dept. CHC
32 Bramble Lane
Riverside, CT 06878

*"The Sculptured Lamps of Donald
McDonald," $1.00 (refundable with
purchase), published annually.*

Handmade sculptured lamps by Donald
McDonald of wildlife such as geese,
quail, pheasants, grouse, marlin, tuna,
dolphins, all in limited editions. The
lamps are unusual and particularly
interesting to wildlife enthusiasts and
retail for approximately $350 to $400.
MO

THE STIFFEL CO.
Dept. CHC
North Kingsbury Street
Chicago, IL 60610

*"From the Stiffel Collection," 50 cents,
updated every 18 months, 40 pages,
color and black and white, illustrated.*

This catalogue has a large array of
traditional table, tray and floor lamps,
torchères and pendant lamps, mostly
brass and metal, but also in
combination with china, crystal, and
wood. One floor lamp is combined
with an étagère. Stiffel also sells
decorative accessories such as clocks,
barometers, wall shelves, and cabinets.
RS/ID   •

STURBRIDGE YANKEE WORKSHOP
Dept. CHC
Sturbridge, MA 01566

*"Sturbridge Yankee Workshop
Handbook and Catalogue," 50 cents, 64
pages, some color, illustrated.*

Many styles of lamps suitable for Early
American rooms are part of the
Sturbridge collection. There is a hobnail
milk-glass pin-up with a cast-iron
bracket for under $30; a combination
ratchet lamp and table in pine with a
burlap shade for under $70; several oil
lamps, hanging and table models; and a
five-arm blue-and-white Delft-and-
pewter chandelier, 22" across, for under
$100.
MO

Japanese-style bathroom, *Kohler*

EQUIPMENT, HARDWARE, AND FITTINGS

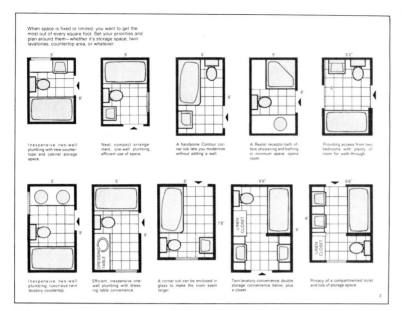

When space is fixed or limited, you want to get the most out of every square foot. Set your priorities and plan around them—whether it's storage space, twin lavatories, countertop area, or whatever.

Inexpensive two-wall plumbing with new counter-tops and cabinet storage space.

Neat, compact arrangement, one-wall plumbing, efficient use of space.

A handsome Contour corner tub lets you modernize without adding a wall.

A Restal receptor-bath offers showering and bathing in minimum space, opens room.

Providing access from two bedrooms with plenty of room for walk-through.

Inexpensive two-wall plumbing, luxurious twin lavatory countertop.

Efficient, inexpensive one-wall plumbing with dressing table convenience.

A corner tub can be enclosed in glass to make the room seem larger.

Twin lavatory convenience, double storage convenience below, plus a closet.

Privacy of a compartmented toilet and lots of storage space.

Bathroom planning kit, *American Standard*

BATHROOM AND KITCHEN EQUIPMENT

Catalogue cover, *Elkay*

AMERICAN STANDARD
Dept. CHC
P.O. Box 2003
New Brunswick, NJ 08903

"Bathroom Planning Kit," $2.00, large envelope of booklets, brochures, a paperback, color, illustrated.

A complete and thorough package for planning all kinds of bathrooms from modest to luxurious. One booklet, "So You're Planning a Bathroom," colorfully illustrates the latest ideas in building, remodeling, and redecorating bathrooms with American-Standard bath fittings. Another booklet, "The Art of Using Unused Spaces," shows you how to tuck in a bath under the stairs, in a basement or attic, and provides working drawings for your plumber. Fixture cutouts and grids for preplanning are part of the kit, along with yet another booklet of floor plans for every conceivable type and size bathroom. A 192-page paperback, "The Homemakers Guide to the Bathroom and the Kitchen," by William Laas and Evelyn Conti, is crammed full of valuable tips on maintenance, repairs, emergencies, as well as plans, designs, and color schemes for these areas. Separate brochures illustrate in color the complete line of fixtures, including the new "Ellisse" sculptured pedestal lavatory from Europe.
RS

ARTISTIC BRASS
Dept. CHC
3136 East 11th Street
Los Angeles, CA 90023

"Elegance Is Artistic," "The Gem Collection," "The Tomorrow Line," no charge, color, illustrated.

Three catalogues that comprise the beautiful line of lavatory, tub, and shower sets designed and manufactured by Artistic Brass. The first lists and illustrates the complete line, including the Gem and Tomorrow groups, with accessory items—towel bars, soap dishes, toilet-paper holders, Roman tub spouts and shower heads—with specifications and details at the back. "The Gem Collection" is a handsome array of the bath sets in gold and semiprecious stones such as malachite, rhodonite, and aventurine, with a brief history of each stone and its source. "The Tomorrow Line" illustrates contemporary, clean-lined bath fittings in satin chrome, antique and satin brass and pewter. As these lines are sold through wholesalers only, you must write for prices and the name of the nearest dealer.
RS/ID

ELJER PLUMBINGWARE
Dept. CHC
3 Gateway Center
Pittsburgh, PA 15222

"The Eljer Plan . . . for a Better Bathroom," $1.00, 35 pages, color, illustrated; "Everything You Need to Know about Bathrooms," no charge, 23 pages, color, illustrated; "Eight Great Cures for the Common Bathroom," no charge, 22 pages, color, illustrated.

"The Eljer Plan" booklet describes and shows different bathroom designs and fixtures. There's an enclosed reply card for additional information. "Everything You Need to Know about Bathrooms" is a guide to selecting the right fixtures and tells how they differ in cost and convenience. "Eight Great Cures" has eight fully illustrated decorating schemes for a typical 5' x 8' bathroom, based on the varied shapes and colors of the Eljer fixtures. All products and materials used are listed and identified.
RS

ELKAY MANUFACTURING COMPANY
Dept. CHC
2700 South Seventeenth Avenue
Broadview, IL 60153

"Choose Elkay: Stainless Steel Sinks, Faucets, Accessories," catalogue CS-6, no charge, 51 pages, black and white, illustrated.

The catalogue comprises the complete line of Elkay stainless-steel sinks for kitchen, bar, laundry, and commercial installations, plus fittings and accessories. Detailed pictures, drawings, specifications, and an index by model number are included.
RS

KitchenAid dishwasher, *Hobart*

Mixer with grain-mill attachment, *Hobart*

ELON INCORPORATED
Dept. CHC
964 Third Avenue
New York, NY 10022

"Carillo Tile Handmade in Mexico," no charge, published annually, 15 pages, color, illustrated.

In addition to their collection of charming rustic floor and wall tiles, many of which would add a decorative touch to a kitchen or bathroom, Elon has hand-decorated basins, towel and soap holders, hooks, door pulls, outlet and switch plates in several delightful patterns. The basins come in round or oval shapes with optional matching corners and cost from about $160 to $205. The set of six decorated bath accessories (towel rack, toothbrush-and-tumbler holder, toilet-roll holders, and two recessed soap dishes) is about $217. Sizes and prices are given.
MO/RS/ID

HOBART CORPORATION
KitchenAid Division
Dept. CHC
Troy, OH 45374

"KitchenAid Appliances," no charge, 8 pages, color, illustrated.

The folder, which is updated periodically as product changes are made, shows the clean-up and food-preparation appliances made by this reliable company (the KitchenAid mixer is standard equipment in the kitchens of many well-known cooks). In addition to the heavy-duty mixer, with its impressive collection of attachments (among them, ice-cream and sausage makers), Hobart's KitchenAid Division makes dishwashers, trash compactors, waste disposers, hot-water dispensers, and coffee mills. Other individual product literature is available at dealers, who will supply prices.
RS

KOHLER COMPANY
Dept. CHC
Kohler, WI 53044

"Great Bathroom Ideas Begin with Kohler," 25 cents, published annually, 31 pages, color, illustrated.

Color illustrations of unusual, luxurious bathrooms, large and small, give you ideas for doing over your own bathroom. Kohler makes the works, from bathtubs to bidets, in china, cast iron, and fiberglass and a range of beautiful colors, all of which are shown here for your temptation. There are even colorful kitchen sinks.
RS

MARLITE
Division of Masonite Corp.
Dept. CHC
Dover, OH 44622

"Marlite Guide to Beautiful Interiors," no charge, 11 pages, color, illustrated.

Two bath kits, "A Complete Package for Tub-Area Remodeling" and "A Complete Bath-in-Box" tub recess kit, designed for do-it-yourself installation, are part of the brochure on "Marlite." All necessary materials and complete installation instructions are included in each kit. There is a regional listing of sales offices and warehouses for further information and prices.
RS

ROPER SALES CORPORATION
Dept. CHC
1905 West Court Street
Kankakee, IL 60901

Catalogue, no charge, 35 pages, color, illustrated.

The catalogue shows this manufacturer's line of gas and electric ranges, cooktops, range hoods, wall and microwave ovens, dishwashers, compactors, grills and disposers, with specifications, illustrations, descriptions, and dimensions. Prices through dealers.
RS

Custom kitchen, *St. Charles*

Shower door kit, *Tub-Master*

**ST. CHARLES MANUFACTURING
  COMPANY**
Dept. CHC
1611 E. Main Street
St. Charles, IL 60174

*"St. Charles Custom Kitchens," 40
pages, and "The Choice Is Yours," 9
pages, mailed as a pair, $2.00 (no
charge at dealer showrooms), published
every two or three years, color,
illustrated.*

"Custom Kitchens" follows the story of
one family, showing how you choose
your kitchen design and add all the
special features when you work with St.
Charles. The elements that make a total
design are explained, with many
alternative selections shown in sketch
and photograph. "The Choice Is Yours"
shows, in photographs, one kitchen in
six different styles from Early American
to contemporary.
RS/ID

THERMADOR
Dept. CHC
5119 District Boulevard
Los Angeles, CA 90040

*"Thermador's Thermatronic Microwave
Ovens for a Whole New World of
Quick & Easy Cooking," no charge,
updated as required, 8 pages, color,
illustrated.*

A folder showing the cooking
appliances of this well-known kitchen-
equipment manufacturer—specifically,
microwave ovens and combinations of
microwave, warming, and conventional
ovens, plus a line of cooktops, all with
specifications.
RS

TUB-MASTER CORPORATION
Dept. CHC
P.O. Box 6115
Orlando, FL 32803

*"The Decorator Bath," 35 cents, 18
pages, color, illustrated.*

An "idea" booklet of different types of
colorful bathrooms, each with a floor
plan showing placement of equipment
and listing the manufacturers. A
standard-size contemporary bath has a
molded two-seater shower with walls
covered in overscaled floral vinyl. A
small bathroom with shower stall is
done in neutral tones to make it seem
larger. There are many, many tips on
color, wall treatments, and bath
accessories.
RS

SHERLE WAGNER, INTERNATIONAL
Dept. CHC
60 East 57th Street
New York, NY 10022

*"Sherle Wagner Catalogue," $5.00, 82
pages, color, illustrated.*

The Sherle Wagner name in bath
fittings and designs is the equivalent of
Rolls-Royce—the finest and most
expensive. This stunningly beautiful
catalogue presents the full line,
arranged in groups of basin sets, tub
sets, lavatory bowls, chaises percées,
wallcoverings, lighting fixtures, with
photographs of some complete
bathrooms. The firm will design a
whole bathroom to your taste or just
provide the handsome fittings. Prices
on request.
MO/RS/ID

WHIRLPOOL CORPORATION
Marketing Communications
Dept. CHC
Benton Harbor, MI 49022

*Six appliance brochures, no charge,
some color, illustrated.*

The brochures illustrate and describe
the major Whirlpool appliances:
electric ranges with self-cleaning ovens,
room air-conditioners and
dehumidifiers, undercounter and
portable dishwashers, food waste
disposers and compactors, automatic
washers and clothes dryers, no-frost
upright and chest freezers, and
refrigerator-freezer combinations.
Specifications and dimensions are given
for each appliance so that you can
preplan your kitchen before
purchasing. Write for the brochures
that interest you and for the nearest
dealer.
RS

Washer and dryer combination, *Whirlpool*

Hand-carved wooden doors, *Acme Hardware*

Twenties ceiling fan, *Windyne*

CEILING FANS

DECORATIVE DOORS AND GATES

THE CEILING FAN COMPANY
Dept. CHC
108 East 82nd Street
New York, NY 10028

Folder, no charge, 6 pages, black and white, illustrated.

The ceiling fan is now the "in" way to cool a room naturally—and decoratively. A 52" fan with Adaptair (a lever to adjust the angle of the four blades) is under $280, under $240 without Adaptair. The 36" fan (no Adaptair) is $159. If you want to add a globe light, there is a light adapter kit for just $16. All fans have two speeds and a five-year guarantee.
MO

GARGOYLES, LTD.
Dept. CHC
512 South 3rd Street
Philadelphia, PA 19174

"Gargoyles, Ltd.," $4.00 (refundable with purchase), updated monthly, 32 pages, some color, illustrated.

Gargoyles, a company that seems to have just about everything in decorative nostalgia, has ceiling fans for Western, Victorian, tropical, or eclectic settings in two sizes: 36" fans with metal blades and 52" fans with wooden blades, some models fitted with lights. Prices on request.
MO

WINDYNE COMPANY
Dept. CHC
Box 9091
Richmond, VA 23225

"Windyne Company Ceiling Fan," no charge, black and white, illustrated.

The brochure presents four good reasons for investing in handcrafted reproductions of the Twenties ceiling fan: They lower electricity bills (presumably by replacing air conditioning); circulate fresh air, thus helping house plants thrive; and add to the decorative interest of a room or a screened porch. The fans have wooden blades and come in two sizes, 39" for about $170 and 53" for about $225, with motor controlled by a 20" gold silk pull cord with tassel. A really practical piece of nostalgia.
MO

ACME HARDWARE COMPANY, INC.
Dept. CHC
150 South LaBrea Avenue
Los Angeles, CA 90036

"Hand Carved Doors and Panels," $1.00, published annually, 41 pages, black and white, illustrated.

Beautiful imported hand-carved mahogany doors to fit every decorating style, in a variety of sizes. If by any chance you can't find what you desire in the over 80 styles offered, custom doors can be ordered to your specification. A delightful door called "Chalet," with the floral carving found on Swiss chalets, 36" x 80" and 1¾" thick, costs about $445. There is also a collection of hand-carved wood panels that you can apply to doors or furniture, priced from $16 to $38.
MO

Ornamental iron door, *Collins-Hanna Iron*

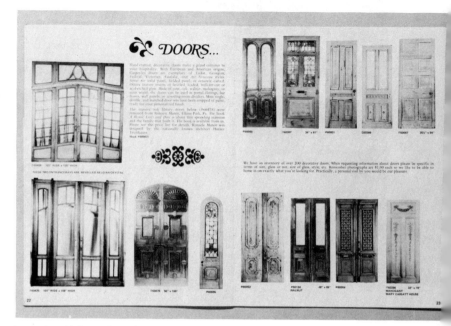

Interesting old doors, *Gargoyles*

CLOPAY
Dept. CHC
Clopay Square
Cincinnati, OH 45214

"Clopay Folding Doors and Room Dividers," booklet, no charge, 8 pages, color, illustrated.

Where door-opening space is limited or to soundproof space between rooms, Clopay's prefinished folding doors are the answer. They come in many colors to match or contrast with wall color or wood grains, with instructions for easy installation.
RS

COLLINS-HANNA IRON COMPANY, INC.
Dept. CHC
450 North Decatur
Memphis, TN 38105

"Ornamental Iron Doors, Gates and Decor Items," no charge, published quarterly, 12 pages, black and white, illustrated.

Ornamental iron doors in eight elaborate designs, fitted with tempered safety glass, automatic door closer, hammer-finish door handle and key lock, come weather-stripped and with full installation instructions. The price for the Spanish Flower design door, standard size (35¾" to 36¼" width by 80" to 81¼" high) is $200. Custom sizes, special width, and special height are $30 more.
MO

GARGOYLES, LTD.
Dept. CHC
512 South 3rd Street
Philadelphia, PA 19174

"Gargoyles, Ltd.," $4.00 (refundable with purchase), updated monthly, 32 pages, some color, illustrated.

Gargoyles has an inventory of over 200 decorative doors from old houses in a variety of styles—Tudor, Georgian, Victorian, and Art Nouveau—and almost any wood you can think of, some with stained-glass panels or iron grilles, singles or pairs, for interior or exterior use. So that they can zero in on what you want, when you request information about doors be specific as to size, style, size of glass, and so on, as the photographs they send you cost $1.00 each, which is applied to the sale. Such decorative architectural details as fretwork, balusters, turnings, corbels, beading, and newel posts, in Tudor, Jacobean, or Georgian styles, or from Victorian houses, are also part of the inventory.

They are into wrought iron, too—19th-century ornamental ironwork with intricate patterns and bold designs, elaborate wrought-iron gates, over-gates, balconies, fountains, and planters for indoor and outdoor use, some of which are shown in the catalogue. All one-of-a-kind, prices on request.
MO

HOUSE OF IRON, INC.
Dept. CHC
3384 Long Beach Road
Oceanside, NY 11572

"House of Iron Gates," folder of leaflets, $1.00 (refundable with purchase), published quarterly, black and white, illustrated.

Wrought-iron gates for archways, doors, room dividers, window guards, fireplace doors are handcrafted by House of Iron, who will make gates to your design. The brochure shows just a few of the hundreds of designs that can be ordered. In addition to gates, the factory makes almost everything conceivable in wrought iron—table bases, shelf brackets, headboards, chairs, legs, chandeliers, mirrors—you name it. Prices range from around $70 to $1,500.
MO

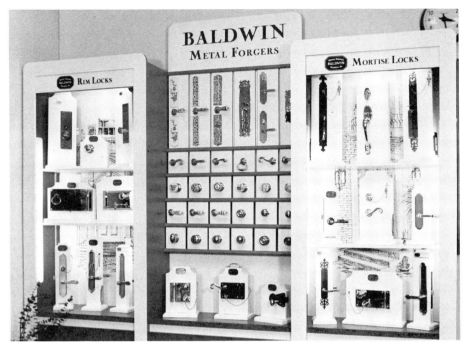

Door pulls and locks, *Baldwin Hardware*

DECORATIVE HARDWARE

ACME HARDWARE COMPANY, INC.
Dept. CHC
150 South LaBrea Avenue
Los Angeles, CA 90036

*"Catalogue of Decorative Hardware,"
$2.00, 206 pages, black and white,
illustrated.*

Every type of door pull, knocker, door
plate, rosette, lock, knob, furniture pull,
hook, push plate, bracket that you can
imagine is to be found in this giant
catalogue, ranging from authentic
Spanish wrought-iron cabinet hardware
to painted porcelain or crystal door
pulls, in styles to fit every decorating
scheme and pocketbook. There is even
a selection of beautiful (and expensive)
Porcelaine de Paris bath fittings, in
color, at the back of the catalogue. All
sizes, finishes, and prices are included.
MO

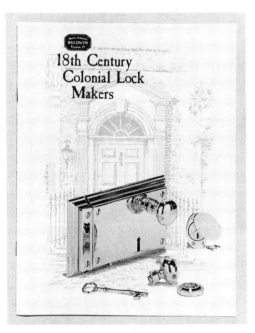

BALDWIN HARDWARE
MANUFACTURING CORP.
Dept. CHC
841 Wyomissing Boulevard
Reading, PA 19603

*Folio of catalogue sheets, no charge,
some color, illustrated.*

Baldwin manufactures forged brass
hardware, mortise and rim locks, letter-
box plates, door knockers, knobs and
fasteners, and cabinet hardware. The
James River and Georgetown
Collections of brass accessories
reproduce Colonial 18th-century brass
and hand-forged black iron hooks,
latches, ring pulls, and brackets as part
of "Collector's Choice." Price list
included.

*"18th Century Colonial Lock Makers,"
no charge, 8 pages, black and white,
illustrated.*

Authentic reproductions of forged
solid-brass locks from the more elegant
homes of 18th-century America—
different types of rim locks, brass,
beveled edge, Dutch elbow, and door
latches. On the back is a guide to
installation and handling of these
unusual locks.
MO/RS

Brochure cover, *Baldwin Hardware*

BALL AND BALL
Dept. CHC
463 West Lincoln Highway
Exton, PA 19341

*"Fine Quality Reproductions by Ball
and Ball," $1.00, 52 pages, black and
white, illustrated.*

Full line of hand-wrought brass
reproductions of original 18th-century
pieces, including cabinet hardware,
house hardware, lighting fixtures, door
knockers, hooks, ornaments, etc., with
descriptions where required. Price list
and order blank included with
catalogue.
MO

CRAFT HOUSE
Dept. CHC
Colonial Williamsburg Foundation
Williamsburg, VA 23185

*"Williamsburg Reproductions—Interior
Designs for Today's Living," $2.95, 232
pages, color and black and white,
illustrated.*

Brass hinges and rim locks with knob or
drop handle and Colonial key or
covered key escutcheon and cylinder
lock, in classically simple shapes, are
crafted by Folger Adams for the
Williamsburg Reproduction program.
The rim lock with two drop handles
and Colonial key is around $194. There
are also door knockers in brass, a
graceful "S" shape for $32.50, an urn
shape for $26.
MO/RS

Catalogue cover, *P.E. Guerin*

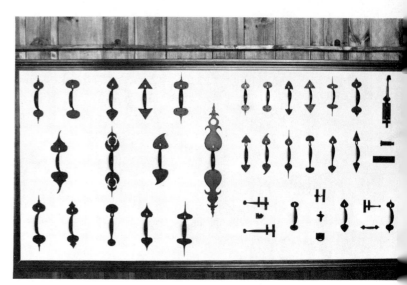

Hand-forged Colonial hardware, *Old Smithy Shop*

P. E. GUERIN, INC.
Dept. CHC
23 Jane Street
New York, NY 10014

"Artistic Hardware," $2.00, 54 pages, revised as required, black and white, illustrated.

Everything in builder's and furniture hardware, bathroom fittings, and accessories. If you can't find what you are looking for in the catalogue, you can have it made to order or duplicated. The hardware comes in many finishes—polished brass, satin steel, pewter, bronze, and gold plate, to list a few, and is priced accordingly. For instance, a 6" bamboo-motif door pull in polished brass is just $12.50; in gold plate, $17.50. The price list is complete with all dimensions, finishes, recommendations for finishes and maintenance. The firm boasts that it has never willfully discarded a model since its founding in 1857.
MO/ID

HORTON BRASSES
Dept. CHC
P.O. Box 95
Cromwell, CT 06416

"Horton Brasses," $1.00, 42 pages, published annually, black and white, illustrated.

A family firm that makes authentic reproductions of 18th- and 19th-century cabinet hardware. The catalogue is divided into sections by style periods—Hepplewhite, Chippendale, Queen Anne, and Victorian—then by materials—forged iron, tin, etc. They offer cupboard hardware and such unusual items as clock parts and forged-iron slide bolts for French or Dutch doors. Prices seem reasonable. A hard-to-find Victorian black wood teardrop pull with stamped brass back plate, 1½" wide by 3" long, is $2.50. Minimum order, $7.50; anything under will be returned.
MO

MEXICO HOUSE
Dept. CHC
Box 970
Del Mar, CA 92014

"Mexico House," 25 cents, 40 pages, black and white, illustrated.

Among the many hand-forged ironwork items offered by Mexico House is a handsome oversized door pull at $10.95 (two for $20) and a 12" wall bracket for hanging flowerpots, lanterns, or a birdcage at $5.95 (two for $10). Dimensions, prices, and handling charges included with each item listed.
MO

OLD SMITHY SHOP
Dept. CHC
P.O. Box 226
Milford, NH 03055

"Colonial Iron Hardware," 25 cents, 7 pages, black and white, illustrated.

Colonial wrought-iron exterior and interior door latches, door cabinet hinges, cabinet hardware, door knockers and bolts, bathroom accessories, and miscellaneous hand-forged hardware, black finished. Price list and order blank included.
MO

OLD WORLD FOUNDRY GUILD, INC.
Dept. CHC
1612 Decatur Street
Ridgewood, NY 11227

"Metal (Brass) Reproductions," no charge, 30 pages, black and white, illustrated.

A fine collection of solid-brass door knockers—a Medusa head, 7" high by 6" across, about $22; a Federal eagle with ball, 11" high by 8¾" across, about $25—with about 25 styles to choose from. An unusual brass wall-hung horse bracket, 24" long by 14" high, is about $93. There are hooks of all descriptions and sizes, from butcher hooks to those made of heavy brass keys. Dimensions, weight, and prices are given on a separate sheet.
MO

Contemporary stereo equipment, *Advent*

Stereo systems for the entire house, *Boulton*

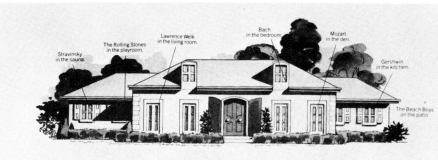

The only stereo system designed for your entire home.

A Boulton stereo system is like no other high fidelity music system you can own. Dad can be listening to Mozart in the den, mother to Gershwin in the kitchen, the kids to the Stones in the playroom. All on the

Boulton radio systems are all electronic, permitting stations to be pre-tuned and selected with the push of a button, anywhere. Their high sensitivity (1.4 mv) brings in more stations clearly than is possible with any other

any time to include additional rooms and a wide variety of special options. Among them: computer-controlled automatic tape recorders, automatic volume reduction when the telephone is used, automatic 50-record player

SOUND SYSTEMS

STURBRIDGE YANKEE WORKSHOP
Dept. CHC
Sturbridge, MA 01566

"Sturbridge Yankee Workshop Handbook and Catalogue," 50 cents, 64 pages, some color, illustrated.

Among the 1,000 items for an Early American home are hand-forged iron hardware such as h-l and strap hinges, latch and lock sets and door knocker, and brass or antique pewter cabinet hardware. Among the many other unusual hardware pieces are cabinetmaker's brass eagles, from 65 cents to $1.20.
MO

W. T. WEAVER AND SONS
Dept. CHC
1208 Wisconsin Avenue
Washington, DC 20007

"Decorative Hardware," $1.50, published annually, 74 pages, black and white, illustrated.

Just about every item imaginable in decorative hardware, from authentic reproductions of Early American locks, knockers, hinges, latches, and signs to contemporary, French, Spanish, and Oriental hardware for a wide range of applications. Also weathervanes and wall sconces. Prices are moderate to expensive.
MO

ADVENT CORPORATION
Dept. CHC
195 Albany Street
Cambridge, MA 02139

Free literature on individual products, illustrated.

Advent product lines include an FM radio, speaker systems, tape decks, microphones, noise reduction units, and color TV. Brochures and product folders provide descriptions, prices, and specifications.
RS

BOULTON STEREO SYSTEMS
Dept. CHC
380 Madison Avenue
New York, NY 10017

Brochure, no charge, 12 pages, black and white, illustrated.

The brochure describes the various Boulton sound systems available, how they work, relative costs and features, performance, installation, and service. Prices range from $700 to $3,500. Included are a no-obligation questionnaire with postage-paid reply envelope and a Boulton stereo demonstration record.
RS/ID

EMPIRE SCIENTIFIC CORP.
Dept. CHC
1055 Stewart Avenue
Garden City, NY 11530

"Empire Guide to Sound Design," no charge, published annually, 14 pages, color, illustrated.

This brochure provides specifications and prices for a line of cartridges, the company's Troubador Turntable, and speakers.
RS

HEATH COMPANY
Dept. CHC
Benton Harbor, MI 49022

"Heathkit," no charge, 88 pages, black and white, some color, illustrated.

Although this company specializes in electronic kits of all kinds, you can buy stereo components fully assembled and ready to use and still save money. The Heath/BSR changer, for $89.95, includes base and dust cover. Prices, dimensions, and all necessary descriptive information are given, along with a convenient order form.
MO

118

Corner speaker and turntable, *KLH Research & Development*

"Total Dispersion" speaker, *RTR Industries*

**KLH RESEARCH & DEVELOPMENT
    CORP.**
Dept. CHC
30 Cross Street
Cambridge, MA 02139

*"KLH," no charge, single-page flyers
and individual product brochures of
varying lengths and sizes; new
brochures are published for new
products.*

The flyers cover the "Research X
Division" line of speakers and
turntables. Each gives specifications but
not price. The brochure describe
speakers, receivers, and other products
of the KLH Research & Development
Corp., including a new digital clock
radio for $149.95.
RS

KLIPSCH AND ASSOCIATES, INC.
Dept. CHC
P.O. Box 688
Hope, AR 71801

*"Klipsch Loudspeaker Systems," no
charge, updated with product changes,
14 pages, black and white, illustrated.*

The booklet describes the Klipsch
speaker systems with emphasis on the
three matched-horn corner speakers
that come in a choice of three cabinet
styles and in a variety of solid woods—
maple, walnut, blonde primavera, light
or dark mahogany or veneers, and the
decorator's model, without decoration,
unfinished or painted black, for
individual expression. There are other
styles too. Prices range from about $250
to $1,441. Descriptive price list and
cross-country dealer list included.
RS

THE MUSIC BOX, INC.
Dept. CHC
58 Central Street
Wellesley, MA 02181

*A 12-page newsletter, no charge,
published at intervals on a regular
basis, black and white.*

An informative report by the owners of
The Music Box on the latest and best
stereo equipment—receivers, speakers,
record changers, tape decks,
amplifiers—with savings to their
readers. In the issue we have they are
offering a DUAL-Shure 1228 record
changer for $189.95 (the regular
component price is $259.95).
MO/RS

MUSIC MACHINE ALMANAC
Dept. CHC
One Embarcadero Center
San Francisco, CA 94111

*"Music Machine Almanac," $6.00,
published quarterly, 128 pages, color,
illustrated.*

A handy reference guide to the
selection and buying of quality stereo
equipment made by the leading
manufacturers, from Altec to Thorens to
Watts record-case equipment. Detailed
information, specifications, and prices
are included. Written to inform the
less-experienced buyer.

RTR INDUSTRIES
Dept. CHC
8116 Deering Avenue
Canoga Park, CA 91304

*Single sheet, no charge, black and
white, illustrated.*

A description of RTR's new "Total
Dispersion" speaker (Model 280 DR)
with transparent speaker enclosure and
hand-rubbed walnut veneer base. To
achieve this "Total Dispersion," six
high-frequency drivers were joined
with four woofers to produce the
incredibly uniform polar energy
response. When writing, ask for the
nearest dealer and the price.
RS

Catalogue cover, *Warehouse Sound*

Victorian mantels, *Gargoyles*

Iron fireplace grate, *Garden Way Research*

STOVES AND FIREPLACES

U.S. PIONEER ELECTRONICS CORP.
Dept. CHC
75 Oxford Drive
Moonachie, NJ 07074

"Pioneer Stereo Components," no charge, published annually, 25 pages, color, illustrated.

Complete description, including specifications and photograph, but no prices, of each item in the famous Pioneer line of stereo components: four-channel receivers, preamplifier, amplifiers, and phono cartridge; eight models of stereo receivers, five turntables (belt and direct drive), matched speaker systems, amplifiers and tuners, electronic crossover network, reverberation amplifier, headphones and accessories, tape decks and cassette decks, and microphones.
RS

WAREHOUSE SOUND CO.
Dept. CHC
Railroad Square
P.O. Box S
San Luis Obispo, CA 93405

"Warehouse Sound Co. Music Systems, Stereo Components, Accessories," no charge, 62 pages, color and black and white, illustrated.

Warehouse Sound Co. offers its own 14 or so stereo sound systems (from $297 to $2,017) of well-known components put together and tested in their sound rooms. Individual components and accessories are offered at special prices. All prices and an order form are included.
MO

CRAFT HOUSE
Dept. CHC
Colonial Williamsburg Foundation
Williamsburg, VA 23185

"Williamsburg Reproductions—Interior Designs for Today's Living," $2.95, 232 pages, color and black and white, illustrated.

Reproductions of antique fireplace accessories by The Harvin Company for Craft House are as attractive an addition to fireplaces today as they were in the 18th century, the heyday of beautiful design. There are handsome claw-and-ball brass andirons, 24" high and 22½" deep, for $236.50; graceful fire tools of brass and polished steel with ball finials for $168.50 a set; a serpentine brass fender with pierced pattern and scalloped edge for $275; even an authentic iron kettle that would make an unusual planter for porch or patio.
MO/RS

GARDEN WAY RESEARCH
Dept. CHC
P.O. Box 26
Charlotte, VT 05445

"Garden Way Fireplace Grate," folder, no charge, black and white, illustrated.

The folder lists 12 reasons why Garden Way's new design of grate can increase your enjoyment of your fireplace and cut air pollution. Specifications are given for three sizes priced from $30 to $35. They also have a high-efficiency, double-walled, Franklin-type stove and the Puff-Poker—a fireplace tool with two uses. Order form, prices, and shipping charges are included.
MO/RS

GARGOYLES, LTD.
Dept. CHC
512 South 3rd Street
Philadelphia, PA 19174

"Gargoyles, Ltd.," $4.00 (refundable with purchase), updated monthly, 32 pages, some color, illustrated.

Gargoyles' wide-ranging catalogue boasts seven pages of mantels of all types, sizes, styles, and materials, from massive marble or carved wood Tudor and Victorian ones to simple pine and mahogany Federal and Georgian styles. No two are alike; most have been salvaged from old homes. The overall and opening sizes are given; prices on request.
MO

120

Center-of-the-room fireplace, *Majestic*

Cast-iron Shaker stove replica, *Guild of Shaker Crafts*

GUILD OF SHAKER CRAFTS
Dept. CHC
401 Savidge Street
Spring Lake, MI 49546

"Guild of Shaker Crafts," $2.50, 28 pages, some color, illustrated.

A unique item in the Guild's collection is the cast-iron Shaker stove with hand-wrought hardware. Faithful in every detail to one of the first stoves made by the Shakers at New Lebanon, New York, it costs about $225.
MO/RS

KRISTIA ASSOCIATES
Dept. CHC
P.O. Box 1461
Portland, ME 04104

"JØTUL," $1.00, published semiannually, 50 pages, black and white, illustrated.

Norwegian cast-iron wood stoves and fireplaces sold through dealers. The catalogue provides information on what to look for, how to install, type of stovepipe, how to start a fire in stove or fireplace, comparative heating efficiency of JØTUL versus other makes, and a list of dealers in Eastern states.
RS

LEMEE'S FIREPLACE EQUIPMENT
Dept. CHC
815 Bedford Street
Bridgewater, MA 02324

"Lemee's Fireplace Equipment," 35 cents, published annually, 36 pages, black and white, illustrated.

A collection of selected artifacts handcrafted by skilled artisans; 17th- and 18th-century Colonial designs, in copper, brass, and iron. All brass is polished and lacquered to preserve the beauty. There are firescreens (folding and curtain types), firesets, andirons, cast aluminum weathervanes, baskets, wall ornaments, candlesticks, etc., with descriptions, including size and weight. Prices are moderate, and an order form is included.
MO

THE MAJESTIC COMPANY
Dept. CHC
Huntington, IN 46750

"Fireplace Ideas," $3.00, 89 pages, some color, illustrated.

This book offers some sound ideas for selecting the right style of fireplace for your room, choosing the right location or adding fireplaces to rooms. Examples of all the different styles and types—prefabricated wood-burning, gas, free-standing, and wall-hanging—are included. Nearest dealer's name on request.
RS

MEXICO HOUSE
Dept. CHC
Box 970
Del Mar, CA 92014

"Mexico House," 25 cents, 40 pages, black and white, illustrated.

Although lanterns and chandeliers of hand-forged iron are the main wares sold by Mexico House, they also have some good-looking fireplace tools and log baskets in the traditional Moorish designs executed since the days of Cortez. Dimensions, prices, and handling charges are included.
MO

PORTLAND STOVE FOUNDRY CO.
Dept. CHC
57 Kennebec Street
Portland, ME 04104

"Wood Stoves," 25 cents, black and white and color, illustrated.

A collection of descriptive folders covering individual product lines of stoves, including the Norwegian "Trolla," coal- and wood-burning kitchen ranges, camp stoves, Franklin stoves, potbelly stoves, and accessories (pipe, elbows, dampers). Price sheet is current but subject to change.
MO/RS

Wood-burning kitchen range and wood-burning stove, *Portland Stove Foundry*

Catalogue cover,
Lemee's Fireplace Equipment

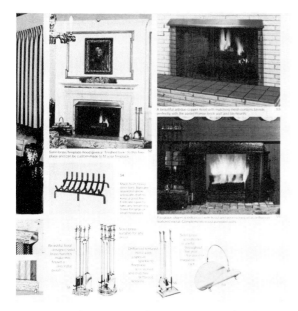

Fireplace screens and equipment, *Portland Willamette*   "The Igloo" Firepot, *Strawberry Bank Craftsmen*

WINDOWS

PORTLAND WILLAMETTE CO.
Dept. CHC
6404 N. E. 59th Place
Portland, OR 97218

"Fireplace Ideas," 25 cents, 15 pages, color, illustrated.

Beautifully illustrated catalogue of a wide variety of glass and mesh fireplace screens and combinations of both, shown in use, and a large selection of fireplace accessories of all kinds. Directions for measuring and ordering are included.
MO/RS

PREWAY
Dept. CHC
Wisconsin Rapids, WI 54494

"The Preway Style," no charge, 10 pages, color, illustrated.

The folder shows free-standing, wall-hung, and built-in fireplaces fueled by wood, coal, gas, or electricity. The styles range from modern through Franklin, most with color choices, starting at $325 for basic unit and chimney. Some are available in kit form.
RS

STRAWBERRY BANK CRAFTSMEN, INC.
Dept. CHC
Box 475
Little Compton, RI 02837

"The Strawberry FirePot," no charge, 6 pages, black and white, illustrated (color brochure in the works).

This brochure on the "FirePot," a free-standing ceramic fireplace in a choice of four glazes and six styles, also has drawings of flues and answers to questions about where and how FirePots can be used. Prices range from $250 to $550. Also available are basket grate and andirons.
MO

STURBRIDGE YANKEE WORKSHOP
Dept. CHC
Sturbridge, MA 01566

"Sturbridge Yankee Workshop Handbook and Catalogue," 50 cents, 64 pages, some color, illustrated.

The catalogue has two pages of fireplace equipment, from a Cape Cod lighter to a Connecticut fireplace screen to Pilgrim hand-wrought iron fire tools and forged loop andirons. There's even a black iron kettle on a hook for fireplace cookery.
MO

ANDERSEN CORPORATION
Dept. CHC
Bayport, MN 55003

"Andersen Windowalls, an investment in beauty . . . and better living," no charge, 35 pages, color, illustrated; "How to Get Good Windows and Gliding Doors When You Buy, Build, Remodel," no charge, published annually, 22 pages, color, illustrated.

Andersen has been making windows and gliding doors for almost 70 years, and they certainly know their business. The first booklet, "Andersen Windowalls," gives basic information about their insulated, weathertight, double-glazed windows and gliding doors, the types available, the features and options (such as Perma Shield), and a window-planning guide. The "How to Get" booklet tells you what to look for when you buy windows—top-grade materials, precision manufacturing, good design, and proper glazing; how to make sure you buy the right windows by preplanning, checking size and proportion, and selecting the appropriate style. Every type of window or gliding door is shown in use, in color, and a table of sizes is given at the back of the booklet.
RS

Window shapes and sizes, *Andersen*

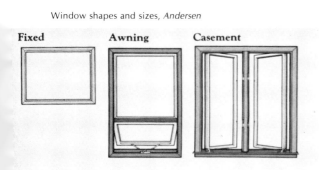

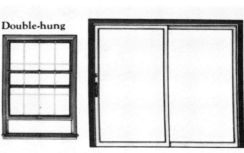

DECORATING IDEAS AND GUIDES

124

Convex mirror, *Syroco*

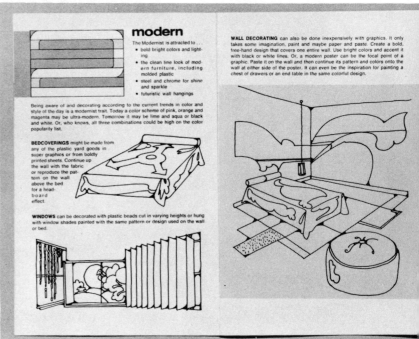

Decorating ideas from "How to Redecorate Your Room,"
Consumer Services Center, Johnson Wax

ACCESSORIES

SYROCO
Attention Mr. Peter Penizotto
Dept. CHC
Syracuse, NY 13201

*"All About Walls," 95 cents, 183 pages,
some color, illustrated.*

Syroco's guide to decorating with
accessories, by John Elmo, ASID, has 24
full-color room settings and a wealth of
drawings that show furniture
arrangements and wall treatments.
Color, lighting, wall arrangements,
accessories, and styles of decorating are
discussed, and there is also a glossary
of decorative motifs and terms, plus an
index.
RS

CREATIVE DECORATING

CONSUMER SERVICES CENTER
Johnson Wax
Dept. CHC
P.O. Box 567
Racine, WI 53403

*"How to Redecorate Your Room," no
charge, 14 pages, black and white,
illustrated.*

A booklet crammed with ideas and
information to help you create a new
look in your rooms without spending a
lot of money. Dissertations on four
decorating styles—Traditional, Modern,
Natural, Eclectic—tell you how to
achieve each look with inexpensive and
simple do-it-yourself ideas. For
instance, if the floor in a traditional
room is old and worn, stencil it new
again to match a curtain fabric pattern
or splatter-paint designs. For a modern
room, the bright idea is a wall hanging
of pegboard patterned with various
sizes of empty cans, either spray-
painted in colors or foil-covered.

ETHAN ALLEN, INC.
Dept. CHC
Ethan Allen Drive
Danbury, CT 06810

*"Getting Beauty and Value for Your
Decorating Dollars," 50 cents, 96 pages,
some color, illustrated.*

A valuable book, well worth the small
investment, that provides sensible,
straightforward information on just
about everything you need to know to
make your house or apartment a
reflection of you and your family, from
planning to buying wisely, lighting,
flooring, cleaning, and much more.

SIGNET BOOKS/THE NEW AMERICAN
LIBRARY, INC.
Dept. CHC
1301 Avenue of the Americas
New York, NY 10019

*"Instant-Effect Decorating," by Marjorie
P. Katz, $1.50, Signet paperback, 1972.*

Here's a book with hundreds of easy,
inexpensive ideas, with step-by-step
instructions, to give your home
excitement. Everything from recycling
trash by covering a wall or ceiling with
empty egg cartons, papering a wall with
old wrapping papers, or disguising a
bad ceiling with used juice cans to
what to do with found furniture. A
glossary, called "Getting It All
Together," lists all the materials needed,
along with the techniques.

Ideas with fabric, *Celanese*

DECORATIVE FINISHES

AMERICAN ART CLAY
Rub 'n Buff Division
Dept. CHC
Box 68163
Indianapolis, IN 46268

"Rub 'n Buff Decorative Inspirations and Craft Ideas," $1.25, color, illustrated.

By using the many Rub 'n Buff finishes, singly or in combination, you can achieve hundreds of interesting effects on furniture, picture and mirror frames, ceramics, candles, and découpage, to mention just a few of the possibilities. This book is full of ideas, with step-by-step instructions and materials necessary to complete the job.

DOORS

NATIONAL WOODWORK
**   MANUFACTURERS ASSOCIATION**
Dept. CHC
c/o SR&A
355 Lexington Avenue
New York, NY 10017

"Remodeling with Wood Windows and Doors," no charge, 14 pages, black and white, illustrated.

An informative booklet on the many types of wooden doors and windows, where and how to use them in remodeling and decorating. Some interesting uses for doors as room dividers, headboards, folding screens, or tabletops are illustrated. Tips on painting, decorating, and care of doors are also included.
RS

FABRIC AND SHEETS

CELANESE CORPORATION
Dept. CHC-HF5
1211 Avenue of the Americas
New York, NY 10036

"Room Service," $1.00, 41 pages, illustrated, some color.

"Celanese House" is a beautiful historic house (built by the son of President Lincoln) that was brought up to date by the use of fabric and other furnishings. The booklet takes you through the house, room by room, showing what can be accomplished with fabric as a decorative material and how to do it. There are hints on room arrangement and window treatments, a color guide, sections on period furniture, carpet maintenance, and a stain- and spot-removal chart.

MARTEX
Dept. CHC
P.O. Box 192, Madison Square Station
New York, NY 10010

"The View from the Tub and How to Change It," $1.00, 40 pages, some color, illustrated.

A booklet of decorating ideas with sheets and towels that you can do yourself, mostly for bathrooms, There are shirred shower curtains with terry tie backs, a ruffled sink skirt, an exercise mat made of bath towels, a tissue box covered with a pillow case. There's a yardage chart for sheets, pillowcases, and towels, step-by-step instructions, and lists of the additional materials needed to make each item.
RS

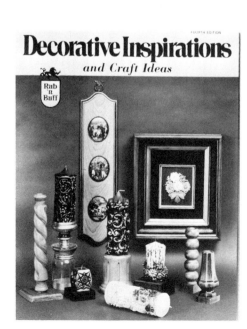

Catalogue cover, *American Art Clay*

Ideas with sheets, *J.P. Stevens*

Catalogue cover, *Hercules*

FLOORS

J. P. STEVENS AND COMPANY, INC.
Domestic and Allied Prod. Adv. Dept.
Dept. CHC
1185 Avenue of the Americas
New York, NY 10036

"Sew and Decorate with Utica's U.S. Mix," 50 cents, 14 pages, color, illustrated.

Many interesting and unusual ways to decorate with sheets—on the walls and ceiling, as a tent, to cover a floor screen, pillows, seat cushions, bolsters, to name a few. Instructions plus sheeting required are given in each case. Great fun.
RS

WAVERLY FABRICS
Dept. CHC
P.O. Box 684
New York, NY 10036

"Waverly's Easy to Do Decorating," $1.25, published annually, color, illustrated.

Hundreds of ideas created by leading interior designers for decorating projects you can carry out yourself. Many of them, naturally, involve the use of fabrics from the extensive Waverly collection, available in fabric stores or through decorators across the country. An interesting section called "The Smart Shopper" discusses buying a sofa, with four steps to take when making a purchase—shopping around, preplanning at home, store testing, and waiting for delivery—and descriptions and illustrations of 13 different sofa types, from canapé to Thirties overupholstered. There are other interesting articles on budget decorating, living with flowers, and new materials for the home.
RS/ID

E. T. BARWICK INDUSTRIES
Attention Mr. Mort Kahn
Dept. CHC
5025 New Peachtree Road
Chamblee, GA 30341

"What You Should Know About Carpet," $1.25, 208 pages, paperback, black and white, illustrated.

Annette Stramesi has written a valuable guide to judging quality and fashion in rugs and carpets with information on how to clean and care for carpeting, what to use where, and a brief history of carpets and a glossary of carpet terms.

HERCULES INCORPORATED
Dept. CHC
910 Market Street
Wilmington, DE 19899

"How to Be a Color Schemer," no charge, updated as needed, 23 pages, color, illustrated.

Ideas based on colorful carpets, used not only on floors but also to provide a wainscot effect, to soundproof and cover the walls of a bedroom alcove, even to display family photos.
RS

Wood flooring ideas, *Hoboken*

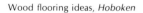

Room arrangements, *Omalon Room Planner*

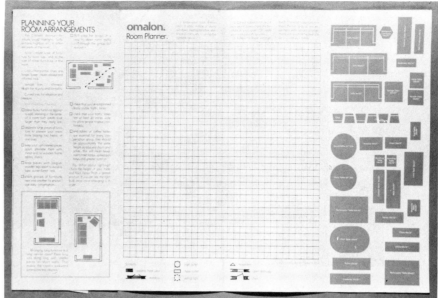

FURNITURE

HOBOKEN WOOD FLOORS
Dept. CHC
100 Willow Street
East Rutherford, NJ 07073

"Custom Design Wood Floors," $1.00,
12 pages, color, illustrated.

Ideas for using wood floors in different
patterns. Ten rooms are shown, each
surrounded by a wheel that gives eight
different choices of patterns, such as
parquet, herringbone, domino, plank,
and block, in different woods. Wood-
tone finishes and designer colors are
suggested as well.
MO

MAGEE CARPET COMPANY
Dept. CHC
919 Third Avenue
New York, NY 10022

"Decorating Color Ideas That Make
Your House a Home," 25 cents, 12
pages, color, illustrated.

Color schemes that start with six color
families—green, blue, orange, yellow
and gold, brown, beige and earth tones,
and red—with four choices in each
category, all based on carpets and wall
paint colors. One scheme in each
group is shown as a completed room.
Helpful up to a point, but a lot of
information necessary to the room
planner is left out.
RS

OMALON ROOM PLANNER
Dept. CHC
P.O. Box 456
Mount Vernon, NY 10551

"Omalon Room Planner, ' 25 cents, 8
pages, some color, illustrated.

A booklet that tells you how to
decorate from the floor up, starting
with the carpet underlay. There are
brief descriptions with sketches of
furniture types, upholstery fabrics, then
advice on room planning, starting with
carpet color, construction (woven,
tufted, knitted), and cushion, or
underlay. To help you plan your room
arrangement there's a room-planner
grid with scaled cutouts of furniture
and a guideline check list. This is a
helpful, straightforward little decorating
guide.
RS

PAINE FURNITURE COMPANY
Dept. CHC
81 Arlington Street
Boston, MA 02116

"Paine Furniture Company," $3.50, 230
pages, some color, illustrated.

This colorful catalogue takes you on a
decorating tour of America, from early
Colonial times to the natural look of
today, with room settings showing the
lines of the many American furniture
manufacturers the company represents.
Several pages are devoted to American
period rooms and how you can achieve
this look with reproductions; how to
mix traditional and contemporary styles
for a timeless eclectic look; and how to
give the clean-lined architectural look
of contemporary decorating your
personal touch. There are ideas for
furniture arrangements, window
treatments, and floor coverings and a
glossary of decorating terms. Paine
offers a complete decorating service
too. Tear-out cards at the back can be
marked for specific information on
merchandise and decorating service.
MO/RS

128

Decorating ideas, *Simmons*

RIVERSIDE FURNITURE CORP.
Dept. CHC
P.O. Box 1427
Fort Smith, AR 72901

"Bring Beauty to the Home," no charge, 14 pages, black and white, illustrated.

A guide to eclectic decorating with advice on mixing and matching tables, pointers on important features to look for in furniture construction and upholstery, and suggestions on using accent pieces.
RS

ROCHE-BOBOIS USA, LTD.
Dept. CHC
200 Madison Avenue
New York, NY 10016

"Roche-Bobois," $5.00, published annually, 132 pages, color, illustrated, with 52-page illustrated price list.

If you lean toward contemporary design with an international flavor, this catalogue will give you lots of ideas. Based on the vast collection of Roche-Bobois imports from Europe and England, the catalogue is packed with colorful decorating inspirations for every room in the house, plus ideas for table settings, window treatments, and floor treatments. The company offers a complete decorating service too.
MO/RS

SIMMONS CO.
Dept. CHC
2 Park Avenue
New York, NY 10016

"Simmons Guide to the Great Indoors," $1.00, 15 pages, color, illustrated.

The guide has five general divisions: 1) decorating basics for you to follow; 2) young ideas for your city apartment; 3) grassroots decorating for your country home; 4) decorating your vacation house; and 5) budget decorating for your first home.

Practical decorating ideas and down-to-earth, inexpensive solutions for common problems are given in the sections, each of which has one large and four small color pictures. At the back of the guide you'll find information about and pictures of Hide-A-Bed sofas and a map of the 67 Simmons Service Centers.
RS/ID

THOMASVILLE FURNITURE INDUSTRIES, INC.
Dept. CHC
P.O. Box 339
Thomasville, NC 27360

"Founders Guide to Modern Decorating," $2.00, 96 pages, some color, illustrated.

A breezily written, basic, and informative little paperback book by three home-furnishings experts—Frances Heard, Harriet Burket, and Joann Francis Gray. It gives a brief history of 20th-century furniture and design and proceeds to tell you how to decorate in the modern way, with sketched floor plans and photographs of Thomasville's "Founders" contemporary furniture.
RS

Paperback book cover, *Thomasville*

Decorating ideas with mirrors, *Bassett Mirror*

LIGHTING

MIRRORS

WENDELIGHTING
Dept. CHC
9068 Culver Boulevard
Culver City, CA 90230

*"Wendelighting," $1.50, 28 pages,
published annually, color, illustrated.*

This handsome brochure, dramatically
illustrated with color plates, shows the
importance of controlled area lighting,
now, more than ever, an important
consideration in interior and
architectural design. The Wendelighting
systems are custom-designed for the
individual object or area. Art objects
are completely engulfed in bright, even
light without any obvious source; the
light in a dining room is confined to
the table top; the illusion of real
moonlight is created in a garden
through clever distribution of light and
shadow.
RS/ID

BASSETT MIRROR CO., INC.
Dept. CHC
P.O. Box 627
Bassett, VA 24055

*"Carleton Varney's Alphabet of
Decorating Ideas," $1.00, 32 pages,
color, illustrated.*

Interior designer and columnist
Carleton Varney has put together this
interesting booklet crammed full of
decorating ideas and tips that
incorporate Bassett's alphabetized
collection of traditional and
contemporary mirrors, occasional
tables, chairs, and étagères, with sizes
and finishes listed at the back of the
booklet.
RS

LIBBEY-OWENS-FORD CO.
Dept. CHC
811 Madison Avenue
Toledo, OH 43695

*"Decorating with Mirrors," 10 cents,
special issue, 11 pages, color, illustrated.*

The illusory and magical effects that
can be achieved with mirrors are
explored in this idea booklet. It shows
how to expand space visually, reflect
natural light, give depth and dimension
to dark areas, play up furniture and
art—all done with mirrors.
RS

PPG INDUSTRIES, INC.
Dept. CHC
One Gateway Center
Pittsburgh, PA 15222

*"All American Homes," no charge,
published every three years, 39 pages,
color, illustrated.*

Decorating ideas with mirrors and glass,
window decorating ideas, and some
general advice on planning a home.
The booklet covers four major types of
all-American homes: Builder, Custom,
Manufactured, and Resort.
RS

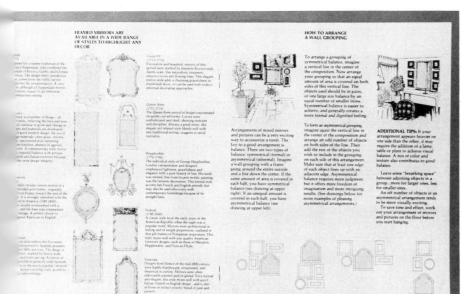

Decorating with mirrors, *Libbey-Owens-Ford*

Ideas with paint, *PPG Industries*

PAINT

PHOTOGRAPHS

BORDEN CHEMICAL
Dept. CHC
P.O. Box 266
Medina, OH 44256

"How to Decorate with Krylon," 25 cents, 12 pages, color, illustrated.

How-to techniques of spray painting with Krylon, plus many decorating ideas for walls, floors, and furniture.
RS

COTTER & CO.
Dept. CHC
Chicago, IL 60614

"Let's Live Color," 50 cents, 32 pages, color, illustrated.

A clutch of decorating ideas, using the brilliant colors of Tru-Test paints, to help you color-plan each room.
RS

PPG INDUSTRIES
Dept. CHC
One Gateway Center
Pittsburgh, PA 15222

"The Naked House," $1.95, 128 pages, color, illustrated.

An amusing but informative paperback by Anne Cain, full of ideas on how to color your home from top to bottom, inside and out, with the emphasis on paint. It shows you how to paint circles and stripes, tells about leafing and gilding, sponging, stenciling, graining, antiquing, and how to make découpage. There are artful ways with color, such as putting a colorful frame around fabric mounted as a painting; using color as a focal point in built-in bookcases with a collection of one-color objects and a stenciled motif on the case itself; painting a front door or planter boxes a brilliant hue.
RS

EASTMAN KODAK CO.
Dept. CHC—841
Rochester, NY 14650

"How to Decorate with Photographs," no charge (on receipt of a self-addressed business envelope with "AM-14" marked on back), 24 pages, color, illustrated.

This booklet of ideas on decorating your home with your own photographs gives suggestions for displaying them in unusual ways: on paperweights, planters, place mats, mobiles, swinging pictures, free-standing frames, and room dividers. Do-it-yourself information includes discussions of materials for mounting and edging, frames, and ways to change the display backgrounds of your photographs.

Decorating with photographs, *Eastman Kodak*

Wallcovering ideas, *Clopay*

WALLCOVERINGS

LUSTRO-WARE DIVISION
  BORDEN CHEMICAL CO.
Dept. CHC
Columbus, OH 43223

"Ideas with Lustro-ware Wall-togethers," no charge, 11 pages, color, illustrated.

Fifteen ways to gain storage in every room with easy-to-install Lustro-ware Wall-together storage units. There are eight different units, ranging from 12" x 12" pegboard panels to three sizes of shelves to two clocks and a mirror, two sets of storage and spice jars on individual shelves. All are wall-hung.
RS

BORDEN CHEMICAL
Dept. CHC
P.O. Box 266
Medina, OH 44256

"Tips with Tape," 25 cents, 12 pages, color, illustrated.

All kinds of ideas with Mystik tape, from making a supergraphic to creating a montage to decorating a window shade to trimming a lamp base and shade. One page shows all the different types of Mystik tape, which comes in a range of colors and widths, with prices per roll.
RS

ETHAN ALLEN, INC.
Dept. CHC
Ethan Allen Drive
Danbury, CT 06810

"Getting Beauty and Value for Your Decorating Dollars," 50 cents, 96 pages, some color, illustrated.

Ethan Allen's decorating and shopping guide has a section on interesting uses of wallcoverings of vinyl, fabric, and wood.

CLOPAY CORPORATION
Homewares Division
Dept. CHC
Clopay Square
Cincinnati, OH 45214

"Decorative Coverings Idea Book," $1.00, 29 pages, color, illustrated.

Ways to decorate indoors and out with Clopay self-adhesive decorative coverings that come in a range of colors and patterns from wet-look vinyls to suedelike, flocked patterns. Ideas for walls, furniture, for revitalizing old rooms and pieces, for games and crafts, and special occasions. Some unusual ideas include supersized graphics. Illustrated how-to's and helpful decorator tips are also given.
RS

Supergraphic with Mystik tape, *Borden Chemical*

"Star Spangled Banner" wallcovering, *Jack Denst Designs*

THE JACK DENST DESIGNS, INC.
Dept. CHC
7355 South Exchange Avenue
Chicago, IL 60649

"The Great American Happy Birthday Book," 50 cents, limited edition, 16 pages, color, illustrated.

Ideas for all rooms using Jack Denst's latest collection of red, white, and blue wallcoverings, from the all-American Hot Dog mural to combos of stars and stripes to mix or match in a dozen ways. There are both way-out designs and simple, conservative American motifs that will go with any style or period of furniture and accessories.
RS/ID

IMPERIAL WALLCOVERINGS
Dept. CHC
23645 Mercantile Road
Cleveland, OH 44122

"Secrets That Decorators Don't Always Tell You About Wallcoverings," 75 cents, 35 pages, color, illustrated.

Such decorator ideas as how to give a room architectural interest, how to pair off patterns in bedrooms, and how to mix contemporary furnishings with traditional patterns in wallcoverings are just a few of the many inspirations shown with Imperial's exciting new designs. There is a page of decorating do's and don'ts and basic information on wall preparation, how to hang prepasted papers, and a quick wallcovering estimate chart.
RS

WALLCOVERING INDUSTRY BUREAU, INC.
Dept. CHC
969 Third Avenue
New York, NY 10022

"Think Wallcoverings," no charge, color, illustrated.

You'll find lots of good ideas and tips in this industry brochure on color scheming, pattern picking, space shaping, and furniture flattering with all types of wallcoverings for all types of rooms. A wallcovering room-analysis chart to take when you go shopping is included.

Strippable wallcovering ideas, *Imperial*

132

Window shade ideas,
Window Shade Manufacturers' Association

WINDOW SHADES AND BLINDS

CLOPAY
Dept. CHC
Clopay Square
Cincinnati, OH 45214

"Clopay Window Shades," no charge,
20 pages, color, illustrated.

Decorative window ideas using Clopay
window shades in a variety of styles
and materials, one with matching
valance, another a do-it-yourself shade
of self-adhesive fabric that permits you
to apply a matching curtain, bedspread,
or lightweight upholstery fabric to the
shade.
RS

WINDOW SHADE MANUFACTURERS'
ASSOCIATION
Dept. CHC
230 Park Ave
New York, NY 10017

"Window Shade Primer" and *"The
Decorative Window Shade,"* each 25
cents, each 16 pages, black and white,
illustrated.

Both booklets are full of ideas that
prove there's a shade for every window
by showing all kinds of window
treatments, using shades to control light
or to enhance a room scheme.

LEVOLOR LORENTZEN, INC.
Dept. CHC
720 Monroe Street
Hoboken, NJ 07030

"Window Magic," 50 cents, 40 pages,
color, illustrated.

Ideas for decorating with Levolor's
standard and slat blinds and woven
aluminum blinds, available in decorator
colors. To link the blinds with a room
scheme, coordinated fabric may be
laminated to the slats, or designs can
be painted on them. Ideas are shown
for using blinds to control light and
sun, to conceal storage, shelving, and
unsightly areas.
RS/ID

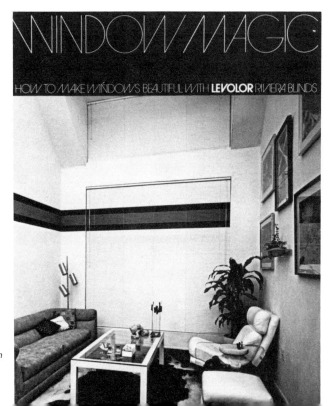

Catalogue cover, *Levelor Lorentzen*

Decorating with sculpture and graphics (courtesy *Family Circle*)

ART: ORIGINALS AND REPRODUCTIONS

Wall sculpture, *Addison Greene Gallery*

Wire horse sculpture, *Barr Art Studio*

CARVINGS AND SCULPTURE

ADDISON GREENE GALLERY, LTD.
Dept. CHC
1093 Second Avenue
New York, NY 10022

"Handcrafted Metal Sculpture," no charge, published annually, 16 pages, black and white, illustrated.

Some 50 of Louis Fajardo's sculptures are shown in this brochure. The complete collection is exhibited in the New York gallery, new designs are constantly being created, and the company welcomes special commissions. All designs can be scaled to specification, and most finishes are interchangeable. There are wall, table, and standing sculptures; wall console and mirror; sculptured fountains and cocktail-table bases of brushed, stainless, natural oxidized, gold- and silver-leafed steel with copper, brass, and bronze accents. The sculptures include abstract designs, "junk" art, and figures ranging in price from $35 to $1,500.
MO

ALVA MUSEUM REPLICAS, INC.
Dept. CHC
30-30 Northern Boulevard
Long Island City, NY 11101

"Alva Sculpture Replicas," $3.50, 80 pages, black and white, illustrated.

Alva, a subsidiary of the New York Graphic Society Ltd., produces authorized replicas of famous and valuable museum pieces, both old and contemporary, which are shown and described in their catalogue. The replicas are handcast in Alvastone and, with a few exceptions, are of the same size as the originals. A table of contents, an index, and a cross-reference of special subject matter facilitates use of the catalogue. Prices range from $2 to almost $500.
MO/RS

ARTIQUES, LTD.
Dept. CHC
P.O. Box 3999
Swormville, NY 14146

Pamphlet, no charge, black and white, illustrated.

Pre-Columbian and pre-Hispanic reproductions from the diverse meso-American cultures, exact even to the patina, which reproduces the effect of centuries. Prices range from about $18 to $60.
MO

BARR ART STUDIO
Dept. CHC
109 Ladder Hill Road
Weston, CT 06880

"Wire Horse Sculptures," no charge, black and white, illustrated.

The flyer illustrates four wire sculpture horses individually handcrafted by Mary Ann Barr, each mounted on a base of weathered wood from the Rocky Mountains. Specifications, prices, and order form are included. Prices range from $125 to $140.
MO

DESIGN MATRIX
Dept. CHC
2424 Esplanade
Bronx, NY 10469

Price list, no charge, illustrated.

Sculptures of delicate metal flowers and trees, in antique gold or green patina finishes, are the specialty of Design Matrix. There are several of each at reasonable prices.
MO

Pre-Columbian figure, *ARTiques*

Catalogue cover, *Museum Collections*

Wall sculptures, *The Sculpture Studio*

CARL FORSLUND, INC.
Dept. CHC
122 East Fulton Street
Grand Rapids, MI 49502

"Timeless Furniture Made by Carl Forslund," $2.00, revised every two to three years, 97 pages, color, illustrated.

Hand-carved by Len Vander Zand and hand-painted by Len Nowicki, "Folk Art" birds are for the serious collector or the sportsman. The set of eight can be bought for less than $300 or individually, from $38 for the pheasant, jacksnipe, woodcock, or quail to $50 for the handsome fantailed ruffed grouse. A most interesting and charming collection.
MO

Cast-bronze group, *Heredities*

HEREDITIES LIMITED
Dept. CHC
P.O. Box 585
Bristol, PA 19007

"Heredities," $3.00 (refundable with purchase), published annually, 42 pages, some color, illustrated.

Small sculptural bronzes by contemporary international artists of people, animals, birds, produced by the cold-cast method. Some are limited editions.
MO

MUSEUM COLLECTIONS
Dept. CHC
Box 999, Radio City Station
New York, NY 10019

"Museum Collections," 50 cents, published annually, 16 pages, color, illustrated.

These sculpture and jewelry replicas from many of the world's greatest museums range from ancient to contemporary, encompassing Egyptian, Chinese, Greek, Roman, Etruscan, and African pieces—and more. All are authentic reproductions, and the history of the original is given along with the picture, description, and price (from about $5 to $500). Order forms are enclosed.
MO

THE SCULPTURE STUDIO, INC.
Dept. CHC
202 East 77th Street
New York, NY 10021

"William Bowie, The Sculpture Studio, Inc.," no charge, published seasonally, color, illustrated.

This brochure (which is being expanded) includes only part of the collection, which can be viewed in its entirety at the studio of William Bowie, who will design sculptures for homes and businesses. His designs include birds, trees, flowers, and abstracts in polished, copper-coated, stainless, gold- and silver-leafed steel with black, brass, copper, silver, and red accents. One standing sculpture of fish is executed in cast aluminum on a lucite base. Wall, standing, and table sculptures are included (some on wood bases), as well as cocktail tables—either the base or the entire table. Some sculptures are available for immediate delivery; some are limited editions. Prices range from about $60 to $1,000.
MO/RS

138

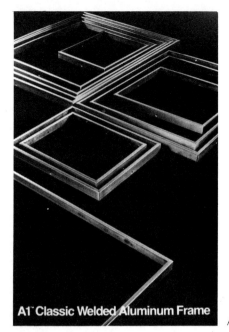
A1™ Classic Welded Aluminum Frame

Aluminum picture frames, *Kulicke Frames*

Metropolitan Opera posters, *Fiesta Arts*

PAINTINGS AND PORTRAITS

J. N. BARTFIELD ART GALLERIES, INC.
Dept. CHC
45 West 57th Street
New York, NY 10019

"The American West," $2.00, published annually, 32 pages, color, illustrated.

A catalogue offering of original, signed paintings, etchings, pen-and-ink drawings, and sculpture of the American West, each shown and described. Prices given on request.
MO

C. C. PRICE, INC.
Dept. CHC
15 East 48th Street
New York, NY 10017

"The Unique Portrait Gallery," no charge, published annually, about 25 pages, black and white.

Portraits, painted from photographs or from life, and portrait sculpture, by over 100 staff artists, in styles ranging from traditional to expressionist, abstract, surrealistic.
MO/RS

PICTURE FRAMES

KULICKE FRAMES, INC.
Dept. CHC
636 Broadway
New York, NY 10012

"Kulicke Catalogue," $1.00, published periodically, 12 pages, black and white, illustrated.

Kulicke, a leading supplier of frames to museums, galleries, collectors, and artists, puts out a folder of six loose sheets, each describing one or more types of frame, complete with assembling instructions and prices (moderate to expensive), order and delivery information.
MO/RS

POSTERS

FIESTA ARTS, INC.
Dept. CHC
Greenvale, NY 11548

Brochure, no charge, published semiannually.

Metropolitan Opera collection of first-performance posters (in color) reproduced from the original programs at $1 each and Siamese temple art panels, $15 each, are the current offerings.
MO

BUCK HILL ASSOCIATES
Dept. CHC
Garnet Lake Road
Johnsburg, NY 12843

"Posters and Handbills from America's Past," 25 cents, published annually, 18 pages, black and white.

Reproductions of over 1,000 posters, handbills, broadsides, prints, and advertisements that trace the political and social history of America from earliest times to the recent past make interesting and unusual wall decorations. Most of the reproductions are black and white and cost from 35 cents up, but there are also six important American documents on tan parchment ($1.50 per set) and eight Civil War battle portfolios, etched by Currier & Ives, each containing six 15" x 11" hand-colored silk-screen engravings ($3.95 per portfolio). Order form included. Minimun order $3.95.
MO

Sports sculpture, *American Gallery of Sports Arts*

Theater poster, *Triton Gallery*

Llama woodcut, *Associated American Artists*

PRINTS

POSTER ORIGINALS LIMITED
Dept. CHC
16 East 78th Street
New York, NY 10021

"American Posters" and "European Posters," $2.00 each, each 16 pages, illustrated.

The European art posters are in black and white, the American art posters in full color. Many are lithographed, several silk-screened, available framed and unframed. A special collection of serigraphs by Braque and Matisse is available for the first time. Also of special interest are the Super Environmental graphics (three panels each) by Rauschenberg and Lindner. Prices are reasonable.
MO

TRITON GALLERY
Dept. CHC
323 West 45th Street
New York, NY 10036

"Triton Poster Catalogue," 25 cents, 20 pages, black and white, illustrated.

Triton lists several hundred film, theater, concert, opera, and ballet posters, plus some miscellaneous subjects, with a separate list of Broadway theater showcards. Most of the posters are for recent events; some are in color, some in black and white. The catalogue includes sizes and prices, which range from about $3 to $10.
MO

AMERICAN GALLERY OF SPORTS ARTS
Dept. CHC
Box 20004
Dallas, TX 75220

"Limited Editions," no charge, published as new editions are offered, color, illustrated.

Four-page mailers of the limited editions offered by this gallery are sent without charge to the enthusiast or collector interested in the sports field of art. Sculpture and prints of such famous sports figures as Hank Aaron and Arnold Palmer, as well as Gilbert Duran's Game Birds of America, are available at present. A fine source for the sports collector.
MO

Marine print, *Bluejacket Ship Crafters*

ASSOCIATED AMERICAN ARTISTS
Dept. CHC
663 Fifth Avenue
New York, NY 10022

Catalogue, 50 cents, published annually, plus three pamphlets and a special patron's supplement, published quarterly, black and white, illustrated.

A collection of signed, limited-edition, original etchings, lithographs, serigraphs, and woodcuts by American and international artists, captioned to provide artist's name, number of impressions, size, price, and shipping cost. There is also a framing service. AAA claims to have America's largest collection of original prints.
MO

BLUEJACKET SHIP CRAFTERS
Dept. CHC
145 Water Street
South Norwalk, CT 06854

"BlueJacket Ship Crafters," 75 cents, 64 pages, black and white, illustrated.

A fine collection of marine prints by the most distinguished marine artists are offered in this catalogue. Among them, Samuel Walters' "The Independence," the well-known 19th-century New York–Liverpool packet, 20" x 29½" plus margins, about $12, and Charles Vickery's "Sunlight and Surf," 36" x 34" plus margins, just $16.50, and many others of equal interest.
MO

American Revolution prints, *Fife and Drum*

Birds of North America prints, *Griggsville Wild Bird Society*

CRAFT HOUSE
Dept. CHC
Colonial Williamsburg Foundation
Williamsburg, VA 23185

"Williamsburg Reproductions—Interior Designs for Today's Living," $2.95, 232 pages, color and black and white, illustrated.

Some interesting reproductions of early 18th-century hand-tinted prints of birds by Fnglish naturalist Mark Catesby and flowers and fruits by English nurseryman Robert Furber are part of the Craft House collection. The prints are $12.95 unframed, $38 framed. There are also some Rowlandson prints, military prints, and historical maps of early Virginia and Williamsburg.
MO/RS

FIFE AND DRUM
Dept. CHC
Valley Forge, PA 19481

"How to Celebrate Our 200th Birthday," no charge, black and white, illustrated.

The brochure describes 20 authentic costume prints of the Revolution by artist Raymond Desvarreux Larpenteur, including the predominating colors of each military uniform. The prints are 16" x 10½" with ample margins for framing. "First-proof," strictly limited editions of 500 copies on diploma parchment paper are $5 and an unlimited edition on dull white woven stock, $3. Flags, 13-star or 50-star, 3' x 5' in long fiber cotton, are also available at $11.50 and $8.50.
MO

FRAME HOUSE GALLERY
Dept. CHC
110 East Market Street
Louisville, KY 40202

"Frame House Gallery Collector Prints," $1.00, 27 pages, published semiannually, black and white, illustrated.

Fine, limited-edition prints of the works of 11 of America's leading wildlife artists, sold through authorized dealers. An additional series, the Fleur-de-Lis Collection, which includes artists of other countries as well as Americans, deals with a variety of subjects. Included is a brief sketch of each artist, along with the size, edition, and price of the print.
MO/RS

GRIGGSVILLE WILD BIRD SOCIETY
Dept. CHC
Purple Martin Junction
Griggsville, IL 62340

"Works of Maryrose Wampler, Richard Timm, and Richard Sloan," 4 pamphlets, 50 cents, published semiannually, color, illustrated.

Limited-edition collector prints of flowers, mammals, and birds by American nature artists, done in water color, acrylic, casein, and gouache. Some state birds and flowers are featured, a series of North American birds, and one of exclusively North American mammals. Prices on request.
MO

Catalogue cover, *Frame House Gallery*

Catalogue cover, *Lambert*

Larry Zox graphic, *Harcus-Krawkow Rosen Sonnabend Gallery*

HAGERTY COMPANY
Dept. CHC
38 Parker Avenue
Cohasset, MA 02025

*"Cohasset Colonials by Hagerty," 50
cents, published annually, 32 pages,
some color, illustrated.*

Included in the catalogue is a selection
of prints, copies of original ship prints
such as the "Saxony of Boston," done
about 1835, $15; some fruit and flower
still-life designs taken from old
theorems and stencils; a sizable (38" x
35") copy of "The Game Cock Inn"
sign; and a charming replica of a 19th-
century hand-colored family register,
$10.
MO/RS

HARCUS-KRAKOW ROSEN
SONNABEND GALLERY
Dept. CHC
7 Newbury Street
Boston, MA 02116

*Color portfolio, $1.25; price list, no
charge.*

The gallery annually compiles a
catalogue of prints available and invites
inquiries about exhibitions or offerings
in any area of contemporary art
(paintings, tapestries, and sculptures). A
subsidiary company, HKL/LTD.,
publishes limited-edition graphics,
primarily large in size and
commissioned for public spaces, some
of which are reproduced in color in the
HKL catalogue. Slides are available on
request. Prices range from around $125
to several thousand dollars.
MO

HORCHOW COLLECTION
Dept. CHC
P.O. Box 34862
Dallas, TX 75234

*"Horchow Collection of Graphics," no
charge, 20 pages, color, illustrated.*

Among the specialized collections of
this top-echelon mail-order company
are graphics in a wide range of styles
and prices (from $60 to $5,000). All
pertinent information is given below
the photograph in the color catalogue,
including the media—wood engraving,
etching, aquatint, serigraph,
lithograph—and there is a section of
biographical sketches of the artists.
Prints are unframed.
MO

LAMBERT STUDIOS, INC.
Dept. CHC
910 North La Cienega Boulevard
Los Angeles, CA 90069

*"The Magnificent World of Art," 50
cents, 20 pages, color, illustrated.*

The Lambert Studios catalogue
illustrates in full color over 200 different
art masterpieces reproduced on canvas.
Hundreds of subjects ranging from
Renaissance masters to contemporary
art posters are available, as are the
Cameo Classic Edition, Canvas Mini
Edition, Decorator Deluxe Edition with
brushstroking. Some subjects are also
available as fine art cards. Frames are
also shown in the catalogue, which
includes price lists and order forms.
Canvas reproductions range from $1 to
about $40.
MO/RS

OESTREICHER'S PRINTS, INC.
Dept. CHC
43 West 46th Street
New York, NY 10036

*"Oestreicher's Reference Book of Fine
Art Reproductions," $5.50, 160 pages,
published every two years, color,
illustrated.*

Oestreicher may well have, as the
catalogue states, "the world's largest
collection of fine color art
reproductions." The catalogue alone
contains 1,100 illustrations of the more
than 500,000 prints, which embrace the
entire spectrum of art, from old masters
to present-day names. The prints are
listed alphabetically by the artist's
name, with title, size, and price
(moderate). There is also an order page
and prices for permanizing the prints.
MO

142

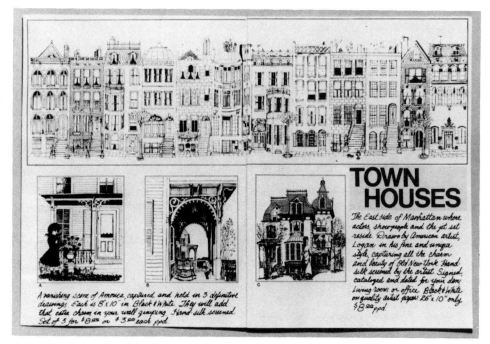

Hand-screened prints, *Something New*

Block prints, *The Tattered Boot*

ORIGINAL PRINT COLLECTORS GROUP
Dept. CHC
120 East 56th Street
New York, NY 10022

"Original Print Collectors Group, Ltd.," no charge, published quarterly, 3 pages, color.

This membership organization gives you the opportunity to purchase signed, framed prints by well-known artists in limited editions, and the membership fee of $25 is applied to your first order. In the brochure we received there were a dozen prints offered, among them an original black-and-white etching by Bruce Zator, signed edition of 50, framed size 25" x 18½", for $115. This is an interesting collection, catholic in taste.
MO

THE PRINT MINT
Dept. CHC
Bridgewater, VT 05034

"Print Mint," published annually, 14 pages, black and white.

Early lithographs, etchings, engravings; contemporary silk screen, woodblocks; Eskimo, Indian, and Himalyan prints and sculptures. The catalogue lists artists, subject, media, publisher, size, date, and prices, in a wide range.
MO

SOMETHING NEW
Dept. CHC
467 Nod Hill Road
Wilton, CT 06897

"Something New Print Catalogue," 50 cents, published annually, 26 pages, black and white, illustrated.

Along with animal, flower, grass, and herb prints, the catalogue shows a pair of flower prints "for formal balance," kitchen graphics, European scenes, Bicentennial graphics of Colonial days, and a red and orange print "Alphagraphics," all at reasonable prices. Frames can be ordered in a choice of four colors, brass or chrome.
MO

THE TATTERED BOOT
Dept. CHC
Lamont, FL 32336

"A Collection of Original Ideas," 25 cents, black and white, illustrated.

Lithographs, etchings, block prints, wood-engraved relief prints of animals, flowers, and rustic scenes. There's an Alice in Wonderland series of eight in black and white or hand-watercolored, and fanciful mushrooms, butterflies, and clowns. Particularly attractive are the ferns, "shell scapes" and individual sea shells, and black-and-white lithographs copied from an 18th-century herbal. Sets are available and matting to complement the lithographs in a choice of colors or special order at inexpensive prices.
MO

VIGNARI ART ENTERPRISES
Dept. CHC
Main Street
Ogunquit, ME 03907

"Sea, Men and Ships," $1.00, published annually, 36 pages, 140 reproductions in black and white.

Compiled by marine artist John T. Vignari, this catalogue encompasses a span of over 300 years of marine art by artists from Canaletto through English painters and French Impressionists to American painters like Homer, Hopper, and Wyeth. The color prints, ranging in price from $8 to $22, are mailed in tubes and insured by Vignari Art Enterprises.
MO

Marine print, *Vignari Art*

Molas tapestry, *Pan-Am Exhibits*

Rambouillet tapestry, *Allan Waller*

TAPESTRIES

LOVELIA ENTERPRISES, INC.
Dept. CHC
P.O. Box 1845
Grand Central Station
New York, NY 10017

"Tapestries," 80 cents, published annually, 12 pages, color, illustrated.

Tapestries of 100 percent cotton from Belgium, France, and Italy, woven on old looms from original jacquards. Some are copies of masterpieces; several incorporate the signature of the original painter. There is also a page of do-it-yourself ideas for decorating with tapestry: upholstery, headboards, valances, pillows. Prices are moderate.
MO

PAN-AM EXHIBITS
Dept. CHC
3743 Highcliff
San Antonio, TX 78218

"About Molas—Salasacas," no charge, published annually.

Molas are unique tapestries created by the Cuna Indians of San Blas, Panama, each an original, one-of-a-kind artifact depicting animal life, plant life, folklore, or geometrics. The sizes range from 13" x 15" to 16" x 19," and there is one price of $17.95, regardless of selection. Also attached is a pictorial review of authentic Salasaca tapestries, Inca and pre-Inca designs of men, animals, and objects, handwoven by the Salasaca Indians of Ecuador. A 17" x 17" tapestry is $7.95, a 30" x 30" $14.95.
MO

ALLAN WALLER, LTD.
Dept. CHC
3437 Piedmont Road N. E.
Atlanta, GA 30305

"The Rambouillet Tapestry from Allan Waller Ltd.," $5.00, published every four years, 36 pages, color, illustrated.

The catalogue provides a comprehensive history of French tapestry, explains the reproduction processes used, illustrates in full color the beautiful tapestries available for sale, gives descriptions of each piece, and includes a price list. The tapestries copied date from the 15th to the 18th centuries and are in French museums. The reproductions are silk screen-printed onto a canvas of Dacron, flax, and wool made to resemble stitching as nearly as possible. Prices for the reproductions, sold only by Waller, the agent for Editions d'Art Rambouillet, range from $195 to $3,060.
MO

COLLECTIONS AND COLLECTIBLES

Art glass, *Fenton Art Glass*

Glass sculpture, *Steuben Glass*

ART GLASS

BOOKS

THE FENTON ART GLASS CO.
Dept. CHC
Williamstown, WV 26187

"Fenton 1975–76," no charge, 68 pages, color, illustrated.

Beautiful illustrations of the art-glass line of lamps, baskets, serving dishes, vases, miscellaneous pieces of all kinds. Includes price list, moderate to expensive, of glassware sold only through Fenton dealers.
RS

HOLLY CITY BOTTLE
Dept. CHC
Box 344
Millville, NJ 08332

Lists, no charge, published as new items are available, black and white, illustrated.

American handmade, hand-blown commemorative decanters (by Clevenger) with real pontils, each different in design and made in limited editions. A special American Bicentennial Series of decanters will have a different design for each of the original 13 colonies. Paperweights are also available. Prices from $6 to $25.
MO

STEUBEN GLASS
Dept. CHC
Fifth Avenue at 56th Street
New York, NY 10022

"Christmas Catalogue," $3.00, published annually in mid-October, color and black and white, illustrated.

Steuben is famous for lead crystal pieces of the finest design and workmanship, and their catalogue consists of beautiful full-page photographs on fine-quality paper with information about each piece on the facing page. Shown in the catalogue are new designs, Steuben classics, purely ornamental pieces, and more functional ones, such as candlesticks, bowls, decanters, vases, and glasses. Illustrations of glass not shown in the catalogue will be sent on request. Price range from $50 to $31,500.
MO/RS

AMERICAN REPRINTS CO.
Dept. CHC
4656 Virginia Avenue
St. Louis, MO 63111

"Books for Collectors," no charge, published semiannually, 22 pages, black and white, illustrated.

A listing of books of interest to collectors of watches and clocks, antiques, bottles, dolls and toys, glass, china and pottery, guns and rifles, knives and razors. Reprints of "The Good Old Days" include a reproduction of a 1908 Sears, Roebuck catalogue. Each book is described by subject matter, size, and price. Order form included.
MO

J. N. BARTFIELD BOOKS, INC.
Dept. CHC
45 West 57th Street
New York, NY 10019

"Fine Binding Catalogue," $1.00, published annually, 92 pages, black and white, illustrated.

An offering of leather-bound books in singles and sets, newly hand-bound in selected imported leathers. Each book or set is listed, described, and priced. There are very few duplicates. Cloth-bound sets are also available. Single leather-bound volumes range from as low as $7.50 to two blue morocco-bound volumes at $7,500.
MO

Commemorative decanter, *Holly City Bottle*

Antique map, *Kenneth Nebenzahl*

Memorabilia, *Gargoyles*

MAPS

HOTCHKISS HOUSE, INC.
Dept. CHC
18 Hearthstone Road
Pittsford, NY 14534

"Books on Antiques and Collectibles,"
no charge, published annually, 32
pages, black and white, illustrated.

A list of over 1,400 titles of books on
antiques and collectibles, divided and
indexed into sixty recognized categories
of antiques, arts, hobbies, and
collecting, with prices and order form.
MO

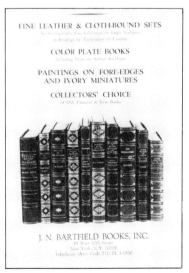

Catalogue cover, *J.N. Bartfield Books*

ELIZABETH F. DUNLAP
Dept. CHC
6063 Westminster Place
St. Louis, MO 63112

"Old Maps and Books," no charge, 18
pages, no illustrations.

A listing of maps of the world, the
individual states and cities of the U.S.,
Canada and its provinces, Mexico,
Central America, and the West Indies.
Most are 19th century, some are in
color, with a price range from around
$3 to $135. There is also an addenda of
old books on Canada and Latin
America.
MO

KENNETH NEBENZAHL, INC.
Dept. CHC
333 North Michigan Boulevard
Chicago, IL 60601

"The Compass for Map Collectors" and
"The Print Collector, 1&2," $2.00,
published quarterly, 30 pages each,
black and white, illustrated.

These three booklets contain
descriptive, illustrated listings of old,
original maps, hand-colored or black
and white, by 16th- through 19th-
century cartographers. Each is in very
good to fine condition, with all faults
or restorations noted. The prints cover
subjects such as ships, politics, scenery,
military, rural America. Rare and
expensive.
MO

MEMORABILIA

GARGOYLES, LTD.
Dept. CHC
521 South 3rd Street
Philadelphia, PA 19174

"Gargoyles, Ltd.," $4.00 (refundable
with purchase), updated monthly, 32
pages, some color, illustrated.

Old posters and ads, pub, street, and
station signs, British Railway signals,
signal arms, lanterns, even dummy
oversized liquor bottles are part of the
memorabilia collection. Almost all are
one-of-a-kind items. The sizes are
included in the catalogue, but the
prices are on request.
MO

PALMETTO ANTIQUES
Dept. CHC
Highway 301
Ulmer, SC 29849

"Collector's Showcase," $1.00
(refundable with purchase), published
semiannually, 70 pages, black and
white, illustrated.

The "discriminating junk" offered by
Palmetto consists mostly of a large
collection of things converted from
their original advertising purpose, such
as beer and soft-drink labels turned belt
buckles for $6.75, or trays ($3 to $10 for
the old ones, $5 for a set of reissues)—
the Coca-Cola Collectibles. Some are
commemorative, some authentic, some
reproduction. Political and war
souvenirs and old Americana bygones
like the red earthenware turpentine
pots and urns from the 1850s ($18.50
each) or stoneware jugs
commemorating South Carolina's
tricentennial ($3.95) are also on the
"junk" list of collectibles.
MO

Butterflies and shells, *Collector's Cabinet*

Fossil, mineral, and shells, *Dover Scientific*

Barite rose rock, *Rose Rock Co. of Oklahoma*

MINERALS, FOSSILS, SHELLS

MINIATURES

THE COLLECTOR'S CABINET
Dept. CHC
1000 Madison Avenue
New York, NY 10021

"Mother Earth Catalog," 50 cents, published annually, 24 pages, color, illustrated; "Exotic Butterflies," supplement, 25 cents, black and white, lists of butterflies mounted in maxi-boxes; "Sea Shell Catalog," 50 cents, black and white, lists over 1,500 specimens.

"Mother Earth Catalog" offers a selection of butterflies, sea shells, minerals, fossils, wildflowers, and other natural-history specimens in curved glass plaques, shadow boxes, paperweights. Lucite and brass specimen holders, Mexican brass-and-glass vitrines and boxes may also be ordered. The other catalogues are devoted, respectively, to butterflies and sea shells.
MO

DOVER SCIENTIFIC CO.
Dept. CHC
Box 6011
Long Island City, NY 11106

"Shell, Fossil and Mineral Catalog," 50 cents, published annually, 43 pages, black and white, illustrated.

In addition to a variety of colorful, exotic, and decorative shells, fossils, and minerals, Dover sells large ceramic Indian sculptures and small clay vessels. Display stands of various designs and brass-and-glass display cases, handmade in Mexico, ranging from a mini-box to a wall case, are also offered.
MO

MALICK'S FOSSILS, INC.
Dept. CHC
5514 Plymouth Road
Baltimore, MD 21214

"Malick's Fossils, Inc. (Artifacts, too)," $3.00, published annually, 105 pages, black and white, illustrated.

A catalogue for knowledgeable collectors or researchers that includes a geological time scale, table of contents, and detailed lists providing name, period, formation, locale. The catalogue covers animals, plants, educational aids, artifacts of early man, minerals, literature available on fossils and artifacts, and a few decorative accessories such as paperweights. Prices are given in some cases and are available on request in others.
MO

ROSE ROCK CO. OF OKLAHOMA
Dept. CHC
Box 6496
Moore, OK 73160

"Beautiful Rose Rocks of Oklahoma," folder, 50 cents, published as needed, color, illustrated.

Central Oklahoma has the only known deposits of good-quality Barite Rose Rocks in the Western Hemisphere. The "roses" are sold singly, in pairs, in clusters (mounted or unmounted), as a bouquet picture (also available in a do-it-yourself kit), from 75 cents to $100.
MO

CHESTNUT HILL STUDIO, LTD.
Dept. CHC
Box 38, RD #2
Churchville, NY 14428

"Fine Miniatures for Collectors," $2.50, 50 cents (refundable coupon with first order), published every five or six years, 44 pages, some color, illustrated.

An amazing collection of over 700 meticulously crafted miniatures, based on fine museum pieces. Twenty-three period rooms with late 16th- to early 20th-century furniture and hundreds of decorative accessories: lamps; oil paintings; hooked, braided, handwoven and petit-point rugs; sterling silver; glassware; wrought iron; pewter; brass; ceramics.
MO

THE COLONEL'S HOBBY
Dept. CHC
8 Shawnee Trail
Harrison, NY 10528

"The Miniature Silver of Guglielmo Cini," no charge with self-addressed, stamped envelope, published periodically, 10 pages, black and white, illustrated.

The catalogue offers seven different miniature reproductions of antique silver museum pieces, authentic in every detail, made to the scale of one inch to one foot, with additional miniatures available but not shown. Each is hallmarked "Cini" and "sterling." Prices range from $5 to $25.
MO

Miniatures collection, *Colonial Craftsmen*

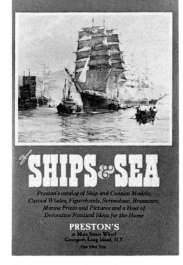

Catalogue cover, *Preston's*

MUSIC BOXES AND MECHANICAL ANTIQUES

NAUTICAL OBJECTS

COLONIAL CRAFTSMEN
Dept. CHC
144 Main Street
Essex, MA 01929

"Colonial Craftsmen: Pewter Workshop, Inc.," $1.00, published seasonally, 9 pages, color, illustrated.

Antique-finish pewter miniatures ranging in price from 60 cents to $700, all items to scale, and tiny home accessories of all kinds, including wallpaper and rugs, are the specialty of Colonial Craftsmen. Complete rooms—assembled or in kit form—are also available. The company also makes three pine handcrafted New England reproduction Colonial cabinets in a choice of finishes.
MO

STEPHEN M. LEONARD
Dept. CHC
P.O. Box 28
Little Neck, NY 11363

"Decorative Mechanical Oddities," weekly newsletter, $3.00 (refundable with purchase).

For the collector of mechanical antiques—music boxes, hurdy-gurdys, old toys, horn-type phonographs, everything from a musical pocket watch to a grand roller organ. Expensive but unique.
MO

BLUEJACKET SHIP CRAFTERS
Dept. CHC
145 Water Street
South Norwalk, CT 06854

Catalogue, 75 cents, 64 pages, black and white, illustrated.

The catalogue, notable for its meticulous layout and editing and interesting copy, reflects the fact that Bluejacket is the enterprise of a family with a seagoing heritage and a respect for fine craftsmanship. Their specialties are ship models and 39 kits of clippers, schooners, frigates, tankers, freighters, with a complete line of exact-scale ship fittings, as well as plans and modeler's tools. The catalogue also offers books about ship-making and the history of ships, whale carvings, marine gifts (linens, glassware, lamps, weathervanes), and a series of full-color reproductions of famous marine prints.
MO

PRESTON'S
Dept. CHC
116 Main Street Wharf
Greenport, NY 11944

"Of Ships and Sea," 25 cents, published semiannually, 144 pages, black and white, illustrated.

As the catalogue title suggests, its pages are filled with things having to do with the sea: ship models (finished and kits), cannons, famous marine pictures, and hundreds of decorative nautical items such as carved whales, figureheads, scrimshaw, brassware, etc.
MO

Antique gramophone, *Stephen M. Leonard*

Paperweight collection, *L.H. Selman*

Folk-art birds, *Carl Forslund*

PAPERWEIGHTS

PORCELAIN FIGURINES, PLATES, AND SCULPTURES

L. H. SELMAN, LTD.
Dept. CHC
407 Cliff Street, Suite 38
Santa Cruz, CA 95060

"Catalogue and Price Guide of Collectors' Paperweights," $3.00, published semiannually, 46 pages, color, illustrated.

Listings of contemporary, limited-edition, and choice antique paperweights (made during the classical period of the 1840s), all separated into categories and completely described. The catalogue offers background on paperweight collecting, lists of relevant books and periodicals, a kit for cataloguing your collection, magnifier, and lucite display stands.
MO

BING AND GRONDAHL, INC.
Dept. CHC
111 North Lawn Avenue
Elmsford, NY 10523

"Collector's Items," $1.00, published annually, 29 pages, color, illustrated.

A representative selection of Copenhagen handmade porcelain figurines, vases, and trays. No prices or particulars are given—just illustrations of about 150 figurines and dozens of vases and plates with identifying numbers. You must write for nearest retail source.
RS

BURGUES PORCELAINS
Dept. CHC
183 Spruce Street
Lakewood, NJ 08701

"Burgues—Porcelains of Limited Edition," $3.00, published annually, color.

Less a catalogue than a collection of 40 full-color glossy prints (themselves handsome enough for framing) of Burgues' porcelains. Mainly intricate and realistic detailing of birds, animals, and flowers in their natural settings, the porcelains range in size from 4" x 3½" to 18" x 9½" x 11" and in price from $125 to $3,500. The edition limits vary from 30 to 950, and some are already fully subscribed. A number of the porcelains are represented in the permanent collections of museums.
MO/RS

CARL FORSLUND, INC.
Dept. CHC
122 East Fulton Street
Grand Rapids, MI 49502

"Timeless Furniture Made by Carl Forslund," $2.00, revised every two to three years, 97 pages, color, illustrated.

"Folk Art" birds, hand-carved by Len Vander Zand and hand-painted by Len Nowicki, an interesting and charming collection, are for the serious collector or sportsman. The set of eight can be bought for less than $300 or individually from $38 for the pheasant, jacksnipe, woodcock, or quail to $50 for the handsome fantailed ruffed grouse.
MO

Porcelain sculpture, *Ispansky Porcelains*

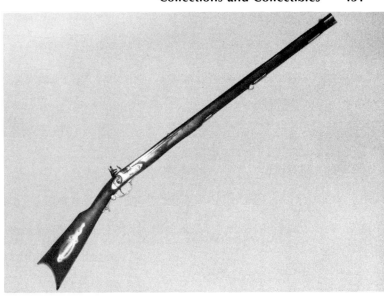

Kentucky rifle, *Muller*

WEAPONRY

ISPANSKY PORCELAINS, LTD.
Dept. CHC
Route 31
Pennington, NJ 08534

"Ispansky Fine Porcelains," $2.00, 48 pages, published annually, black and white, illustrated.

Fine porcelain sculptures by noted Hungarian-born sculptor Laszlo Ispansky. Fifty-five of his beautifully executed figures and flower porcelains are shown in this catalogue, although many more are available. They range in price from $35 for a piece entitled "White Serenity" from the Open Editions to $2,500 for the "Emerald Dragon" from the Special Editions. All editions are limited.
MO/RS

McDONALD'S
Dept. CHC
P.O. Box 1422
Manhattan Beach, CA 90266

List, no charge with #10 stamped, self-addressed envelope, changed seasonally.

A comprehensive list for collectors of commemorative plates by Royal Copenhagen and Bing & Grondahl dating as far back as 1895. Also included are Christmas, Easter, Bicentennial, Mother's Day, and other plates by such famous firms as Arabia, Capo di Monte, Crown Staffordshire, Dresden, Georg Jensen, Gorham (to name a few), and Hummel, noted for collector figurines.
MO

MY GRANDFATHER'S SHOP
Dept. CHC
940 Sligo Avenue
Silver Spring, MD 20910

"Collector's Guide," $1.00 subscription fee (refundable with $25 purchase), published annually, plus three or four price lists during the year, 42 pages, black and white, illustrated.

An unusual catalogue in that it includes a library of 21 other catalogues that you can borrow or buy for $1 each, a glossary of terms helpful to the collector of plates, figurines, and bottles, histories of glass, porcelain, and silver, and background information on Wedgwood. The "Guide" also has a collector's exchange, gift certificates, a repair-service department, and personalized wedding and birth plates by Delft, Noritake, and Fenton Art Glass Company.
MO

WAKEFIELD-SCEARCE GALLERIES
Dept. CHC
Shelbyville, KY 40065

"Wakefield-Scearce Galleries," $2.00, published annually, 56 pages, black and white, illustrated.

A large section of this handsome catalogue is devoted to the porcelain figures of famed artists—Dorothy Doughty, Doris Lindner, Bernard Winskill, Ronald Van Ruyckevelt, Boehm, Cybis, Ispansky, and Burgues—with dimensions and number of the edition but no prices. They also offer some limited contemporary collectibles such as the U.S. Bicentennial Society "Double Eagle" plate at $125 or "Washington Crossing the Delaware," one of four pewter sculptures designed by Robert W. Sullivan for Wallace Silversmiths at $400.
MO

THE MULLER CO.
Dept. CHC
Dogwood Hollow Lane
Miller Place, NY 11764

"Fine Decorative Weaponry," 25 cents, 12 pages, black and white, illustrated; also color catalogue for $1.00

Authentic replicas of old guns and pistols, some fireable, are hand-assembled by this company. For the collector of antique firearms for display there is an 18th-century British blunderbuss for about $130 or a Civil War Colt pistol for under $30, true in every detail. There are also decorative swords such as a replica of a Crusader's scimitar, about $25; wall plaques of crossed swords and armor; miniatures of antique cannons that actually fire caps; and a complete line of gun racks.
MO

CLOCKS AND MIRRORS

Mantel and case clocks, *Ethan Allen*

Pier mirror and table, *Bassett*

Bamboo-motif mirror, *Chapman*

ETHAN ALLEN, INC.
Dept. CHC
Ethan Allen Drive
Danbury, CT 06810

"The Treasury of Ethan Allen American Traditional Interiors," $7.50 (no charge at showrooms), published every two years, 408 pages, color, illustrated.

Traditionally styled wall and floor clocks, some with stencil decorations, others with different finishes, are part of the Ethan Allen home-furnishings collection. The mirrors are even more varied in style—sunbursts, trumeau mirrors, Chippendale, Queen Anne, Federal, bamboo motif, with a good selection of small mirrors from 11" to 22" high in attractive diamond, shield, and octagon shapes.
RS

BASSETT MIRROR COMPANY, INC.
Dept. CHC
P.O. Box 627
Bassett, VA 24055

"Carleton Varney's Alphabet of Decorating Ideas," $1.00, 32 pages, color, illustrated.

Carleton Varney, noted interior designer and columnist, has filled this delightful booklet with ideas for unusual decorating looks combining Bassett's collection of traditional and contemporary mirrors and other furnishings in alphabetized fashion. The sizes and finishes of all pieces are listed at the back.
RS

CAROLINA MIRROR CORPORATION
Dept. CHC
Box 548
North Wilkesboro, NC 28659

"Carolina Mirror #973," $1.00, published every two years, 31 pages, color, illustrated.

Reproductions, pier sets, and mirrors in all sizes, styles, finishes, and shapes: rectangular, oval, and shaped, framed and unframed. The deluxe arch-top plate-glass mirror may be used singly as a door mirror or in multiples as a wall mirror.
RS

CHAPMAN
Dept. CHC
481 West Main
Avon, MA 02322

"Lamps and Accessories," 50 cents, published annually, black and white, illustrated.

Chapman has some unusual mirrors. Particularly handsome are the 52" x 34" white lacquer bamboo-motif mirror, a stripped pine fan-topped mirror, and one with a brass frame and beveled glass in the Queen Anne style. Equally out of the ordinary are Chapman's reproduction clocks, all meticulous copies of the originals. There's a large (47" x 24" x 5") wall-hung Act of Parliament clock in antique black finish with gold-leaf trim; a narrow, 12"-wide by 72"-tall mahogany case clock; and a stripped pine wall-hung 17th-century Dutch pendulum and weight clock. Prices of both mirrors and clocks are on request, but style numbers and dimensions for retail-store shopping identification are included.
RS/ID

LAURA COPENHAVER INDUSTRIES, INC.
Dept. CHC
Box 149
Marion, VA 24354

"Rosemont," 50 cents, 31 pages, published annually, black and white, illustrated.

Among the handmade pieces reproduced by these Virginia mountain craftsmen are two charming and well-priced mirrors—a Chippendale jigsaw frame in solid walnut or cherry, 18½" x 32", under $50, and a shaving mirror with drawer, 21" high, 17" wide, 7¼" deep, in walnut or cherry for under $60.
MO

CRAFT HOUSE
Dept. CHC
Colonial Williamsburg Foundation
Williamsburg, VA 23185

"Williamsburg Reproductions—Interior Designs for Today's Living," $2.95, 232 pages, color and black and white, completely illustrated.

There are some truly beautiful mirrors in the Williamsburg reproductions by Friedman Brothers, among them a two-plate Queen Anne mirror with a black lacquer frame decorated with Chinese birds and plants, about $410, an oval Adam-style mirror framed in gold leaf with an intricate design of urn, flowers, and leaves, about $515, and an eye-catching Federal-style bull's-eye mirror framed in gilt wood and gesso with two candle arms balancing the eagle on top, about $590. There is also a reproduction late 18th-century English bracket clock, the Wythe House clock, of solid mahogany inlaid with holly wood, striking or non-striking, about $432.50 with bracket.
MO/RS

Bracket clock, *Crown Clock*

Gilt mirror, *Hickory Chair*

CROWN CLOCK CO., INC.
Dept. CHC
P.O. Drawer G
Fairhope, AL 36532

"Crown Bracket Clocks," 25 cents (refundable with purchase), published seasonally, color, illustrated.

Chiming bracket clocks designed in early 18th-century style, also "hobby" clocks specially designed for the golfer, chess player, fisherman. Clocks come completely assembled and finished from about $75 to $250, as kits from about $50 up.
MO

EMPEROR CLOCK CO.
Dept. CHC
Emperor Industrial Park
Fairhope, AL 36532

"Emperor Grandfather Clocks," foldout pamphlet, no charge, published annually, color, illustrated.

These grandfather clocks are available three ways: do-it-yourself kit without movement from $100; assembled, unfinished case without movement; completely finished clock from about $270 with movement.
MO

CARL FORSLUND, INC.
Dept. CHC
122 East Fulton Street
Grand Rapids, MI 49502

"Timeless Furniture Made by Carl Forslund," $2.00, revised every two to three years, 97 pages, color, illustrated.

Clocks in the Forslund Collection range from a Schoolroom clock for about $140 to a bracket clock for $63. All are replicas of early 19th-century originals.
MO

GARGOYLES, LTD.
Dept. CHC
512 South 3rd Street
Philadelphia, PA 19174

"Gargoyles, Ltd.," $4.00 (refundable with purchase), updated monthly, 32 pages, some color, illustrated.

The fascinating Gargoyles catalogue includes a section of the now much sought-after pub mirrors, both old and reproduction, in a variety of sizes. The old ones are mostly 19th-century, some are beveled, all are beautifully etched and hand-painted and leafed in burnished gold. Prices on request. The reproductions, naturally, are a fraction of the cost of the old ones.
MO

HICKORY CHAIR COMPANY
Dept. CHC
Hickory, NC 28601

"Furniture Reproductions Inspired by Heirlooms from Historical James River Plantations," $2.00, 100 pages, some color, illustrated.

Along with the over 150 fine 18th-century furniture reproductions are four handsome mirrors, two Queen Anne styles with amber frames, a Federal style with beveled glass, columns, frame in gold finish, and an elaborate gold Chippendale carved style, of rigid polyurethane, each for under $150. They are all of good size and would be a handsome accent in a modern or traditional setting.
RS/ID

Federal mirror, *LaBarge*

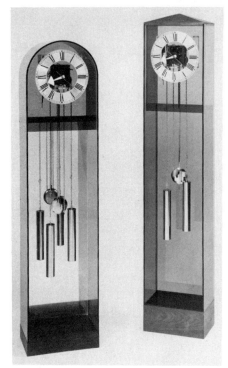

Contemporary case clocks, *Howard Miller*

Electronic mantel clock, *Howard Miller*

LaBARGE CO.
Dept. CHC
875 Brooks Avenue
Holland, MI 49423

"Mirrors," no charge.

Mirrors imported from Italy, Belgium, and Spain in a wide variety of styles, from the simplest contemporary to the most rococo, with most historical styles represented. Also American (including the Henry Ford Museum Greenfield Village reproductions), Oriental, and time-honored European designs.
RS

LIBBEY-OWENS-FORD COMPANY
Dept. CHC
811 Madison Avenue
Toledo, OH 43695

"Decorating with Mirrors," 10 cents, special issue, 11 pages, color, illustrated.

This is an idea booklet that shows the illusory and magical effects that can be achieved with mirrors—how to expand space visually, reflect natural light, give depth and dimension to dark areas, play up furniture and art. There are diagrams on how to arrange wall groupings around a mirror, information on how to install and clean mirrors, a mirror glossary, and a chart of traditional styles of framed mirrors.
RS

MAGNOLIA HALL
Dept. CHC
726 Andover
Atlanta, GA 30327

"World's Largest Collection of Victorian Furniture," $1.00, published quarterly, 63 pages, black and white, illustrated.

An outstanding Victorian Louis XV pier mirror set in gold leaf with the tabletop of cultured marble at $179.95 would be a fascinating addition to the hall of a home where the accent is on Victoriana. Equally elaborate is a deep-carved gilt wall mirror, 43" tall x 25" wide, $99.95, and a triple wedding-band parlor mirror in gold leaf, $189.95, 64" long, 44" high. For the bedroom, a hard-to-find cheval glass, copy of an 1850 one, is only $119.95. Magnolia Hall's Victorian-styled wall clocks with rich fruitwood cases include two by Ansonia, the Banker's Parlor clock at $149.95 and the Country Store clock at $119.95, and the Saw clock with movement copied from an 18th-century brass ratchet clock but housed in a Victorian case at $139.95. A giddy Golden Venus swinging pendulum clock is just $79.95. There are other styles to choose from, including an Eli Terry mantel clock and a cherry case clock with moving Moon dial and Westminster chimes.
MO

HOWARD MILLER CLOCK CO.
Dept. CHC
Zeeland, MI 49464

"Barwick" and *"Howard Miller Clock Company,"* no charge, color and black and white, illustrated.

Historically authentic Barwick clocks derive their inspiration from 18th-century-style periods. Besides the grandfather clocks, which are registered and personalized with a brass plate, Barwick offers special collections: Bicentennial (school, railroad, and calendar clocks), wall and shelf clocks, cottage clocks, chiming clocks, and an illuminated wall clock in a wide range of prices. Howard Miller clocks represent the contemporary line: cylinder, digital, ball, plexiglass, etc., in wall, floor, and table models, again in a wide range of prices.
MO/RS

THOMAS MOSER
Dept. CHC
26 Cobb's Bridge Road
New Gloucester, ME 04260

"Thomas Moser Cabinetmaker," $1.00, 29 pages, black and white, illustrated.

In this catalogue of superbly crafted reproductions of Shaker and Pennsylvania German furniture there are two interesting clocks, a tall, 7'-high case clock of simple design, under $400, and a wall-hung clock, 34" high x 5" deep x 10½" wide, about $225. Both clocks have non-strike, eight-day, spring-driven brass pendulum movements and cherry cases with a beautifully hand-rubbed oil finish.
MO

Mirrored wall, *PPG Industries*

Elaborate mantel clock, *Wilkinson Empire*

PPG INDUSTRIES, INC.
Dept. CHC
One Gateway Center
Pittsburgh, PA 15222

"All American Homes," no charge, published every three years, 39 pages, color, illustrated.

Mirrored walls are one of the best and most traditional ways to expand space visually. This booklet is loaded with ideas for ways to use them on walls, doors, as dividers, shields, and reflectors.
RS

RAINBOW ART GLASS CORPORATION
Dept. CHC
49 Shark River Road
Neptune, NJ 07753

"Rainbow Art Glass Corporation," 50 cents (refundable with purchase), published annually, color, illustrated.

Among its many stained-glass offerings, Rainbow Art has a dozen styles of clocks with leaded stained-glass faces in the Tiffany manner. Each is 13" square, has a Danish walnut frame, may be wall-hung or flush-mounted over a wall opening, and costs about $70 completely finished. If you want to put it together yourself, there are kits for each model, about $38, with the frame kit an additional $6. There is also a selection of six styles and shapes in Art Nouveau-type mirrors in assorted colors, each about 12" overall, from about $30 to $36, ready to hang or easel-mount.
MO

RIDGEWAY CLOCKS
Gravely Furniture Co, Inc.
Dept. CHC
Ridgeway, VA 24148

"Ridgeway Clocks," no charge, 8 pages, color, illustrated.

An informative brochure on the over 50 styles of case, wall, and shelf clocks made by Ridgeway showing how they can be used in living room, entrance hall, study, bedroom, or open-plan room. The emphasis is on case clocks, which range in price from $480 to $3,300, in a size and style for every decorating scheme, from simple Provincial to elaborate chinoiserie black lacquer. Dimensions, finishes, and most price ranges are given.
RS

ROCHE-BOBOIS USA, LTD.
Dept. CHC
200 Madison Avenue
New York, NY 10016

"Roche-Bobois," $5.00, published annually, 132 pages, color, illustrated, with 52-page illustrated price list.

Contemporary mirrors with simple, straightforward frames of polished steel, lacquer, or colored plastic, some with attached shelf units. There's a "woman's-profile" mirror on a stand, Twenties nostalgia, for about $85, a pivoting wall mirror for about $82. Dimensions, in inches and meters, and prices are given.
MO/RS

STURBRIDGE YANKEE WORKSHOP
Dept. CHC
Sturbridge, MA 01566

"Sturbridge Yankee Workshop Handbook and Catalogue," 50 cents, 64 pages, published annually, some color, illustrated.

A good source for reproductions of American clocks, whether it be a pine battery-operated wall clock with a bullfinch and redbreast inlaid into the clock face, about $50, or a 72"-high case clock with Westminster chimes for under $400. There is also a Sturbridge clock with painted scene on the lower half and "Sturbridge, Masstts" on the clock face, about $80. There are several mirrors, too. A large gilt Federal convex, 29" high x 18" wide with 14" mirror, at around $35, is a good buy.
MO

WILKINSON EMPIRE
Dept. CHC
9850 Park Street
Bellflower, CA 90706

"Decorative Gifts for the Home," 50 cents (refundable with purchase), published annually, color.

These distinctive and beautiful clocks from Europe (among them a variety of cuckoo clocks) are mailed directly to the customer from overseas. Prices are reasonable. The company also has other decorative accessories such as swords and sword wall plaques and has just added a line of ivory statues, the latter priced from $400 to $1,150.
MO

DECORATIVE ACCESSORIES

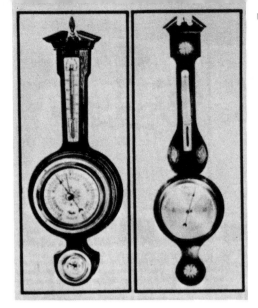

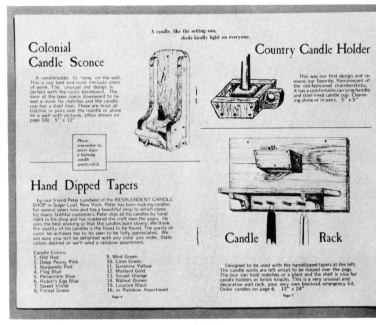

Handmade wooden objects, *Carriage House Woodshop*

FROM BAROMETERS, BASKETS, AND BOXES TO PLANTERS, VASES, AND UMBRELLA STANDS

BLUEJACKET SHIP CRAFTERS
Dept. CHC
145 Water Street
South Norwalk, CT 06854

"BlueJacket Ship Crafters," 75 cents, 64 pages, black and white, illustrated.

Many marine decorative accessories are included in this catalogue. For about $35 you can get a polished brass ship's clock, a barometer, or a stormoscope barometer. A Sheraton-style reproduction barometer is about $160. There's a very good-looking 12" brass porthole mirror for about $45 and scenes of the seas captured in glass by a sand-carving process done on the back of a polished block by Michael Yates from about $30 to $80, depending on size and subject matter.
MO

CAPE COD CUPOLA CO., INC.
Dept. CHC
78 State Street
N. Dartmouth, MA 02747

Catalogue, 50 cents, 47 pages, published biannually, black and white, illustrated.

The company claims that it offers the largest assortment of cupolas and weathervanes in the U.S. The weather vanes are made of cast aluminum, all aluminum, copper, and gold leaf. One is a cast-aluminum whale. "Full-bodied" weather vanes are handmade from rare, over 100-year-old molds. Accessory items, such as flagpole ornaments, chimney letters, script lettering, post signs, and antique cast-aluminum scroll brackets, are also pictured. The catalogue has an assortment of wall decorations and plaques for indoor or outdoor use: eagles, seagulls, a Colonial horse.
MO

THE CARRIAGE HOUSE WOODSHOP
Dept. CHC
Black Meadow Farm
Chester, NY 10918

"The Carriage House Woodshop," no charge, published annually, 12 pages, black and white, illustrated.

This brochure presents rustic designs for the home, handmade from authentic weathered barn siding. The objects include trays, planters, shelves, racks, candleholders, frames, and pegs. Each one is fully described. In addition, hand-dipped tapers are available and dried flowers in a wall holder. The prices range from $2 to $45.
MO

CHAPULIN
Dept. CHC
Route 1, Box 187
Santa Fe, NM 87501

"Southwestern Primitive Crafts," $1.00, published every 18 months, 14 pages, black and white, illustrated.

Papugo baskets, pottery figures from Cochiti and Acoma pueblos, and small wall hangings of all types, some of which may be used as pillow and hassock covers, are offered.
MO

Accessories from the Williamsburg collection, *Craft House*

THE COASTAL TRADER, INC.
Dept. CHC
423 15th Avenue East
Seattle, WA 98112

*"Presentations from the Coastal Trader,"
25 cents, published annually, 16 pages,
black and white, illustrated.*

The Coastal Trader has an interesting
and unusual selection of decorative
accessories for the home. Boxes of
cedar and black lacquer are about $19;
handmade cedar boxes, one square,
about $15; and a hexagon, with
perfectly mitered corners, about $16. A
raffia basket of 25 note cards and
envelopes of five printed designs of
Pacific Northwest oyster shells,
barnacles, snail shells, mussels, and
crabs in pen and ink by a Seattle artist
is under $10. There is a hand-carved
red-lacquered wooden carp, 32" long, a
Japanese antique, circa 1870, for under
$300, subject to prior sale, and
handsome trays of hand-wrapped
cedar, inlaid with cherry bark bindings
and lined in red lacquer, in three sizes.
Japanese folk toy birds carved from a
single piece of wood and handpainted,
from about $3 to $15, would make an
interesting group. So would white
ceramic square-based candlesticks in
three heights or as a set of four
modules (the four, about $26) on a
dining table.
MO

THE COUNTRY LOFT
Dept. CHC
552 Forest Street
Marshfield, MA 02050

*"The Country Loft: Unique Antique
Reproductions by Mail," 25 cents, 3-
page folder, black and white,
illustrated.*

Shaker woodenware, handcrafted from
sheets of clear maple stock, and Early
American tinware (canisters, salt boxes,
teapots), the poor man's silver of the
19th century, at reasonable prices.
MO

CRAFT HOUSE
Dept. CHC
Colonial Williamsburg Foundation
Williamsburg, VA 23185

*"Williamsburg Reproductions—Interior
Designs for Today's Living," $2.95, 232
pages, color and black and white,
illustrated.*

Many of the unusual and beautiful
objects in the Williamsburg collection
of decorative items would be perfectly
at home in the most modern house or
apartment. Especially charming are the
Delft jardinière ($28.20, $54.50 the pair),
4" high, and the Delft bricks, 2½" and
3½" high, which make delightful
containers for low flower arrangements.
A gorgeous polychrome brick in subtle
shades of soft blue and purple is $29.95;
a pair, at $58, could double as
bookends. Also noteworthy are the
graceful brass candlesticks, mahogany
serving trays, handsome mahogany tea
caddies that might be used as jewel
boxes, a Wedgwood Monteith, or
punch bowl, and a chess or checkers
gaming board in parquet squares of
rich, contrasting woods, $58.90.
MO/RS

FRAN'S BASKET HOUSE
Dept. CHC
Route 10
Succasunna, NJ 07876

*"Fran's Basket House," 25 cents, 46
pages, black and white, illustrated.*

Baskets, bird cages, umbrella stands,
planters, plant stands, hanging
shelves—all of rattan or wicker—are to
be found in this enormous collection,
at prices for every pocketbook.
Decorative and useful baskets in all
sizes and shapes that may be used for
fruit, flowers, mail, crackers, or bread
start around $4.95. There are many at
this price.
MO

Stained-glass triptych, *Glass Masters*

Wooden accessories, *Guild of Shaker Crafts*

GLASS MASTERS
Dept. CHC
621 Avenue of the Americas
New York, NY 10011

Brochure, 50 cents (refundable with purchase), published semiannually, 3 pages in color, 6 pages of retail price lists, illustrated.

This stained-glass studio that claims to follow "the tradition of those unsurpassed craftsmen and painters" who created the medieval stained-glass windows recreates details of 11th- to 16th-century medieval windows, made for hanging (except for diptyches and triptyches), with display bases generally extra. Art Nouveau ornaments and glass with American birds and wildflowers are also among their work.
MO

GREEK ISLAND, LTD.
Dept. CHC
215 East 49th Street
New York, NY 10017

"Greek Island Ltd.," no charge, published annually, 39 pages, black and white, illustrated.

Although Greek Island, Ltd. specializes in handmade Greek clothes, there are also a few distinctive decorative accessories, such as a cast-metal, silver-finished cigarette box with double-headed Byzantine eagle, a heavy brass Venetian lion door knocker, and terra-cotta roofline tiles, salvaged from razed buildings in Athens, that make handsome shelf or garden ornaments.
MO

GUILD OF SHAKER CRAFTS
Dept. CHC
401 Savidge Street
Spring Lake, MI 49546

"Guild of Shaker Crafts," $2.50, 28 pages, some color, illustrated.

Among the interesting offerings of the Guild are thirteen sizes of lidded oval storage boxes from 3¼" x 2¼" x 1¼" up to 15" x 11" x 7", $8 to $35, and many sizes and types of serving trays—a rimmed, cherry serving tray, a dining-room tray for flatware in pine, a charming oval herb carrier in maple, a pine candle box—all with many uses for today. There are also a few interesting candlesticks based on early Shaker designs.
MO

HOUSE OF ONYX
Dept. CHC
Rowe Building
Greenville, KY 42345

Lists, no charge.

All kinds of carved Mexican onyx objects: figurines, miniature animals, fruits, idols, ashtrays, and bookends. Some Tonala Mexican ceramics are offered as well as a variety of chess sets and boards, all at very low prices.
MO

MARTHA M. HOUSE
Dept. CHC
1022 South Decatur Street
Montgomery, AL 36104

"Southern Heirlooms," $1.00 (refundable with purchase), published annually, 44 pages, black and white, illustrated.

On page 20 of the latest catalogue there's a collection of the hand-decorated Imari porcelain that originated in 17th-century Japan, from temple and ginger jars to covered cigarette boxes to vases and ashtrays. Page 37 has elegant accessories of cut crystal and 24-kt gold plate—ashtrays, cigarette holders, candleholders, a footed covered candy dish, and a flower vase. There are some inexpensive items, such as a white bisque urn or pin box with raised flowers, a Florentine covered box in blue with red and gold trim, or a Capo di Monte candleholder.
MO

Wooden storage boxes, *Shaker Workshops*

Unusual bookends, *Sarreid*

THE PATIO
Dept. CHC
550 Powell Street
San Francisco, CA 94108

"Spring/Summer Sunny Thoughts,"
$1.00, some color, illustrated;
"Fall/Winter San Francisco Gift Book,"
$1.00, some color, illustrated.

As one would suspect, there are some unusual decorative accessories in these catalogues, mostly in the "Gift Book." Planters of all kinds range from a woven reed cache pot on macramé hanger, 5½" diameter x 7" high, for $5, to a set of square white wicker tubs from 7¼" to 11" square, the set of three $28. A double-ended mirror, hand-carved from solid California pine, 44" long x 11¼" wide, with delicate carving at each end, is $50. There is blue-and-white enamel westernware, picture frames with traditional American Indian motifs in enamel and goldtone, handcrafted wind bells in the shape of kachina dolls, each $7.95, and from the Peaceable Kingdom collection amusing ceramic animal vases by Jon Carlos Lopez of a raccoon or squirrel, 8" high, each $7.95.
MO

ROCHE-BOBOIS USA, LTD.
Dept. CHC
200 Madison Avenue
New York, NY 10016

"Roche-Bobois," $5.00, published annually, 132 pages, color, illustrated, with 52-page illustrated price list.

Art Deco accessories, such as hand-painted silk, down-stuffed pillows and pouffes, china boxes, bowls and vases, and shades-of-the-Twenties boxes in colored Perspex are just a few of the hundreds of contemporary accessories in a wide price range shown in this catalogue. It would be well worth a visit to the showroom, where there are many more.
MO/RS

SARREID, LTD.
Dept. CHC
P.O. Box 3545
Wilson, NC 27893

"Sarreid, Ltd.," no charge, color.

Along with the interesting accent furniture, Sarreid makes decorative accessories with a one-of-a-kind look, such as a 10"-high magnifying glass on adjustable stand, hand-polished brass with German lens, that is almost like an antique (about $62); a pair of heavy brass duck bookends that, singly, could act as doorstops (about $60); and a series of cut and hand-forged country roof ornaments (cow, hen, and pig) mounted on wood bases as decorative sculptures (about $50 each).
RS/ID

SHAKER WORKSHOPS, INC.
Dept. CHC
P.O. Box 710
Concord, MA 01742

"Shaker Furniture," 50 cents, published semiannually, 30 pages, some color, illustrated.

In addition to the kits of their handsome, functional Shaker furniture, the Workshops sell, finished and ready for use, a set of pine fruit trays in several sizes from about $6 to $7.50, two sizes of square wooden berry boxes (the deeper one at $4.50 would be ideal for a plant, the shallower one, $4, for sewing articles or dried flowers), and a series of five oval lidded boxes, for storage, priced from $15 to $25 or the set for $95. There are also wooden bowls for salad or fruit and two tin candleholders, one with hurricane shade.
MO

164

STAINED GLASS SUNDIAL

During the 17th Century Puritanical prejudice against windows in churches forced glasspainters to turn their craftsmanship in other directions. Heraldry formed their principal employment while many turned their hand also to sundial making. Few have survived the years since drilling the very thin glass made it particularly susceptible to fracture. Our stained-glass sundial is an exact replica of one of these early dials. It is not intended to tell accurate time in this country but is for ornamentation only. Of special interest is the fly which was the craftsman's way of adding his touch of humor. Since it is third dimensional it appears to move as you're looking at the dial. Comes complete with eyelets for hanging and removable stand for a table display as well as gnomon (shadow arm). An unusual gift with a delightful story. (9" x 7").

Stained-glass sundial, *Sundials & More*

Decorative weathervane, *E.G. Washburne*

SPANISH VILLA
Dept. CHC
Building 1101, L.A.F.B.
Laredo, TX 78040

"Spanish Villa," $1.00 (refundable with purchase), published annually, 34 pages, black and white, illustrated.

Spanish Villa offers an interesting, although limited, collection of decorative accessories. Two wall medallions, one a handsome cast sun head, 23" across, the other a lacy, hand-forged wrought-iron classic, 27" across, each $38.50, can be used indoors or out. Several bird cages, in bamboo or wrought iron, start at $9.95. A handsome onyx chess set with Aztec carved figures and 14½"-square board retails for $56.50. Other items include black Oaxacan and gaily painted Mexican pottery, carved wood bookends and figures, some interesting bark paintings, and candlesticks of hand-wrought iron in swirling or scroll designs. Two Colonial tinware pieces, a 16"-tall candleholder with glass sides, like a slender lantern, at $12.95 and a 9"-tall lantern for $6.95, are unusual in their simplicity.
MO

THE STIFFEL CO.
Dept. CHC
700 North Kingsbury Street
Chicago IL 60610

"From the Stiffel Collection," 50 cents, updated every 18 months, 40 pages, black and white, illustrated.

In addition to its vast collection of table and floor lamps, Stiffel offers an interesting selection of decorative accessories, replicas of antiques, such as clocks, barometers, wall shelves, and cabinets.
RS/ID

SUNDIALS & MORE
Dept. CHC
P.O. Box H
New Ipswich, NH 03071

Catalogue, no charge, 32 pages, some color, illustrated.

This catalogue contains a few pages of handcrafted stained-glass panels, each one painted on hand-blown glass, bordered in lead, with lead eyelets cast into the top for hanging. The stained glass comes in different shapes and sizes and a variety of designs: flowers, birds, animals, a 15th-century zodiac.
MO

SYROCO
Dept. CHC
Syracuse, NY 13201

"Syroco Decorative Accessories," $1.00, published annually, 51 pages, color, illustrated.

A comprehensive collection of decorative accessories for every room in the house, from a reproduction Winthrop pendulum clock (about $65) to Art Deco planters ($27 to $42) to a wall plaque of shore birds in chrome, about $25. There are pieces in almost every design style—Early American, French Provincial, Rococo, Art Deco, Spanish, Italian Renaissance, to mention a few. There are pages of planters and lavabos, sconces, wall brackets, and plaques at prices that anyone can afford, also many decorating ideas to help you select the right accessory.
RS

Early American spoon rack, *Syroco*

Handwoven baskets, *West Rindge Baskets*

Quilted pillows, *Patricia Wing*

AKE TUGEL
Dept. CHC
266 Sea Cliff Avenue
Sea Cliff, NY 11579

Folio of color photographs, 50 cents, revised at random.

Artist/cabinetmaker Ake Tugel produces hand-finished and hand-painted lidded boxes based on Swedish traditional designs. A child's ride-a-toy-box, 9" x 9" x 22", costs about $60. Dimensions and prices on a separate list.
MO

E.G. WASHBURNE & CO.
Dept. CHC
85 Andover Street
Danvers, MA 01923

Catalogue, no charge, 20 pages, black and white, illustrated.

Copper weather vanes, hand-hammered from original old cast-iron molds. Balls, cardinals, and spires are available separately. Custom designs, full body or silhouette, are made to your idea or specifications, and finishes include antique verdigris patina, natural polished copper, paint of any color, and—at extra cost—23-kt gold leaf. A price list is included.
MO

WEST RINDGE BASKETS, INC.
Dept. CHC
Box 24
Rindge, NH 03461

"Hand Woven New England Baskets," no charge, published annually, illustrated.

Baskets of ash with oak hoops and handles in about two dozen different types and sizes, handcrafted to last two generations. Minor variations and irregularities make each basket unique.
MO

PATRICIA WING, LTD.
Dept. CHC
Birdwood
Mathews, VA 23109

Brochure, $1.00 (refundable with purchase), published periodically.

Patricia Wing, designer of the first velvet-framed, linen-backed pillow, has pillows for every room and interest, with designs of birds, botanical and hunting prints, and so on. Prices range from $25 for an 18" x 18" pillow to $150 for a 26" x 32" floor cushion.
MO

Carving a wooden bowl, *Appalachian Fireside Crafts*

HANDCRAFTED ACCESSORIES

Handmade quilt, *Appalachian Fireside Crafts*

Navajo rug, *Chapulin*

REGIONAL, PRIMITIVE, IMPORTED

APPALACHIAN FIRESIDE CRAFTS
Dept. CHC
Box 276
Booneville, KY 41314

"Appalachian Fireside Crafts," a series of leaflets, $1.00, black and white, illustrated.

An organization of eastern Kentuckians who, seeking to reflect their pioneer heritage in their crafts, make and market quilts (for children and adults), cornshuck dolls, angels, flowers and mats, needlecraft pillows, and woodcraft birdhouses, trays, bowls, baskets, cutting boards, and candleholders. Particularly appealing are the cornshuck flowers that can be bought in single sprays, or bouquets, from $3 to $12 a dozen. A sunflower is $1.75.
MO

BEREA COLLEGE STUDENT CRAFT
INDUSTRIES
Dept. CHC
CPO #2347
Berea, KY 40403

Craft catalogue, 25 cents, 24 pages, color, illustrated.

The students of Berea College not only make and sell handcrafted furniture but also a wide variety of other handcrafts. Ceramics, hand-loomed wall hangings, pillows and place mats, wastebaskets, brooms, colorful and decorative toys, and some big handsome games such as skittles and table hockey, all made by the students, are at reasonable prices.
MO

CHAPULIN
Dept. CHC
Route 1, Box 187
Santa Fe, NM 87501

"Southwestern Primitive Crafts," $1.00, published every 18 months, 14 pages, black and white, illustrated.

In addition to the handsome collection of Navajo rugs and hangings, Chapulin has handwoven Papago baskets and bowls from southern Arizona made of exotics such as beargrass, devil's claw, and yucca root. They range in price from $22 for an 8" bowl to $130 for large covered baskets.
MO

Handmade brooms, *Berea College Student Craft Industries*

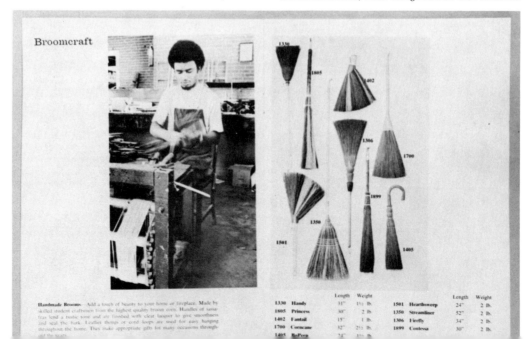

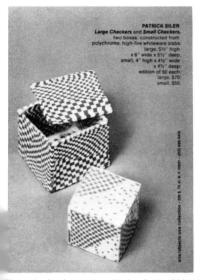

One-of-a-kind ceramics, *Circle of Arts/Objects*

PATRICK SILER
Large Checkers and *Small Checkers,*
two boxes: constructed from
polychrome, high-fire whiteware slabs:
large, 5½" high
x 6" wide x 5½" deep;
small, 4" high x 4½" wide
x 4½" deep;
edition of 50 each:
large, $70;
small, $55

Japanese handcrafts, *The Coastal Trader*

FOR THE BIRDS
Japanese folk toys (left)
are hand carved from a
single piece of wood and
delicately hand painted.
Shown: Small owl T-16
(3½" tall), Medium hawk
T-17 (7" tall), Large hawk
T-18 (12" tall).

T-16 2.95 (.50)
T-17 8.95 (1.00)
T-18 14.95 (1.50)

Our captivating quail
(upper right) is 2½" tall
and hand cast of matte
black solid iron.
P-10 8.95 (1.00)

"My little chick-a-dee"
is our small chick, 2 5/8"
high (lower right) is also
cast by hand and finished
carefully of matte black
solid iron.
P-14 8.95 (1.00)

Gift Ideas for Special People

WE HAVE RECENTLY
REDISCOVERED
some fine examples of the
ancient art of cherry bark,
such as this beautiful box
(8 1/4" x 5 1/4" x 1 1/8")
made of hand applied
cherry bark to a solid wood
core, that would make a
decorative and unique
holder for your stationery.
T-19 24.95 (2.00)

Handcrafts, *Heather Hill Crafts*

CIRCLE OF ARTS/OBJECTS, INC.
Dept. CHC
140 East 81st Street
New York, NY 10028

"Arts/Objects: USA," $1.00 (refundable
with purchase), 80 pages, color,
illustrated.

This brochure illustrates over 100
examples of the creative work of
contemporary artist-craftsmen. Each
page identifies the artist, the title of the
object, the media, and the edition of
the work. Some are one of a kind; most
are in editions. Various craft media are
represented: porcelain, clay, enamel,
blown and stained glass, metal, jewelry,
and hooked, woven, knitted, and
sculptured fibers. The objects range
from functional to purely decorative,
from "weed" pots and platters to chess
sets, paperweights, and plaques. A
sheet with a thumbnail description of
each artist is enclosed. Prices range
from $15 to $6,500.
MO

THE COASTAL TRADER, INC.
Dept. CHC
423 15th Avenue East
Seattle, WA 98112

"Presentations from the Coastal Trader,"
25 cents, published annually, 16 pages,
black and white, illustrated.

The Coastal Trader was formed to
import quality contemporary Japanese
handcrafts and claims to select
personally Japanese antiques and
accessories such as hand-cast sculpture,
cedar and lacquerware, and articles
made from cherry bark: ashtrays,
coasters, salad bowls, trays, boxes.
MO

THE COUNTRY LOFT
Dept. CHC
552 Forest Street
Marshfield, MA 02050

*"The Country Loft: Unique Antique
Reproductions by Mail,"* 25 cents, 3
pages, black and white, illustrated.

Handcrafted tinware, the "poor man's
silver" of 19th-century America, is ideal
for stenciling, hand-painting,
découpage, or left natural to acquire
the primitive look of antique pieces.
Prices range from $1.75 for a seven-inch
round plate to $18 for a deed box. Also
available is a fine handmade collection
of Shaker woodenware boxes and
piggins.
MO

HEATHER HILL CRAFTS
Dept. CHC
4312 West 178th Street
Torrance, CA 90504

Booklet, no charge, published
semiannually, 12 pages, black and
white, illustrated.

A whole compendium of crafts from
leaded glass window ornaments to
terrariums, calico flowers, hand-painted
eggshells, decorative stoneware,
pottery, and wooden items for the
home.
MO

IROQRAFTS
Dept. CHC
RR2
Ohsweken, Ontario, Canada

"Crafts Catalogue," 50 cents, published
semiannually, 40 pages, black and
white, illustrated.

A large selection of traditional and
ceremonial Iroquois crafts and arts
from the Six Nations reservation,
among them Iroquois watercolors and
paintings, Mohawk paintings and
ceremonial jewelry, carvings, Eskimo
art, stone sculptures, masks, and
musical instruments. Many are
collectors' items, some of souvenir
status. Also available: craft supplies,
books, graphics. Wide range of prices
from 50 cents to hundreds of dollars.
MO

Early American Tinware
"POORMAN'S SILVER"

HINGED-TOP CANISTER (1)

TINKER'S MEASURE (2)

TIN SALTBOX (3)

TIN PLATES (4)

TIN TEAPOT (5)

DOCUMENT BOX (6) AND
DEED BOX (7)

Handcrafted tinware, *The Country Loft*

170

Tinware collection, *Irvin's Craft Shop*

Patchwork, *Puckihuddle Products*

IRVIN'S CRAFT SHOP
Dept. CHC
RD 1, Box 58
Mt. Pleasant Mills, PA 17853

"Handcrafted Tin and Copper Reproductions," 25 cents, published annually, 3-page folder, black and white, illustrated.

Irvin's pieces, most of which are available in either country tin or antique copper, range from candle boxes to pie-safe panels—exact reproductions of Early American pierced tin panels from Grandma's pie cupboard. Gingerbread boy and girl and angel or rabbit cookie cutters make attractive wall decorations. Reasonable prices.
MO

PUCKIHUDDLE PRODUCTS
Dept. CHC
Oliverea, NY 12462

"Craftskills from the Catskills," 50 cents (refundable with purchase), published annually, 26 pages, some color, illustrated.

A charmingly illustrated catalogue of handcrafted decorative and practical wares ranging from Humpty Dumpty dolls to tea cozies, with some nostalgic and unusual creations. Noteworthy are quilts, tablecloths, patchwork lap blanket, and tunic aprons for at-home entertaining. Prices range from around $3 to $200.
MO

NAVAJO ARTS AND CRAFTS
ENTERPRISE
Dept. CHC
Drawer A
Window Rock, AZ 86515

"Navajo Arts and Crafts Enterprise," $1.00, 20 pages, color, illustrated.

A beautifully illustrated collection of high-quality, authentic Navajo arts and crafts. Weaving, jewelry, basketry, sand paintings, hand carving, and medicine pots are shown, and the catalogue describes the rug-making process. A price list gives a general idea of price ranges, as handcrafting makes price fixing difficult. Items range from $2 up, with rug prices usually beginning around $300.
MO

Cover, *Navajo Arts and Crafts*

REEVES KNOTIQUE
Dept. CHC
Box 5011
Riverside, CA 92507

"Macramé and Other Handicrafts," 10 pages, black and white, illustrated.

The booklet includes many ready-made macramé items such as a jute wall hanging with wooden beads and earthenware plaque in two color combinations, 10" wide x 32" long, for about $30; a large (18" x 24") natural jute cross, $11; or a handsome bell pull in three colors of polypropylene macracord with olivewood beads and a 2" Indian brass bell for $13. A hanging planter pot, $12, and a hanging plant platform, 11" x 11" with a 5" depression in the center for the pot, $13, for indoor or outdoor use, are among the many other interesting items.
MO

Macramé hangings, *Reeves Knotique*

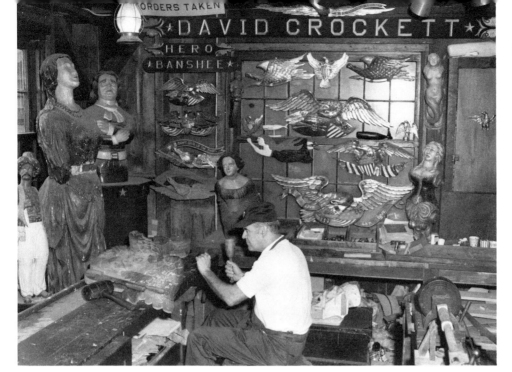

Individual wood carvings, *Willard Shepard*

WILLARD SHEPARD
Dept. CHC
Jordan Cove
Waterford, CT 06385

"Shep's Ship Shop," no charge.

One of the best woodcarvers in the country, Willard Shepard can, will, and does carve practically anything, from simple name boards to cigar-store Indians, although the latter are by special order only. He will send you an illustrated price list (ranging from $9 for a 8" whale carving to over $600 for a 72"-long gold-leafed Louisburg Eagle) of his standard works and will confer on special orders if you desire something out of the ordinary.
MO

SHOPPING INTERNATIONAL
Dept. CHC
800 Shopping International Building
Norwich, VT 05055

"Shopping International," 25 cents, about 45 pages, color, illustrated.

Handcrafted gifts from over 30 lands are illustrated and described in this catalogue, which offers you a "tour of the world's exotic bazaars." Among things for the home are glasses, decanters, Oxted pitchers, prints, candleholders, alabaster wares, Kiri and Namako vases, ginger and temple jars, and a Jumna footed bowl. There is also the "Artists Collection" of selected pieces made by gifted international artisans. Prices and order form are given.
MO

TREASURE-HOUSE OF WORLDLY
WARES
Dept. CHC
1880 Lincoln Avenue
Calistoga, CA 94515

Lists, no charge, published periodically, illustrated with black-and-white pencil sketches (color photographs of items may be obtained on request for 50 cents each).

Folk art from all over the world, especially American Indian art, old and new. Included are Navajo sand paintings, pottery from various pueblos, baskets, beadwork, leathercraft, rugs, and wall hangings. From other parts of the world come masks, tapestries, large drums, Javanese batik sarong lenths, wood carvings, dolls. Wide range of prices.
MO

WAKE'DA TRADING POST
Dept. CHC
P.O. Box 19146
Sacramento, CA 95819

"Wake'Da Trading Post," 25 cents, 21 pages, black and white, illustrated.

The Trading Post specializes in American Indian crafts of all kinds—beads, bells, feathers, shawls, moccasins, to name a few. The catalogue lists hundreds of items, illustrates some, gives details of each, including prices, with order blank.
MO

Hand-loomed wall hanging, *Treasure-House of Worldly Wares*

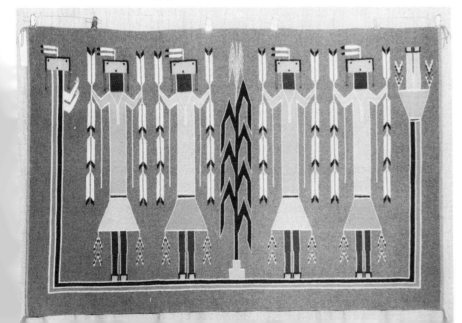

Contemporary table setting, *iittala*

TABLEWARE AND TABLE ACCESSORIES

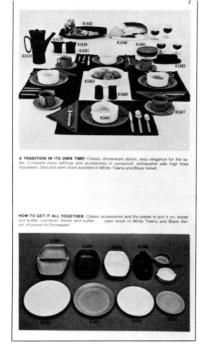

A TRADITION IN ITS OWN TIME! Classic dinnerware above, easy elegance for the table. Complete place settings and accessories in ovenproof, dishwasher safe high fired stoneware. Sets and open stock available in White, Tawny and Black Velvet.

HOW TO GET IT ALL TOGETHER. Classic accessories and the plates to put it on, bread and butter, luncheon, dinner and buffet . . . open stock in White, Tawny and Black Velvet, of course its Stoneware!

Contemporary pottery, *Bennington Potters*

Williamsburg reproductions, *Craft House*

CHINA AND POTTERY

BACCARAT, INC.
Dept. CHC
55 East 57th Street
New York, NY 10022

"Ceralene China," 50 cents, color, illustrated.

The brochure gives a brief description of the different types of china—bone, American and Continental, of which one is Limoges Ceralene, the hardest glaze of all, fired at nearly 2500°F. Each pattern is shown in color. Simplest is the all-white Osier (French for "wicker"), a basket-weave theme popularized by the Meissen factory of Germany in the 18th century. A three-piece place setting (dinner plate, tea cup and saucer) costs $30, one of the less expensive patterns. The gold-encrusted Imperial pattern, an exact replica of the Prud'hon design for Napoleon at Malmaison, perhaps the richest and most formal dinnerware made today, is $224 for a three-piece setting. Complete price list for each pattern and list of accessories available.
MO/RS

BALDWIN HARDWARE MFG. CORP.
Dept. CHC
841 Wyomissing Boulevard
Reading, PA 19603

Folio of catalogue sheets, no charge, some color, illustrated.

Two types of pottery: earthenware in vivid Chinese blue glaze on hand-formed shapes—bowls, bird flower holder, candleholder—and French faïence, decorated in traditional 18th-century patterns on classic forms such as the Monteith bowl, bulb pot, and cache pot, are part of the "Collector's Choice" line.
MO

BENNINGTON POTTERS, INC.
Dept. CHC
324 County Street
Bennington VT 05201

"Bennington Potters," 50 cents, published annually, 12 pages, color, illustrated.

Unusual design and imaginative styling are the forte of this old-established pottery studio, which makes complete place settings and accessories in ovenproof, dishwasher-safe stoneware. There are oven-to-table casseroles, coffee services, ashtrays that are windproof, plates, mugs, pitchers, planters, tiles, and trivets. Prices moderate.
MO/RS

CRAFT HOUSE
Dept. CHC
Colonial Williamsburg Foundation
Williamsburg, VA 23185

"Williamsburg Reproductions—Interior Designs for Today's Living," $2.95, 232 pages, color and black and white, illustrated.

The Wedgwood company of England, famous for porcelain since the late 18th century, makes for Williamsburg bone china in five traditional patterns—Colonial Sprays, Chinese Flowers, Bianca, Cuckoo, and Chinese Tiger—and also the familiar creamy-colored Queen's Ware in Potpourri, a fruit-and-flower pattern taken from an antique fabric. A five-piece place setting of the china ranges from $61.75 to $66.75 for Bianca; the Queen's Ware, less expensive, is $29.60 for a five-piece place setting. Equally attractive, though sturdier, and engagingly rustic in quality, is the Williamsburg pottery inspired by fragments excavated in Williamsburg and at Jamestown, which is handmade by local craftsmen. These are single pieces, jugs, pitchers and mugs, pie plates, bowls, jars, and molds made by traditional techniques—gray saltglaze mugs have cobalt-blue decoration, yellow and brown soup bowls are decorated with sgraffito. Particularly stunning are the marbleized slipware pie plate, 10¼" diameter ($5.95), and the large, 16 ¾"-long yellow-and-brown slipware trencher with typical 18th-century comb decoration ($16.75), which makes a super serving dish and is ovenproof to boot. There's also a small 8¼" trencher for $3.75. A tiny charmer is the ovenproof white saltglaze star mold ($2.35), 3½" in diameter by 1½" high, perfect for individual baked desserts.
MO/RS

Plantation Colonial china, *Carl Forslund*

Blown and cut crystal, *Baccarat*

CRYSTAL AND GLASSWARE

CARL FORSLUND, INC.
Dept. CHC
122 East Fulton Street
Grand Rapids, MI 49502

"Timeless Furniture Made by Carl Forslund," $2.00, revised every two to three years, 97 pages, color, illustrated.

Although primarily a furniture source, Carl Forslund stocks several china patterns, including Mason's Plantation Colonial, based on Spode's discontinued Seasons, in blue, Vista ironstone, and Green Strathmore china, and Mary Hadley pottery. All patterns are open stock or sold as complete services. A page of the catalogue is given to the lovely reproductions of 19th-century pressed glass in such colors as amber, blue, pink, amethyst and cranberry, vaseline and ruby, and patterns like "Daisy & Button," "Thumbprint," "Three-face," "Thistle," and "Hobnail." Prices range from about $2.50 for Double Wedding Ring salt in amber, blue, or green to about $20 for an Embossed Rose Fairy Lamp in ruby.
MO

HAVILAND & CO., INC.
Dept. CHC
11 East 26th Street
New York, NY 10010

"Haviland," 25 cents, color, illustrated.

The brochure gives a brief history of Haviland china and illustrates in color 24 of the current patterns with description and background of each. Four generations of Havilands, all Americans, are still making the china styled in America and crafted in Limoges, France, since 1842. Prices range from under $40 to over $300 for a five-piece place setting.
RS

BACCARAT, INC.
Dept. CHC
55 East 57th Street
New York, NY 10022

"Baccarat, The Crystal of Kings," two brochures, 50 cents each, black and white, illustrated.

There are two brochures of this truly beautiful crystal. One has photographs of each of the stemware patterns, from the simple Montaigne Plain, created in 1890, $13.50 a glass, to the richly ornate Empire design with gold leaf baked over the entire bowl, $69 a glass. The second brochure is the Baccarat collection of gift items: brick-cut crystal vases designed by Van Day Truex from $54 to $240; "Bistro" individual wine carafes for $35; classic Louis XIV and traditional design crystal candelabrum and candleholders from $55 to $850. Each brochure includes a complete price list and a delightful history of Baccarat, one of the oldest names in crystal.
MO/RS

BALDWIN HARDWARE MFG. CORP.
Dept. CHC
841 Wyomissing Boulevard
Reading, PA 19603

Folio of catalogue sheets, no charge, some color, illustrated.

Hand-blown and hand-formed bubble glass with a rustic quality, part of the "Collector's Choice" collection, includes tumblers and goblets, pitchers, footed bowl, and covered cheese dish.
MO/RS

CRAFT HOUSE
Dept. CHC
Colonial Williamsburg Foundation
Williamsburg, VA 23185

"Williamsburg Reproductions—Interior Designs for Today's Living," $2.95, 232 pages, color and black and white, illustrated.

Williamsburg glass reproductions are made by the skilled artisans of Royal Leerdam, one of the few glass manufacturers continuing the tricky art of off-hand glass blowing, evidence of which can be seen in the airtwist, teardrop, and baluster patterns of the stemware. With their timeless simplicity of shape and design, these glasses are as appropriate to contemporary as to traditional tables, although they are not inexpensive—airtwist wineglasses are around $20 each, whereas a plain wineglass is $14.55. There are also decanters in three shapes, tumblers and tavern glasses, glass candlesticks and hurricane shades, and, perhaps the most interesting to glass collectors, reproductions of antique wine flasks, pitchers, and wine rinsers (deep, lipped bowls which today we use as finger bowls, flower bowls, or to serve fruit or ice-cream desserts) in glowing colored glass—amber, sapphire, emerald, and amethyst. The wine rinsers or finger bowls are $12.30 each, the wine flasks $14.25, and the pitchers, 5" high, $15.05, or $11.30 for the miniature size, 3⅝" high.
MO/RS

Hand-blown goblet, *iittala*

Cover, *Jacques Jugeat*

J. G. DURAND INTERNATIONAL
Dept. CHC
Wade Boulevard
Millville, NJ 08332

"Elegance in French Glassware," folder
of leaflets, no charge, published
seasonally, some color, illustrated.

From France, Crystal d'Arques, an
extraordinary collection of lead crystal
stemware in traditional and
contemporary patterns, from $3 to $5
per stem. Also shown are complete
lines of crystal items—vases, ashtrays,
decanters, break-resistant glass
dinnerware, bowls and tumblers,
stemware in colors, even the
"luminarc" canning and storage jars.
Items are handsome and well priced.
RS

FOSTORIA GLASS CO.
Dept. CHC
Moundsville, WV 26041

"Heavenly Fostoria Crystal," no charge,
9 pages, color, illustrated.

A colorful catalogue of all the latest
patterns in Fostoria stemware. Some are
embellished with gold or platinum
braids, deep cuttings, delicately etched,
or are individually molded, like the
reproductions of pressed glass from the
Henry Ford Museum. Prices range from
about $7.75 to $16.75.
RS

iittala USA ltd.
Dept. CHC
225 Fifth Avenue
New York, N.Y. 10010

"We're having a party . . . ," 34 pages,
and *"Setting your table with Solaris,"* 6
pages, 25 cents, color, illustrated.

"We're having a party . . . ", a booklet
of entertaining ideas with the complete
glass collection of iittala, covers events
from a wedding reception with the
slim, brilliant clear champagne flutes to
a sauna party with beer in clear glass
tankards. The complete line is shown at
the back with a round-the-world listing
of where they can be seen and
purchased.
   "Setting your table with Solaris" is a
folder with suggestions for table
settings using the textured glass plates
and bowls designed by Tapio Wirkkala.
RS

JACQUES JUGEAT, INC.
Dept. CHC
225 Fifth Avenue
New York, NY 10010

"Lalique, a Tradition in Elegance" and
"Saint Louis Cristal de France," no
charge, black and white, illustrated.

The Lalique brochure shows some of
the famous satin-finished lead crystal
pieces created by René Lalique in the
early 1900s and now made by his son,
Marc. In addition to the well-known
sculpture pieces and bowls, which
range in price from around $45 to over
$300, there are three lines of elegant,
expensive stemware.
   The manufacture of Saint Louis
Cristal dates back to 1586, when the
Compagnie des Cristalleries de Saint
Louis was founded. Since that time the
factory has produced beautiful
handcrafted crystal stemware and
decorative items, handsomely cut or
shaped. Depending on pattern and cut,
the glasses cost from about $13.25 to
$55 each. Price lists are included with
both brochures, but you will have to
write for the name of the nearest
dealer.
RS

Wine decanter and glasses,
Marjorie Lumm's Wine Glasses

Candle lantern, *Viking Glass*

Handcrafted pewter, *Colonial Casting*

PEWTER

MARJORIE LUMM'S WINE GLASSES
Dept. CHC
P.O. Box 732
Sausalito, CA 94965

"Wine Glasses," 25 cents, published annually, 30 pages, black and white, illustrated.

Top-quality wine glasses of all types, from six-ounce Rhine wine to 22-ounce magnum. The catalogue shows wine goblets, champagne flutes, brandy glasses, glass mugs for Irish coffee, sherry glasses in the hard-to-find classic shape, decanters, sherry shaker (for seasoning soups, English style), plus wine accessories such as silverplated coasters, drip-stopper, cork-puller. An excellent source for wine connoisseurs. Reasonable prices.
MO

VIKING GLASS CO.
Dept. CHC
New Martinsville, WV 26155

"Beauty Is Glass from Viking," 25 cents, 42 pages, color, illustrated.

An interesting story with pictures of the making of the well-known American handmade glass by Viking, with color catalogue of the latest Viking collection of glassware and objects, including the Biccentennial red and blue plates and glasses.
RS

CRAFT HOUSE
Dept. CHC
Colonial Williamsburg Foundation
Williamsburg, VA 23185

"Williamsburg Reproductions—Interior Designs for Today's Living," $2.95, 232 pages, color and black and white, illustrated.

Pewter was one of the most widely used metals in Colonial days, and the pewter pieces copied by the Stieff Company from antiques in the Colonial Williamsburg buildings capture the enduring grace of the originals. There are simple footed bowls ranging in diameter from 5½" to 11" and in price from $15.30 to $81.35, candlesticks, porringers, pitchers, tankards, and spoons. A dressing spoon is $28.45, a berry spoon $7.75. Almost everything conceivable is copied in the pewter line, even a miniature sundial, 3" in diameter, that would make an unusual paperweight, $6.25.
MO/RS

COLONIAL CASTING CO.
Dept. CHC
443 South Colony Street
Meriden, CT 06450

"Hand-Crafted Pewter," 25 cents, published annually, 7 pages, black and white, illustrated.

Handsome reproductions in lead-free pewter of 18th-century pieces such as a 20-ounce Queen Anne tankard with scalloped base, about $15, or a series of scalloped-edge pewter plates from 4½" diameter, under $6, to a 10" one for about $21. There are ladles and spoons, chargers and other serving plates in interesting shapes. Some of the plates have been converted into candle wall sconces. A large selection at sensible prices.
MO

HAGERTY CO.
Dept. CHC
38 Parker Avenue
Cohasset, MA 02025

"Cohasset Colonials by Hagerty," 50 cents, published annually, 32 pages, some color, illustrated.

The pewter collection in the Hagerty catalogue consists of reproductions of original pewter pieces by Danforth, Revere, Boardman, Trask, Yale, and others and includes a six-cup teapot from a Savage original, dated 1834, $48; a 13" fiddle-back ladle for soup or punch, $16.50; and a complete Peterson coffee service, six-or nine-cup pot, creamer and sugar, and 12" tray, individually priced. There are also candlesticks in two sizes and a chamberstick with elevator, $19.
MO

WOODBURY PEWTERERS
Dept. CHC
P.O. Box 4821
Woodbury, CT 06798

Two leaflets, no charge, black and white, illustrated.

One leaflet has the Henry Ford Museum reproductions, including the Dunham Hops lidded pitcher for $45, the Benjamin Day tankard for $27.50, and the Boardman basin (for fruit or serving) for $15—exact reproductions from the museum's collection. The other leaflet shows more reproductions of antique pewter, including electrified candlestick lamps, a small 15½"-high pair for $60 and a 24" single stick lamp and shade for $50. Although Woodbury Pewterers will not sell direct, when you write for their literature they will tell you the nearest store for their wares.
RS

Christofle silver, *Baccarat*

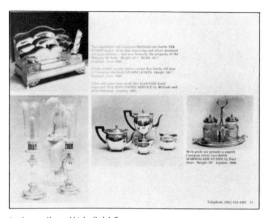

Antique silver, *Wakefield-Scearce*

Stainless-steel holloware, *WMF of America*

STERLING SILVER, SILVERPLATE, AND STAINLESS STEEL

BACCARAT, INC.
Dept. CHC
55 East 57th Street
New York, NY 10022

"Christofle Silver," 10 cents, black and white, illustrated.

The most sought-after name in European flatware, the heavily plated, hand-finished Christofle tableware is reasonably priced. A six-piece place setting in Cluny, a Louis XIV style, or Spatours, Louis XV style, costs $53. There are six patterns shown in the brochure, a complete price list for the two sizes—American or dinner (European)—in place settings, including accessory and serving pieces.
MO

CRAFT HOUSE
Dept. CHC
Colonial Williamsburg Foundation
Williamsburg, VA 23185

"Williamsburg Reproductions—Interior Designs for Today's Living," $2.95, 232 pages, color and black and white, illustrated.

The sterling silver and plated silverware reproductions made for Craft House by Stieff, with their unadorned, 18th-century elegance, are among the most beautiful examples to be found today. There are two superb flatware patterns

that would go with any table setting, the Williamsburg Shell, based on a set of English Georgian silver in the Colonial Williamsburg collection, and the Queen Anne, with pistol-handled knives, rat-tailed spoons, and three-tined forks, probably the most popular of all 18th-century designs. A six-piece place setting of the Queen Anne sterling is $187, the Williamsburg Shell $190. Holloware pieces range from coffee pots, compotes, and bowls to a muffineer, mustard pot, and a delightful little potbellied brandy warmer, inspired by an old English saucepan, that makes a perfect server for melted butter, hot sauces, or for cold vinaigrette. It holds eight ounces and costs $88.50.
MO/RS

JOSEPH H. KILIAN
Dept. CHC
39 Glen Byron Avenue
South Nyack, NY 10960

"Antique Silver & Old Sheffield Plate," $1.00, 14 pages, black and white.

An impressive list of antique silver and gold *objets d'art* that makes fascinating reading. In addition to sterling and Sheffield salvers, tureens and coffee sets, and table appointments there are such items as hard-to-find marrow scoops by Hester Bateman, from $200 to $300; asparagus tongs in fiddle, thread and shell pattern by George Adams, 1867, for $160; a pair of sauce tureens from Gorham, c. 1850, $900. An 1849 18-carat-gold snuff box made in London by John Linnit is $8,000. As these are all one of a kind, the lists vary as things are sold. Each item is fully described, and all measurements and any identifying markings are given.
MO

WAKEFIELD-SCEARCE GALLERIES
Dept. CHC
Shelbyville, KY 40065

"Wakefield-Scearce Galleries," $2.00, published annually, 56 pages, black and white, illustrated.

Part of this catalogue is devoted to the Silver Vault, copied from the old London vaults, which houses a vast collection of 18th- and 19th-century silver, both sterling and Sheffield. There are tea and coffee services by such famed silversmiths as Peter and William Bateman, a two-bottle marmalade stand by Paul Storr, an unusual octagonal bacon dish by T. & J. Cheswick, and a finely engraved footed salver by John Carter. All are one of a kind, with prices on request.
MO

WMF OF AMERICA, INC.
Dept. CHC
85 Price Parkway
Farmingdale, NY 11735

"Fraser's Stainless Flatware," no charge, published annually, 36 pages, black and white, illustrated.

Stainless-steel flatware in distinctive patterns of contemporary and traditional styles, priced from about $19.50 for a five-piece place setting. There are also two silverplate patterns—contemporary, $27.50 for a five-price setting, and traditional, $30 for five pieces, as well as accessory and serving pieces. Dimensions, where necessary, are given and all prices.

"Fraser's Stainless Holloware," no charge, published annually, 65 pages, black and white, illustrated.

Stainless-steel tableware in everything from salad bowls to trays, champagne buckets to a child's porringer. Prices on request.
RS

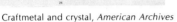

Craftmetal and crystal, *American Archives*

Contemporary tableware, *Roche-Bobois*

Flamefast ovenware, *WMF of America*

TABLEWARE COLLECTIONS

AMERICAN ARCHIVES
Dept. CHC
P.O. Box 1776
Meriden, CT 06450

*"International Silver Company '1776
House Catalogue,'" no charge,
published biannually, 32 pages, color,
illustrated.*

A beautiful catalogue of handsomely
crafted reproductions of genuine
Colonial patterns in sterling, silver
plate, pewter and crystal tableware, and
other household items at reasonable
prices.
MO

THE PFALTZGRAFF CO.
Dept. CHC
Box 1069
York, PA 17405

Brochures, no charge, color.

Specialists in handsome stoneware
table settings, this company will send
you color brochures of tabletop
decorating ideas using their various
lines, such as the Heritage, Gourmet,
and Yorktowne stonewares, Yorktowne
pewterware, and Touchmark and
Buenilum hostess table accessories.
Pfaltzgraff also reproduces china for the
Henry Ford Museum and Greenfield
Village, shown in the museum
catalogue.
RS

ROCHE-BOBOIS USA, LTD.
Dept. CHC
200 Madison Avenue
New York, NY 10016

*"Roche-Bobois," $5.00, published
annually, 132 pages, color, illustrated,
with 52-page illustrated price list.*

Good design in contemporary
tableware—stoneware, china, Limoges
porcelain designed by Marc Held,
enameled china, plexiglass and
stainless-steel cutlery, crystal and
pressed-glass items, none too cheap but
not too expensive either.
MO/RS

STURBRIDGE YANKEE WORKSHOP
Dept. CHC
Sturbridge, MA 01566

*"Sturbridge Yankee Workshop
Handbook and Catalogue," 50 cents,
published annually, 64 pages,
illustrated.*

In this collection of over 1,000 items for
furnishing an Early American home are
authentic reproductions of ruby,
cranberry, and Sandwich glass, several
patterns of ironstone china, crystal with
etched clipper-ship motif, pewter based
on designs by Paul Revere and Ashbil
Griswold, and many designs in
stainless-steel flatware. Dimensions and
prices, which seem quite moderate, are
given.
MO

WILLIAMS-SONOMA
Dept. CHC
532 Sutter Street
San Francisco, CA 94102

*"A Catalog for Cooks," no charge,
published twice a year, black and white
and color, illustrated.*

Although primarily full of all kinds of
great cooking equipment, much of it
imported, the Williams-Sonoma
catalogue also has some very handsome
decorative serving pieces for the table,
wine accessories, and glasses. A post-
paid order form is included.
MO

WMF OF AMERICA, INC.
Dept. CHC
85 Price Parkway
Farmingdale, NY 11735

*"Thomas China and Glass Master Price
Book," no charge, published annually,
32 pages, black and white, illustrated.*

An interesting collection of
contemporary china, pottery, and glass.
Some of the china designs are
stackable, such as the Brushed Colbalt
pattern (five-piece place setting,
$27.50). In ovenproof ware such as
Flammfest, an all-purpose two-pint dish
is $16. The crystal stemware, also
contemporary in design, starts at $2.50
for a wineglass in the "Rumba" pattern.
The pottery, all white, consists of vases,
ashtrays, and table dishes in interesting
shapes and textures.
RS

Shop interior, *Gargoyles*

ODDITIES AND CURIOSITIES

Hooded cradle, *Cornucopia*

FROM BELL PULLS TO
POOL TABLES TO
SPINNING WHEELS

Wicker screens, *Deutsch*

ADLER BILLIARD
Dept. CHC
820 South Hoover Street
Los Angeles, CA 90005

"Pool Tables by Adler," $1.00 (refundable with purchase), published periodically, 10 pages, black and white, illustrated.

All kinds of pool tables, from standard run-of-the-mill models to some that are highly unusual and fanciful, with elaborate bases and amusing names. The Adler Heirloom series consists of authentic replicas of the old Brunswick and English Thurston tables built prior to 1900. There are also some completely restored antique billiard tables. Adler pool tables are individually handcrafted, with a choice of finish, cloth frieze, and pocket treatment, in a wide range of prices.
MO/ID

CORNUCOPIA, INC.
Dept. CHC
43 Waltham Street
Lexington, MA 02173

"The Second Cornucopia Catalogue," $1.25, published periodically, price lists published quarterly and mailed on request, 19 pages, black and white, illustrated.

Among the unusual items found in this catalogue is an authentically detailed and working spinning wheel that comes complete with spinning instructions. It's 37" high and costs $120. A charming pine hooded cradle that can be rocked or locked in place, 48" high on stand, is $160 without stand, $215 with, in several finishes. For the collector of whaling items, there are four reproductions of harpoons copied from those in New Bedford's whaling museum, about 7' long, priced about $40 each.
MO

DA-LITE SCREEN COMPANY, INC.
Dept. CHC
Road 15 North
Warsaw, IN 46580

"DA-Lite Slide and Movie Projection Screens, Tripod, Wall-Ceiling & Automatic Electric" brochures, no charge, color, illustrated.

The ultimate for home-movie buffs is a disappearing electric movie screen that can be concealed behind a beam, rolled up to the ceiling, or mounted in a wall box. The company offers more conventional slide and movie screens, with a guide to selecting the right screen for your purposes and room. Write for prices and nearest dealer.
RS

DEUTSCH, INC.
Dept. CHC
196 Lexington Avenue
New York, N.Y. 10016

Catalogue, $1.00, published annually, 64 pages, black and white, illustrated.

Fanciful screens of wicker and rattan to divide or decorate space, in five patterns, are to be found in the Deutsch catalogue. The tulip pattern would look well with Art Deco; the peacock and sweetheart designs are wildly Victorian; the stick rattan and simple cane weave would go equally well with contemporary or traditional styles. Each screen has three panels, and prices range from $110 to $135.
MO/RS/ID

Pool table, *Adler Billiard*

Magazine cover, "Heirloom Treasures from Antique Trunks," *Dorothy Mae's Trunks*

English pub pieces, *Gargoyles*

DOROTHY MAE'S TRUNKS, LTD.
Dept. CHC
Box 536
Spearman, TX 79081

"Heirloom Treasures from Antique Trunks," $2.50, 24 pages, color, illustrated.

That old trunk Grandmother left in the attic can become an heirloom, believe it or not. The booklet tells you how to restore antique trunks, including miniatures, to their original state, with illustrations of rejuvenated pieces. Everything needed for repairing, cleaning, painting and varnishing, replacement parts, and outer and inner refurbishing and decoration is covered. A free eight-page repair-parts catalogue shows such essentials as trunk hardware, studs, tacks, locks, handles, and ornaments, all described and priced. Should you really wish to delve into the subject, $1.00 more will bring you an eight-page "History of Antique Trunks."
MO

GARGOYLES, LTD.
Dept. CHC
521 South 3rd Street
Philadelphia, PA 19174

"Gargoyles, Ltd.," $4.00 (refundable with purchase), updated monthly, 32 pages, some color, illustrated.

Among the many offbeat items and objects in the Gargoyles catalogue are massive sideboards—from medieval "serving tables" to a Victorian waitress station—and old-time bars and bar fittings. Dimensions and materials are given. Among the miscellaneous items are old posters and ads, pub, street, and station signs, dummy oversized liquor bottles, and British Railway signals, signal arms, and lanterns. Almost all are one of a kind. Sizes are given. Prices of all items are on request.
MO

THE GREAT PHONE COMPANY
Dept. CHC
5404 Northfield Road
Cleveland, OH 44137

"The Great Turn-a-Round in Telephone Fashion," no charge, 8 pages, color, illustrated.

Tired of that clunky old phone? This catalogue of telephone fashions ranges from a giddy ivory-and-gold reproduction French phone, the kind Colette might have used, for under $80, to a way-out plexiglass "Apollo" for avant-garde life-styles, around $125. There are antique telephones from Denmark, France, and Italy; phones in leather, onyx, rosewood; colors from demure pastels to flaming red. The price list covers all the accessories you might need for do-it-yourself installation.
MO

GREEK ISLAND, LTD.
Dept. CHC
215 East 49th Street
New York, NY 10017

"Greek Island Ltd.," no charge, published annually, 39 pages, black and white, illustrated.

Terra-cotta roofline tiles, salvaged from razed buildings in Athens, are among the unexpected offerings in the Greek Island catalogue. You might use them as garden or shelf ornaments.
MO

Catalogue cover, *Great Phone Company*

Hand-blown decanters, *Holly City Bottle*

Gun cabinet, *Jasper Cabinet*

HOLLY CITY BOTTLE
Dept. CHC
Box 344
Millville, NJ 08332

Lists, no charge, published as new items are added, black and white, illustrated.

American commemorative handmade, hand-blown decanters by Clevenger, each different in design and made in limited editions. A special Bicentennial Series, with a different design for each of the 13 colonies, will be available in various colors. Prices range from $6 to $25.
MO

MARTHA M. HOUSE
Dept. CHC
1022 South Decatur Street
Montgomery, AL 36104

"Southern Heirlooms," $1.00 (refundable with purchase), published annually, 44 pages, black and white, illustrated.

A handsome dictionary stand, complete with Webster's Unabridged Dictionary, with a second shelf for books, comes in fruitwood, maple, or antique finish, measures 23' wide, 15' deep, 37½" high, and is reasonably priced.
MO

HUNTING WORLD
Dept. CHC
16 East 53rd Street
New York, NY 10022

"Hunting World & Anglers World," $1.00 (refundable with first purchase), 116 pages, some color, illustrated.

A fun catalogue to browse through whether or not you are a big-game hunter or fisherman. In addition to all types of sporting gear, some unusual items for the home include hand-blown Bavarian crystal, each piece copper-wheel-engraved with African, European, or American animals or birds. A series of exciting game prints by wildlife artist Guy Coheleach range in price from $80 for a tree-perched leopard to $190 for the fox den. A handsome 29"-high cast-bronze giraffe by the late Dr. James L. Clark of the American Museum of Natural History is limited to 50 copies at $5,000 each. There are two supersized ostrich eggs, one completely covered with ring-neck pheasant feathers on either a clear lucite ring base or handmade gilded brass stand, unique but expensive.
MO/RS

JASPER CABINET CO.
Dept. CHC
P.O. Box 69
Jasper, IN 47546

"Quality Accent Furniture," $5.00, published annually, color, illustrated.

For the sportsman or collector, Jasper has a handsome gun display cabinet with a choice of eight burned-in designs such as mallard ducks, doves, grouse, quail, to personalize the piece. The locked cabinet holds six guns with ammunition storage in the lower section and is priced under $450.
MO/RS

Music or book stand, *Ephraim Marsh*   FIFI dog bed, *M.G.M. Showrooms*

M. H. KLUEVER AND SON
Dept. CHC
1526 North Second Avenue
Wausau, WI 54401

Catalogue, 50 cents, or $1.00 for 4 issues, some color, illustrated.

If you are looking for the unique in decorative accessories, or your passion is collecting Bronze Age weapons, these catalogues will lure you. Kluever describes itself as "purveyors of ancient and medieval armor, swords, battleaxes and poleaxes, plus associated antiques, with the most varied Bronze Age weapons collection in the country." There are fighting axes from India (about $15), a German 16th-century halberd ($50), or daggers and ancient Greek pots. A most fascinating collection.
MO

STEPHEN M. LEONARD
Dept. CHC
P.O. Box 28
Little Neck, NY 11363

"Decorative Mechanical Oddities," weekly newsletter, $3.00 (refundable with purchase).

Mechanical antiques such as hurdy-gurdys, old toys, horn-type phonographs, music boxes—everything from a musical pocket watch to a grand roller organ are listed in this newsletter of mechanical antiques and oddities in the expensive-but-unique category.
MO

MAGELLAN'S
Dept. CHC
21 West 16th Street
New York, NY 10001

Folder, no charge, color, illustrated.

Two cut-velvet butler's bell pulls with leaf and berry design in five color combinations, for about $13, are reproduced actual size (32" x 4") in the folder, which also gives 25 decorating ideas, with drawings, for ways to use the pulls.
MO

M.G.M. SHOWROOMS
Dept. CHC
511 East 72nd Street
New York, NY 10021

"Meyer, Gunther, Martini," $5.00, 91 pages, black and white, illustrated.

Pamper your miniature French poodle with the FIFI puppy bed, in Louis XV style with caned or upholstered sides, that also serves as an ottoman with loose cushion. Write for price of and nearest dealer for this esoteric item.
RS/ID

EPHRAIM MARSH CO.
Dept. CHC
Box 266
Concord, NC 28025

"Catalogue 19," $1.00, published annually, updated with supplement semiannually ("Catalogue 20"), 195 pages, plus 63-page supplement, color and black and white, illustrated.

Among the more unusual of Ephraim Marsh's traditional reproductions is a globe with the latest Replogle political map, 16" in diameter and beautifully mounted in a pine stand with brass casters and finials, for under $200. Also noteworthy are an imported rococo-carved walnut book or music stand, a handsome addition to a music room or library, about $245, and a bamboo-turned easel, ready to assemble and finish, just $52. For silver storage there's a chest resembling a miniature highboy in a choice of Queen Anne, Italian Provincial, and Oriental styles (the Oriental version can be ordered in Chinese red lacquer), with compartmented drawers lined with Pacific cloth, under $350.
MO

Amusing victrola, *Stephen M. Leonard*

Collection of leather-bound trunks, *Phyllis Morris Originals*

Catalogue cover, *Sea and Jungle Imports*

PHYLLIS MORRIS ORIGINALS
Dept. CHC
8772 West Beverly Boulevard
Los Angeles, CA 90048

*"Premiere Collection," $5.00
(refundable with purchase), updated as
necessary, 18 pages, color, illustrated.*

Included in the Phyllis Morris Originals
is a collection of leather-bound, nail-
studded trunks and boxes, each fitted
for a different use—silver chest, liquor
box, trinket case, or spur chest—and a
bride's, stage-coach, or Saratoga trunk
to be used as a foot locker or end
table. There are also eight
reproductions of antique capitals-cum-
tables. Sizes are given, but you have to
write for prices.
RS/ID

OLD WORLD FOUNDRY GUILD, INC.
Dept. CHC
1612 Decatur Street
Ridgewood, NY 11227

*"Metal (Brass) Reproductions," no
charge, 30 pages, black and white,
illustrated.*

Among the brass or other metal pieces
in this unusual collection are such
hard-to-find things as music stands in
three styles, an elaborate portrait easel,
three styles of brass costumers, and a
dictionary or Bible stand for around
$114. Prices plus sizes and weights are
given on a separate sheet.
MO

THE PATIO
Dept. CHC
550 Powell Street
San Francisco, CA 94108

*"Fall/Winter San Francisco Gift Book,"
$1.00, some color, illustrated.*

The "San Francisco Gift Book" has
some offbeat items, such as a two-foot-
high skull of a billy goat mounted on a
painted hardwood base, quite a
conversation piece for $90. Since it's
the real thing, the supply is limited.
Another eye-catcher is the five-foot-
high hand-carved and painted wooden
American Indian for $600, or a 12"-high
desk-top miniature replica for $30.
MO

SEA AND JUNGLE IMPORTS
Dept. CHC
4666 San Fernando Road
Glendale, CA 91204

*"Sea and Jungle Imports," no charge, 24
pages, color, illustrated.*

Sea and Jungle, which calls itself "the
largest Polynesian shop of its kind in
the world," carries exotic and unusual
imports, not all of which are included
in the catalogue. From 22 different
countries come building materials
(panels, matting, poles, thatch, corks,
ropes, fencing), nets, tiles, lamps,
drums, shields, masks, giant clam shells,
birds, fish, tikis, weapons and artifacts,
decorative lighting, and sculptured
stone waterfalls. Items are pictured and
described, different weaves of mats
shown, ordering information is given,
as well as updated price lists. A list of
items not in the catalogue is provided.
MO

Country roof ornaments, *Sarreid*

Hand-carved cigar-store Indian, *Willard Shepard*

Offbeat bar, *Thomasville Furniture*

SARREID, LTD.
Dept. CHC
P.O. Box 3545
Wilson, NC 27893

"Sarreid, Ltd.," color, no charge.

Sarreid has some accessories you are unlikely to encounter anywhere else, among them a pagoda-shaped terrarium and a series of cut and hand-forged country roof ornaments (cow, hen, and pig) mounted on wood bases, for about $50 each.
RS/ID

WILLARD SHEPARD
Dept. CHC
Jordan Cove
Waterford, CT 06385

"Shep's Ship Shop," price list, no charge, illustrated, black and white.

Cigar-store Indians are among the more unusual items of nostalgic Americana carved by Willard Shepard. These are by special order only. He will send you his price list of his standard works, such as whale carvings ($9 for the 8" size), name boards, and eagles and will confer on special orders if you desire something completely out of the ordinary.
MO

THOMASVILLE FURNITURE INDUSTRIES, INC.
Dept. CHC
P.O. Box 339
Thomasville, NC 27360

"Homemaker's Guide," $2.00, 100 pages, color, illustrated.

For offbeat accent furniture pieces, Thomasville has borrowed from the "Four Corners" (name of the group) of the World. From India, an amusing white lacquer elephant occasional table; from the Orient, a brass-bound sea captain's chest or a Korean chest, with elaborate brass hardware, both of camphor and teak woods; a cabinet with Coromandel panels in black lacquer and raised chinoiserie scenes or a reproduction 18th-century English globe on stand that opens to become a bar. All these unusual pieces with a one-of-a-kind look are reasonably priced.
RS

THE WINE VAULT, INC.
Dept. CHC
P.O. Box 6298
909 Park Avenue
San Jose, CA 95150

"The Wine Vault," folder of sheets, no charge, color, illustrated.

Prefabricated and easily assembled, the Wine Vault maintains a constant temperature of 53°–57°F. The six models, capable of holding from 174 to over 2,000 bottles, start at $1,450 and range up to $4,575. The smallest unit, 53" wide and 25" deep, is ideal for recessing in a wall or closet. The other units are like small rooms and can be built in or left free-standing. Sizes and prices are included. If you can't find a size to fit your needs, your own Wine Vault can be custom-designed.
RS

Built-in unit, *The Wine Vault*

Before

After

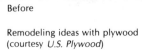

Remodeling ideas with plywood
(courtesy *U.S. Plywood*)

DO-IT-YOURSELF, REMODELING, AND BUILDING

190

ANTIQUING, PAINTING, FINISHING, AND REFINISHING

AMERICAN ART CLAY CO., INC.
Rub 'n Buff Division
Dept. CHC
Box 68163
Indianapolis, IN 46268

"Brush 'n Leaf," no charge, color, illustrated; "Finger or Brush 'n Buff," no charge, color, illustrated.

"Brush 'n Leaf" gold and silver leaf and antique gold metallic finishes are sold for interior use on any dry surface—metal, wood, cloth, glass, plastic, or papier-maché—in a one-step application. They cost about $1.90 a bottle. The exterior finishes in Brass or Old Gold can be applied to mail boxes, lampposts, or any material exposed to weather.

"Finger or Brush 'n Buff" are tubes of color to antique or decorate any surface or material, ideal for picture frames, découpage, casts, furniture, sconces, any item to which you want to give a rich or weathered, bold or subdued look. Instructions are given for highlighting, antiquing, streaking, spattering, weathering, and découpage. You can combine any of the 18 Rub 'n Buff colors to create exactly the color and effect you want. There are also six wood-tone "Stain 'n Buff" finishes for touch up or finishing. A third finish, "Antique n' Glaze" (about $1.50 a bottle), in rich Colonial brown, gives an antique finish over any Rub 'n Buff or Brush 'n Buff finish. Just brush it on and, when tacky, wipe off as much as you want.
RS

BORDEN CHEMICAL
Dept. CHC
P.O. Box 266
Medina, OH 44256

"How to Decorate with Krylon," 25 cents, 12 pages, color, illustrated.

How-to techniques of spray painting, plus many do-it-yourself decorating ideas for floors, walls, and furniture.
RS

SAMUEL CABOT, INC.
Dept. CHC
One Union Street
Boston, MA 02108

"Cabot's Stains," 25 cents, published periodically, 16 pages, color, illustrated.

If you don't know the difference between a stain and a paint, this little handbook on wood and wood stains will tell you. There's information about stains for interiors and exteriors, for weathering, transparency, decks, fences, and cement floors, about bleaching oil, and a one-page guide to successful staining, plus recommendations for finishing or refinishing furniture.
RS

CHEM-CLEAN FURNITURE RESTORATION CENTER
Dept. CHC
Route #7
Arlington, VT 05250

"Furniture Restoration Tips and Home Use Products," 25 cents, some color, illustrated.

Tips on how to use the various Chem-Clean products for bleaching furniture, stripping floors, removing paint and varnish, and cleaning and reconditioning brushes. A separate sheet has ten do-it-yourself tips for refinishing from start to finish and a product price list.
MO/RS

CONSUMER SERVICES CENTER
Johnson Wax
Dept. CHC
P.O. Box 567
Racine, WI 53403

"A Beginner's Guide to Refinishing Furniture," no charge, 15 pages, black and white, illustrated.

One of a series of booklets offered by Johnson Wax. Step-by-step, clear instructions and rules for refinishing are given: cleaning the surface to be refinished, removing the existing finish, preparing the surface for the new finish, applying the new finish, and protecting the new finish.
RS

A roundup of booklets for painting and refinishing

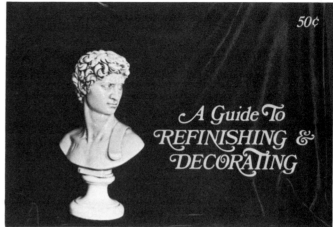

CANING

MINWAX CO., INC.
Dept. CHC
72 Oak Street
Clifton, NJ 07014

"Tips on Wood Finishing," no charge, published annually, 16 pages, black and white, illustrated.

Tips for stripping, sanding, and finishing anything made of wood, with a description of Minwax's various wood-finishing products.
RS

PRATT & LAMBERT
Dept. CHC
Box 22
Buffalo, NY 14240

"How-to-Paint Mini Library," 50 cents, color, illustrated.

This well-known paint company has prepared a neat little folder of seven colorful booklets that tell you all about using paints, stains, varnishes, sealers, and fillers. One booklet tells how to paint supergraphics; others tell how to prepare and paint wood surfaces, walls, doors, ceilings, house exteriors, swimming pools, and how to refinish floors and antique furniture. The information is clear, detailed, and professional.
RS

STAR BRONZE CO.
Dept. CHC
Box 568
Alliance, OH 44601

"A Guide to Refinishing and Decorating," no charge, 15 pages, color, illustrated.

Detailed instructions for refinishing furniture and floors, from tools to finishes. The decorating part has tips on coordinating color and design, selecting curtains, wallpaper, and accessories.
RS

WATCO-DENNIS CORP.
Dept. CHC
1756 22nd Street
Santa Monica, CA 90404

"How to Finish Beautiful Wood" and *"Beautiful Wood Staining and Finishing,"* no charge, black and white, illustrated.

How to use Watco Danish Oil and Watco stains, which range from vivid decorator colors to natural wood tones.
RS

PEERLESS RATTAN AND REED MANUFACTURING CO.
Dept. CHC
97 Washington Street
New York, NY 10006

"Peerless Rattan & Reed Chair Caning Handbook," no charge, published semiannually, 15 pages, black and white, illustrated.

An instruction booklet that shows and tells you how to weave a cane seat or to install a machine-woven one. Step-by-step instructions make it easy for anyone to get the hang of this craft. Included is a price list of the various types of caning, cane webbing, and reeds for the job; also chair-caning kits and tools at moderate prices.
MO

Catalogue cover, *Craft Products*

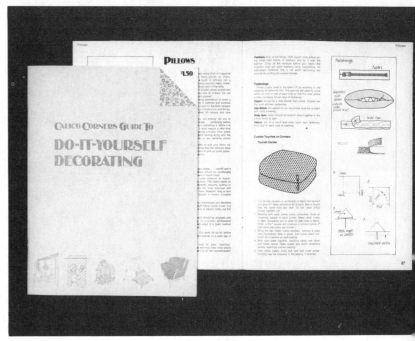

Catalogue cover, *The Calico Corners*

CLOCK-MAKING

DECORATING WITH FABRIC AND SHEETS

CRAFT PRODUCTS CO.
Dept. CHC
Elmhurst, IL 60126

"Clocks and Clockworks," 50 cents, 98 pages, black and white, illustrated.

Clock plans for case, wall-hung, and mantel clocks with cases designed to hold movements that are available from Craft Products. The plans are full-size, easy to follow, and run from about 80 cents for any of the shelf clocks to about $1.60 for grandfather and grandmother clock cases. There are also complete clock kits, some with movements included, offered by Craft Products. Movements for each of the clocks, dial, hands, moldings, and ornamental hardware to complete the clock are available, illustrated and priced.
MO

CALICO CORNERS, INC.
Dept. CHC
Bancroft Estate, Box 670
Wilmington, DE 19899

"Calico Corners Guide to Do-It-Yourself Decorating," $1.50 plus 25 cents postage, 40 pages, illustrated.

Packed with detailed instructions and professional tricks, this clear and informative little book on decorating with fabric is put out by a franchise store with branches all over the country. (Calico Corners sells drapery, slipcover, and upholstery fabric seconds from top design houses at a saving of up to 50 percent on the original "first" price.) The book tells you how to cover walls with fabric, using starch, paste, glue, a staple gun; how to build a frame of furring strips to which fabric can be anchored with staples or brads; how to shirr fabric on rods. Other sections cover applying and sealing fabric on floors; making a shirred, starched, or suspended fabric ceiling; different types of window treatments; fabric wall hangings for instant art; how to make pillows, tablecloths, shower curtains, patchwork, a fabric headboard; and the technique of covering Parsons tables, screens, trunks, shelves, or the panels of a wood door with fabric.
RS

CLOPAY
Dept. CHC
Clopay Square
Cincinnati, OH 45215

"Decorative Coverings Idea Book," $1.00, 30 pages, color, illustrated.

Any room in the house can be transformed by using Clopay self-adhesive fabrics on walls, doors, bookshelves, headboards, furniture, and appliances—and you can even use them to create your own supergraphics. The book gives you plenty of ideas, plus a complete set of instructions for applying the fabrics and some helpful decorating tips.
RS

KENNEY MANUFACTURING CO.
Dept. CHC
1000 Jefferson Boulevard West
Warwick, RI 02887

"Creative Windows," $1.25, published annually, 72 pages, color, illustrated.

Some ten pages of this handsome book show you how to make your own curtains, from lined and unlined draperies to simple café curtains, with a guide to selecting the proper hardware—from Kenney, of course.
RS

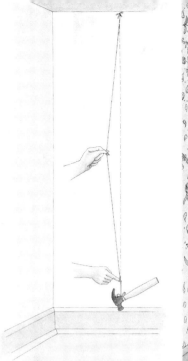
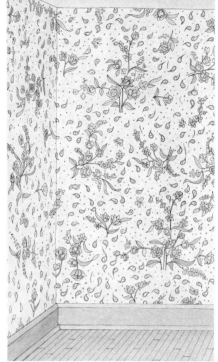

Do-it-yourself decorating ideas, *Martex*

DECORATIVE PROJECTS

MARTEX
Dept. CHC
P.O. Box 192
Madison Square Station
New York, NY 10010

"The View from the Tub and How to Change It," $1.00, 40 pages, some color, illustrated.

A booklet full of do-it-yourself ideas with sheets and towels, mostly for and in bathrooms, such as shirred shower curtains with terry tie backs or a ruffled sink skirt. Some other fun things to make—an exercise mat of bath towels, a tissue box covered with a pillow case. The booklet includes a yardage chart for sheets, pillowcases, and towels, all step-by-step instructions, lists of additional materials needed to complete each item, and gives the ten most important questions and answers about towels.
RS

J. P. STEVENS AND COMPANY, INC.
Domestic and Allied Prod. Adv. Dept.
Dept. CHC
1185 Avenue of the Americas
New York, NY 10036

"Sew and Decorate with Utica's U.S. Mix," 50 cents, 14 pages, color, illustrated.

Unusual and sometimes exotic ideas for decorating with sheets. Walls, ceilings, seat cushions, pillows, even a bed tent, as well as the bed itself, are shown covered with sheets, with instructions on how to make each item and the size and number of sheets required. A lot of bright ideas for the money.
RS

COUNTRYSIDE PRESS
Dept. CHC
200 James Street
Barrington, IL 60010

Handmade Rugs from Practically Anything, by Jean Ray Laury and Joyce Aiken, 1972, $7.95.

Some leftover yarns, old curtains, or even used blue jeans are the makings of an original area rug. This book tells you how to construct and design it. To make your recycled design original, you won't need a loom or any special equipment, just a knowledge of knitting, sewing, or crocheting. There are over 150 interesting ways for using up old materials shown, some in color.

AMERICAN ART CLAY CO., INC.
Rub 'n Buff Division
P.O. Box 68163
Indianapolis, IN 46268

"Decorative Inspirations and Craft Ideas," no charge, 23 pages, color, illustrated.

"Creative decorating magic . . . in your hands" is the way the manufacturers refer to "Rub 'n Buff," "Stain 'n Buff," "Brush 'n Leaf," and "Spray 'n Seal," four decorating, antiquing, and finishing products that can be used on wood, glass, plastic, canvas, plaster, cloth, metal, paper, and leather. The brochure gives ideas and complete directions for these little miracle workers, which are sold in craft supply shops.
RS

Paperback book cover, *Little, Brown*

Paperback book cover,
Simon and Schuster

Brochure covers, *American Cyanimid*

FLOOR TILING

THE FLINTKOTE CO.
Dept. CHC
480 Central Avenue
East Rutherford, NJ 07073

*"Floors, All Styles," no charge,
published annually, 28 pages,
illustrated.*

The adhesive is already on the back of
Peel-and-Stick vinyl floor tiles, so all
you have to do is remove the protective
cover and press the tile in place, and
it's guaranteed to stick for five years. A
separate folder describes and illustrates
the 12 steps to laying the Flintkote tiles
yourself.
RS

FURNITURE-MAKING

THE BERKSHIRE TRAVELLER
Dept. CHC
Stockbridge, MA 01262

*"Berkshire Traveller Press," no charge,
12 pages, black and white, illustrated.*

The catalogue lists two books of special
interest to the amateur furniture
craftsman or collector: *Shop Drawings
of Shaker Furniture and Woodenware*.
Volumes I and II, $3.50 each. The
former contains 80 measured drawings
for reproducing original Shaker pieces
at home. The latter contains 76 more
scaled drawings and photographs of
selected Shaker pieces.

LITTLE, BROWN
34 Beacon Street
Boston, MA 02106

*"Make Your Own Antiques," by Francis
Hagerty, paperback, $5.95.*

This is a complete guide for the
amateur woodcrafter interested in
reproducing American Colonial designs
down to the last detail. Mr. Hagerty
suggests types of wood, finishes;
includes line (working) drawings;
supplies sources for all necessary tools
and materials.

SIMON AND SCHUSTER, INC.
630 Fifth Avenue
New York, N.Y. 10020

*Designer Furniture Anyone Can Make,
by William E. Schremp, paperback,
$2.95.*

The new low-scaled contemporary
furniture the interior designers are
using is shown in simple,
straightforward, easy-to-follow
drawings, from on-the-floor seating to
platform beds to storage ideas.
MO

MACRAMÉ

REEVES KNOTIQUE
Dept. CHC
Box 5011
Riverside, CA 92501

*"Macramé Supplies," 13 pages, and
"Macramé and Other Handicrafts," 10
pages, $1.00, black and white,
illustrated.*

The two booklets come together. The
first is a collection of supplies for do-it-
yourself macramé: stoneware and
porcelain beads, pendants, pots,
macramé cord, and other necessary
items. Each item is described and
priced. You can buy a sample card of
the cords for 50 cents, the beads and
the pendants for $2.50 each. Also
included is a selection of books on
macramé from 15 cents to $1.95. The
second catalogue is a group of ready-
made macramé items and glass tube
bud vases mounted on California
redwood bases from $2.50 to $4.
MO

Catalogue cover, *Flecto*

Staple-gun decorating, *Swingline*

PLASTICS

STAPLE-GUN DECORATING

AMERICAN CYANAMID CO.
Acrylite Sheet Dept.
Dept. CHC
Wayne, NJ 07470

"Working with Acrylite," no charge, color, illustrated; *"Acrylite Glazing Manual,"* no charge, 25 pages, black and white, illustrated.

Two brochures on Acrylite (a cast acrylic plastic in sheet form), its optical and physical properties, characteristics, care, installation, and suggested uses, such as glazing.
RS

THE FLECTO CO.
Dept. CHC
P.O. Box 12955
Oakland, CA 94604

"Decopour Idea Book," $1.25, 27 pages, color, illustrated.

"Do me and dry me" ideas for the do-it-yourselfer using Decopour Deep Glass Plastic, a clear polymer compound that can be applied to almost any surface (simply by pouring it on) to provide a clear, protective coating. The booklet illustrates about ten projects (trays, boxes, plaques, etc.) with step-by-step directions and lists of materials needed. Also included are a list of items that you can seal with Decopour, five pages of do's and don'ts, and a list of products that can be used successfully with Decopour.
RS

ROHM AND HAAS CO.
Dept. CHC
P.O. Box 4480
Philadelphia, PA 19140

"Do It Yourself with Plexiglas," 25 cents, 19 pages, color, illustrated.

Plexiglas, the registered trade name of the Rohm and Haas Company's acrylic plastic, is sold in sheets of transparent tints, translucent and opaque colors as well as the clear, colorless sheets most often seen. This booklet presents almost 60 illustrated ideas for home furnishings made with Plexiglas, from a backgammon board to a telephone table. To get the complete plans, 50 cents a set, just fill in the order card. Also enclosed is an illustrated price list of the accessory products you will need when working with the acrylic sheets— cements, saws, drills, cleaner, and strip heater element for bending Plexiglas. There is also a list of cross-country distributors of the product.
RS

SWINGLINE
Dept. CHC
Box 1484
New York, NY 10010

"Staple Gun Decorating," 25 cents, 10 pages, color, illustrated.

A Swingline Staple Gun is the fastest way to cover chairs, screens, headboards, walls, woodwork, or furniture with fabric. Step-by-step directions, diagrams, and pictures start you off with ten specific decorating jobs ranging from a mirror frame to a "fabric picture." Also included are staple-gun decorating tips and advice on using the gun correctly.
RS

Ideas with vinyl wallcoverings, *General Tire and Rubber*

TRUNK RESTORATION

UPHOLSTERING, WALL, AND WINDOW COVERINGS

DOROTHY MAE'S TRUNKS, LTD.
Dept. CHC
Box 536
Spearman, TX 79081

"Heirloom Treasures from Antique Trunks," $2.50, 24 pages, color, illustrated.

How antique trunks (including miniatures) can be restored to their original state, with many illustrations of rejuvenated pieces. Everything needed for repairing, cleaning, painting and varnishing, replacement parts, and outer and inner refurbishing and decoration is covered. A free eight-page repair-parts catalogue shows such essentials as trunk hardware, studs, tacks, locks, handles, and ornaments, all described and priced. For those who wish to know more, there's an eight-page "History of Antique Trunks" for $1.
MO

FLAIR-CRAFT, INC.
Dept. CHC
P.O. Box 3494
Kimberling City, MO 65686

"Trunks to Treasures," $2.00, illustrated.

Step-by-step instructions and ideas for transforming those old trunks salvaged from attics, basements, and junk shops into useful and decorative blanket chests, hope chests, and toy boxes.

THE GALLERY
Dept. CHC
Amsterdam, NY 12010

"The Gallery," no charge, 32 pages, some color, illustrated.

Giant photomurals in two designs, woodland trees or snow-capped mountains, come with glue and step-by-step instructions for easy installation, $49.95 each.
MO

THE GENERAL TIRE AND RUBBER COMPANY
Dept. CHC
P.O. Box 951
Akron, OH 44329

"Decorator 6 Pack," $1.00, 6 booklets, color, illustrated.

The six booklets cover different aspects of using vinyl wallcoverings in every room of the house. One booklet, "The Hang of It," is a guide to wall preparation, measuring, and hanging vinyl wallcoverings.
RS

IMPERIAL WALLCOVERINGS
Dept. CHC
23645 Mercantile Road
Cleveland, OH 44122

"Secrets That Decorators Don't Always Tell You About Wallcoverings," 75 cents, 35 pages, color, illustrated.

You can be your own decorator and handyman with this handy little booklet that tells you how to hang Imperial's prepasted and pretrimmed and strippable wallpapers and how to use their many patterns in different ways. There are complete instructions for hanging prepasted or unpasted wallcoverings, lining problem walls before papering, a wallcovering estimate chart, and a list of decorating do's and don'ts.
RS

SHIBUI WALLCOVERINGS
Dept. CHC
P.O. Box 1268
Santa Rosa, CA 95403

Samples, 50 cents.

Samples of beautiful and sound-deadening grasscloths and cork will be sent for your selection, with complete do-it-yourself instructions. Necessary tools may also be purchased.
MO

UNIROYAL
Coated Fabrics Dept.
Dept. CHC
Mishawaka, IN 46544

"Upholstering with Naugahyde," no charge, 16 pages, black and white.

A step-by-step upholstery booklet for Naugahyde, the trademark name for Uniroyal's vinyl upholstery, a manmade look-alike for leather. It shows, with clear and detailed illustrations, how to cut, fit, and sew vinyl yard goods, down to the finishing touches. A yardage chart for the basic upholstered pieces is included.
RS

Remodeling ideas, *American Plywood Association*

Catalogue cover, *Craft Patterns*

HOME-IMPROVEMENT PROJECTS

**WINDOW SHADE MANUFACTURERS'
   ASSOCIATION**
Dept. CHC
230 Park Avenue
New York, NY 10017

*"Lam-Eze Pressure Sensitive Laminating
System,"* no charge, with a stamped,
self-addressed #10 envelope, black and
white.

The leaflet gives step-by-step directions,
with accompanying drawings, for
making your own window shades by
applying the fabric of your choice to
shades treated with the Lam-Eze
adhesive laminating system, the easiest,
quickest, and least expensive way to get
a custom-designed shade.

*"Do-It-Yourself Ideas for Window
Shades,"* 25 cents, 16 pages, black and
white, illustrated; *"How to Make
Decorator Window Shades,"* folder, no
charge with a stamped, self-addressed
#10 envelope.

The first booklet is full of do-it-yourself
ideas and instructions for decorating
plain shades with trimmings, appliqué,
stencils and painted designs, and
interesting pulls. The folder shows how
to fabric-cover any shade in four easy
steps, using Stauffer's Tontine brand
shade cloth.
RS

AMERICAN PLYWOOD ASSOCIATION
Dept. CHC
1119 A Street
Tacoma, WA 98401

*"Some Solutions for Clutter," "The Art
of Adding On," "Easy Changes, Large
and Small,"* 50 cents each or three for
$1.00, published annually, 16 pages
each, color, illustrated.

Practical and attractive ideas for adding
space to your home and eliminating
"clutter" through utilizing dead space
and streamlining closets. Projects range
from storage walls to structural
additions of wings, rooms, and second
stories. Ten additional publications are
offered for $1.
RS

BETTER HOMES AND GARDENS
Dept. CHC
Box 384
Des Moines, IA 50336

*"Better Homes and Gardens Guides and
Do-it-Yourself Books,"* $1.00 each, 3 for
$2.00, 7 for $4, 10 for $6.00; about 50
pages each, black and white and color,
illustrated.

At present count there are about 15
current guides and how-to books
covering just about every problem you
will ever encounter around the house,
all generously illustrated and full of
ideas and instructions. Some of the
subjects are floors, walls, and ceilings;
home upkeep and repair; painting,
finishing, and redecorating; patios,
decks, and fences to build; space
saving.

CLOPAY
Dept. CHC
Clopay Square
Cincinnati, OH 45214

*"Clopay Folding Doors and Room
Dividers,"* no charge, 8 pages, color,
illustrated.

Decorative ideas for using Clopay's
prefinished, self-installed folding doors.
They come in many colors and wood
grains, and some have soundproofing
and insulating qualities. Installation
instructions are included with the
doors.
RS

CRAFT PATTERNS STUDIO
Dept. CHC
Route 83 and North Avenue
Elmhurst, IL 60126

"Home Ideas Book," 60 cents, 104
pages, black and white, illustrated.

A catalogue of detailed patterns and
instructions for hundreds of projects,
from Colonial and outdoor furniture to
fences and gazebos. Prices and order
forms are included.
MO

Window-shade ideas, *Window Shade Manufacturers' Association*

Vinyl "Countryside" paneling, *Evans Products*

Paneling ideas, *Georgia-Pacific*

EVANS PRODUCTS COMPANY
Dept. CHC
1121 Southwest Salmon Street
Portland, OR 97205

"Evans Remodeling Paneling Decorating Ideas," $2.50, 35 pages, black and white, illustrated.

Bright-Ons, plywood panels, ready-cut, ready to nail or glue on existing walls, come in the 36 *House and Garden* colors, which means you can color-coordinate them with other merchandise made by manufacturers who match *H & G's* colors. A special directory in the booklet lists these manufacturers. Six pages show decorative uses of Bright-Ons in every room in the house.
RS

GEORGIA-PACIFIC CORPORATION
Dept. CHC
900 S.W. Fifth Avenue
Portland, OR 97204

"The Great American Look in Paneling," 25 cents, 29 pages, color, illustrated; "How to Make Beautiful Things Happen to Walls," 25 cents, 28 pages, color, illustrated.

"The Great American Look in Paneling" shows different styles of prefinished plywood paneling named for such historic areas as the Oregon Trail, Valley Forge, and Portsmouth in six colorful folders that picture American ways of life in different parts of the country, with plywood paneling as part of the background. A how-to-install section is part of the package. "How to Make Beautiful Things Happen to Walls" gives remodeling ideas for practically every room in the house—literally from basement to attic—with prefinished plywood paneling from Georgia-Pacific's handsome collection. The installation instructions are straightforward and easy to follow.
RS

**HARDWOOD PLYWOOD
MANUFACTURERS' ASSOCIATION**
Dept. CHC
P.O. Box 6246
Arlington, VA 22206

List of brochures with price list, no charge, black and white.

The list offers individual brochures relating to plywood: finishing, applications, use as wall paneling and so on, and do-it-yourself plans for such simple projects as a desk, planter, room divider. Prices range from 10 cents to $10.
RS

Plywood projects, *Hardwood Plywood Manufacturers*

SPIRAL STAIR KIT

FEATURES
- ALL STEEL CONSTRUCTION WITH VINYL HANDRAIL.
- FITS INTO SQUARE WELL OPENINGS 2" LARGER THAN THE DIAMETER OF THE STAIR.
- CAN BE INSTALLED AGAINST A BALCONY OR DECK.
- INTERIOR AND EXTERIOR USES.
- CAN BE INSTALLED LEFT OR RIGHT HAND UP
- SAVES FLOOR SPACE.
- EASY TO WALK UP OR DOWN.
- ALL METAL PARTS PREFITTED FOR EASE OF INSTALLATION.
- TREADS AND LANDING PRE DRILLED TO RECEIVE FINISHED WOOD OR CARPET COVERED WOOD STEPS.
- ALL FASTENERS INCLUDED.
- YOU NEED JUST A FEW SIMPLE TOOLS TO INSTALL IT.

BASIC 4'0 DIAMETER KIT WITH OPTIONAL BALCONY RAILING.

BASIC 5'0 DIAMETER KIT WITH OPTIONAL ⅝ FLAKEWOOD TREADS. (Carpet Covering by owner.)

STANDARD KIT INCLUDES:
- 1–12'6" LONG CENTER POLE WITH A 10" DIAMETER BASE PLATE
- 1–TOP LANDING OF 1/8" THICK FORMED STEEL PLATE
- 12–TREADS OF 1/8" THICK FORMED STEEL PLATE
- 12–3/4" SQUARE RAILING SPINDLES
- 1–3/4" SQUARE STARTING POST
- 1–COIL OF 1⅝" ROUND VINYL HANDRAIL
- 1–LANDING RAILING

OPTIONAL ACCESSORIES
- EXTRA TREADS, SPINDLES AND LONGER CENTER POLE (for heights other than standard.)
- 5/4" OAK TREADS AND LANDING
- 3/4" FLAKE BOARD TREADS AND LANDING (inside to receive carpet)
- PAPER TEMPLATES FOR CUTTING YOUR OWN WOOD TREADS
- SELF STANDING WELL HANDRAILS
- CAST IRON SPINDLE DESIGN
- SCROLL DESIGN SPINDLE FILLERS

ALL HARDWARE NEEDED TO ASSEMBLE AND INSTALL STAIR . . . ALL METAL PRIMED FLAT BACK . . . EASY TO FOLLOW ILLUSTRATED STEP–BY–STEP INSTRUCTIONS.

the IRON SHOP
400 Reed Road
Broomall, Pa. 19008

Area Code 215
544-7100

Spiral-staircase kit, *The Iron Shop*

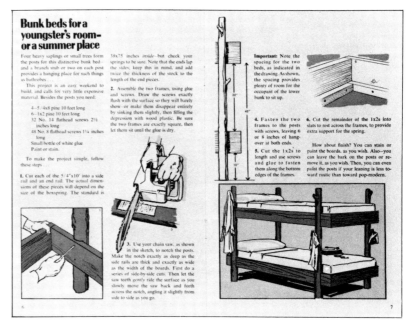

Weekend project, *Homelite*

HOMELITE
Dept. CHC
Riverdale Avenue
Port Chester, NY 10573

"Weekend Projects," $1.25, 25 pages, some color, illustrated.

Twenty-two easy projects that can be completed in a single weekend by the owner of a lightweight chain saw. The brochure provides detailed instructions for constructing a range of useful indoor and outdoor items such as fences, swings, tables, bird feeders, benches, stools, treeless tree houses, planters, bunk beds. Safety precautions for operating a chain saw are thoughtfully included.
MO

THE IRON SHOP
Dept. CHC
400 Reed Road
Broomall, PA 19008

"Spiral Stair Kit," no charge, black and white, illustrated.

If space is limited but access to another area is desired, the do-it-yourself spiral stair kit is the answer. In diameter sizes from 3'6" to 6' for finished floor-to-floor heights of 8'1½" to 9'6", these kits cost from $355 to $495 f.o.b. and come with complete installation instructions. If you want the do-it-yourself instructions and free-estimate sheet, send along 50 cents when you write for the brochure.
MO

MYLEN INDUSTRIES
Dept. CHC
650 Washington Street
Peekskill, NY 10566

"Mylen Industries," no charge, about 30 pages, black and white, illustrated.

The brochure illustrates Mylen's space-saving spiral stair units that are shipped in kit form ready for installation. Assembly and installation are said to be easy, requiring no special skills or tools and just a couple of hours' time. Many stair designs are available for both interior and exterior use in homes and apartments, some pictured in settings. The advantages of the units are detailed, including their decorative value. Questionnaire forms, when filled out and returned to Mylen, are the basis for an estimate that is then sent to you. Prices start at about $300.
MO

NATIONAL PLAN SERVICE, INC.
Dept. CHC
435 West Fullerton Avenue
Elmhurst, IL 60126

Special publications lists, no charge.

On request, the National Plan Service will supply lists of illustrated booklets, catalogues, books of plans, blueprints, and how-to books covering every imaginable home-improvement project, from remodeling, home design, furniture-making, and refinishing to carpentry, painting, gardening, and landscaping. There's a wide range of prices, from under $1, and special discounts. Four 89-cent booklets are devoted to plumbing repairs, hand and power tools, electrical wiring, and decorating ideas. The Sunset how-to and *Better Homes and Gardens* do-it-yourself books are listed.
MO

NATIONAL WOODWORK MANUFACTURERS ASSOCIATION
Dept. CHC
c/o SR&A
355 Lexington Avenue
New York, NY 10017

"Remodeling with Wood Windows and Doors," no charge, 14 pages, black and white, illustrated.

An unusual and informative booklet about the many types of wooden doors and windows that tells you where and how to use them when you are remodeling and decorating. Tips on painting and care of doors are also included.

PRODUCT SPECIALTIES, INC.
Dept. CHC
600 Washington
Eaton, IN 47338

"Product Specialties, Inc," no charge, published annually, color, illustrated.

Similar to the process used by Roman and Egyptian glassmakers, "Cathedralite" is a non-leaded, multicolored glass that comes in sheets. You can use it as decorative light-suffusing panels in doors and windows, as room dividers, as tabletops or mirror frames. Complete do-it-yourself instructions come with each order. Sizes and prices are on request.
MO

200

Catalogue cover, *Brookstone*

Workbench, *Leichtung & Galmitz*

TOOLS FOR THE JOB

WESTERN WOOD PRODUCTS
ASSOCIATION
Dept. CHC
Yeon Building
Portland, OR 97204

"Ideas for the Home Craftsman," list, no charge with stamped, self-addressed envelope.

The list offers plans for 39 do-it-yourself ideas for remodeling or adding to your home. Two garage plans, one for converting the garage into a solarium or family room, the other for utilizing the space above for an indoor-outdoor living room, are each 25 cents. There are storage ideas, ten build-it-yourself projects, paneling ideas, all using Western Wood products.
MO

U.S. PLYWOOD
Dept. CHC
Box 61
New York, NY 10046

"All About Wall Paneling," 50 cents, 27 pages, color, illustrated.

Over 50 illustrations and 26 ways to decorate with plywood, plus a color guide, paneling planning chart, installation instructions for paneling, and examples of different types of moldings are included in this handy little booklet for do-it-yourselfers. A selection index gives name, type, description, and colors of U.S. Plywood Paneling.
RS

ACROPOLIS BOOKS, LTD.
Dept. CHC
2400–17th St. N.W.
Washington, DC 20009

Creative Craftsmanship with Power Tools, by Bernd Kasch, Acropolis Books, Ltd., 1974, $7.50.

For beginner or expert, an excellent complete guide to using power tools for crafts, decorating, home maintenance, remodeling, carpentry. Includes diagrams and drawings of furniture, cubes and wall storage systems, and constructions with plastics.

BROOKSTONE CO.
Dept. CHC
120 Vose Farm Road
Peterborough, NH 03458

"Hard-to-Find Tools and Other Fine Things," no charge, 68 pages, some color, illustrated.

A catalogue of all kinds of tools, clearly illustrated and described in meticulous detail, with suggested uses. If you can't find a tool for a particular job in this catalogue, chances are it doesn't exist. The prices seem reasonable.
MO

LEICHTUNG & GALMITZ, INC.
Dept. CHC
5187 Mayfield Road
Cleveland, OH 44124

"The World's Finest Woodcrafting Tools," no charge, published semiannually, 12 pages, some color, illustrated.

The ultimate in do-it-yourselfmanship is to become a cabinetmaker and carpenter. Anyone with a yen to become a woodworker will be fascinated by this catalogue, which lists, among the many offerings, an 80" beech workbench from Denmark that can hold items as large as a grandfather clock and can be used for marking, finishing, sawing, assembling, veneering and glueing, planing, chiseling, and carving. Unique holding devices can be used individually or in combination to grip almost any kind of workpiece in practically any position to give comfortable access to any side without repositioning. This super workbench costs about $450, but there are others for less. A set of five-piece cabinetmaker's screwdrivers is $14, a six-piece amateur's woodcarving set is $35. Prices are on the order form.
MO

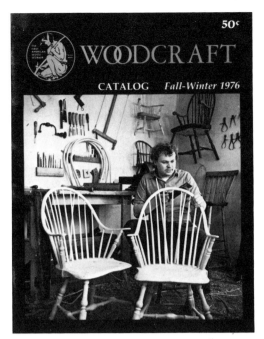

Catalogue cover, *Woodcraft Supply*

Catalogue cover, *IXL Furniture*

PLANNING KITS AND MANUALS

WOODCRAFT SUPPLY CORP.
Dept. CHC
313 Montvale Avenue
Woburn, MA 01801

"Woodcraft," 50 cents, published biannually, 48 pages, color, illustrated.

A catalogue of over 1,000 top-quality hand tools such as planes, carving tools, wood sculptors' tools, rifflers, rasps and files, vises and clamps, saws, chisels, and turning tools, as well as wood supplies, workbenches, a library of books on woodcraft, and over 40 sets of measured drawings of 17th-, 18th-, and 19th-century furniture, each 35 cents. Dimensions, prices, and order blanks included.

AMERICAN-STANDARD
Dept. CHC
P.O. Box 2003
New Brunswick, NJ 08903

"Bathroom Planning Kit" and "The Homemaker's Guide to the Bathroom and Kitchen," $2.00.

For your $2 you get a thick package comprising leaflets, pamphlets, brochures, planning charts, cutouts, and a 192-page paperback handbook on how to decorate, make emergency plumbing repairs, get the proper lighting, and reduce heating bills. There is information on remodeling or redecorating your bathroom and kitchen, how to plan a bathroom, from modest to luxurious, how to put unused space to work.
RS

IXL FURNITURE COMPANY
Dept. CHC
Route #1
Elizabeth City, NC 27909

"How to Install Kitchen Cabinets," 35 cents, 15 pages, black and white, illustrated.

A step-by-step manual that enables even a novice to remove old cabinets and install his own. The manual explains how to find studs, which cabinets to install first, and gives a list of necessary tools. Seven soffit treatments are illustrated and directions given for preserving the wood.
RS

LIFE STYLES GROUP
Dept. CHC
Box 361
Irvington, NY 10533

"Color Scheming Kit," $4.95, plus 50 cents postage.

Plan your color schemes the way interior designers do with this exciting kit. Sixty-four interior-designer color schemes to choose from, each with an offbeat color accent. Color swatches, a text explaining how and where to use each color, with work sheets, are included to let you experiment for professional results before setting out with paint, paper, and fabric.
MO

Catalogue cover, *American Standard*

202

Catalogue cover, *Long-Bell Division, International Paper*

Catalogue cover, *Old House Journal*

PUBLICATIONS ON OLD HOUSE RESTORATION

HOUSE PLANS AND DESIGNS

LONG-BELL DIVISION
International Paper Company
Dept. CHC
P.O. Box 8411
Portland, OR 97207

"Long-Bell Kitchen Planning Kit," $1.00, 4 brochures, color and black and white, illustrated.

The four brochures have 16 pages of ideas using Long-Bell modular cabinets and vanities in kitchens, "dead areas," and throughout the house—for example, a work-and-study center that can be installed in a family room, kitchen, or den. Layout sheets and specifications for the 100 modular cabinet unit sizes are included in the kit.
RS

PLAN-IT-KIT, INC.
Dept. CHC
Box 429
Westport, CT 06880

Folder, no charge, black and white, illustrated.

With this 3-D Plan-It-Kit you will be able to work out many furniture combinations and room arrangements. The kit, which costs $8.95, comes with lightweight styrofoam furniture miniatures, made to scale, an eight-page illustrated booklet with instructions and design pointers.
MO

THE OLD HOUSE JOURNAL
Dept. CHC
199 Berkeley Place
Brooklyn, NY 11217

"The Old House Journal," annual subscription $12, published monthly, black and white, illustrated; "Field Guide to Old Houses," 50 cents, 4 pages, black and white, illustrated.

The "Journal," a monthly newsletter devoted exclusively to pre-1914 antique houses, covers interior and exterior decoration in authentic period styles as well as preservation and restoration of the house itself. There are practical, do-it-yourself techniques and lists of suppliers of authentic period decorating fixtures. A free sample copy will be sent on request. The "Field Guide" provides at-a-glance architectural details of the most common styles.
MO

ACORN STRUCTURES, INC.
Dept. CHC
Box 250
Concord, MA 01742

"Acorn in a Nutshell," no charge, 15 pages, color, illustrated; complete catalogue of designs, $3.

Acorn offers 30 standard, single-family house designs and 28 Cluster (the modern row house) designs in sizes from 725 to 2,500 square feet and prices from $21,000 to $59,000. These manufactured homes come in a variety of designs, from one-story to three-level houses, a few of which are shown in the brochure. Their modular system allows sizes to be increased or decreased, windows added to take in a view, and room layouts to be modified to suit family needs.
MO

Cluster shed homes,
Carolina Log Buildings & Cluster Shed

Geodesic domes, *California Domes*

Contemporary home, *Deck House*

CALIFORNIA DOMES
Dept. CHC
P.O. Box 842
Santa Cruz, CA 95061

"California Domes," $1.00 (refundable with purchase), 16 pages, some color, illustrated.

The catalogue shows the four basic geodesic-design home shells, which can be used separately or in clusters and sell for about $1,700 for 300 square feet, up to $3,500 for 1,400 square feet. All parts come precut, ready to bolt and nail together, with only a hammer and wrench needed for assembly, and the dome shell can be converted to whatever arrangement of kitchen, living room, bathroom, and bedroom you prefer. The catalogue compares the strength, practicality, and economy of the design to that of the conventional house and claims that it represents savings of from 25 to 60 percent over a house of comparable quality. Specific building questions are answered in the back, with prices, order form, and shipping costs.
MO

CAROLINA LOG BUILDINGS & CLUSTER SHED, INC.
Dept. CHC
Fletcher, NC 28732

"Cluster Shed," $2.00, published annually, black and white.

This new form of inexpensive, quality housing that you can build yourself is based on a single 12' x 16' unit, which can be stacked one above the other, connected side by side, or clustered for a residential or commercial complex. This kit includes miniature cutout Cluster Sheds you put together to plan your own home. There are several versions shown for you to experiment with and prices start at under $3,500 for the single unit, with complete construction and optional interior floor plans included. See also Vermont Log Buildings for description of the Log houses.
MO

DECK HOUSE, INC.
Dept. CHC
930 Main Street
Acton, MA 10720

"The Deck House Residential Brochure," $3,00, published annually, 20 pages, black and white.

The Deck House catalogue explains the concept of architectural design in detail. It is beautifully illustrated with several decorated homes and has complete sets of the individual house plans. The styling is contemporary, with a choice of nine models ranging in price from about $13,000 to $99,000. Deck House is a combination of prefab and on-site building termed "pre-engineered."
MO

GREEN MOUNTAIN CABINS, INC.
Dept. CHC
Box 190
Chester, VT. 05143

"Designing Your Own Green Mountain Log Home," $3.00, black and white.

This is a kit that takes you step by step through the planning/designing stage of creating your own log home. Comprehensive instructions, complete with drawn-to-scale appliances, furniture, and fixture sheets are provided. Designing and pricing sheets (each piece is individually priced) will help you to work out exactly what you want and estimate what it will cost. Or you can send for a free brochure, with prices, of typical chalets, homes, and cabins.
MO

204

Vacation house, *Lindal Cedar Homes*

Design Collection guides, *Home Planners*

HOME PLANNERS, INC.
Dept. CHC
16310 Grand River
Detroit, MI 48227

"Home Planners 180 Homes—Multi-Level Designs," $2.25; "Home Planners 250 Homes—One-Story Designs Below 2,000 Square Feet," $2.25; "Home Planners 185 Homes—One-Story Designs Above 2,000 Square Feet," $2.25; "Home Planners 230 Homes—1½ and Two-Story Designs," $2.25; "233 Home Planners Vacation Homes," $2.25; 175 pages each, black and white (some color in the Vacation Homes book), illustrated.

The complete Design Collection of five titles costs $7.95. Altogether the books have over 1,000 home designs by designer Richard B. Pollman and 2,700 illustrations of floor plans. There are houses for all budgets, tastes, and life-styles in Colonial, English, French, Spanish, and Contemporary adaptations. Construction blueprints with complete architectural details are available for all designs in kits that also include a list of materials and an outline of specifications.

LINDAL CEDAR HOMES
Dept. CHC
10411 Empire Way S.
Seattle, WA 98178

"Lindal Cedar Homes Plan Book," $1.00 (refundable with purchase), 42 pages, color.

Lindal houses of precut cedar come in an extensive variety of styles and numerous modifications of each style, offering many possibilities for year-round or vacation living. The descriptions of the construction methods and the important structural elements of the houses plus the color photographs and floor plans in the Plan Book give a clear and detailed picture of the finished product. Prices on request.
MO .

NORTHEASTERN LOG HOMES, INC.
Dept. CHC
Box 126
Groton, VT 05046

"The all season Log Homes complete brochure," $2.00, published seasonally, black and white, illustrated.

Northeastern log homes are designed to provide year-round living with virtually no maintenance, and the double-roof construction of the cathedral ceilings affords maximum insulation. Any conventional heating system may be used. The brochure contains descriptive information, model illustrations, floor plans, and prices, which run from about $9,200 for "The Rockwood," a two-bedroom home, to around $21,000 for the two-story "Cambridge" with garage. Custom design service is also available at no charge.
MO

NORTHERN PRODUCTS, INC.
Dept. CHC
Bomarc Road
Bangor, ME 04401

"An Adventure in Outdoor Living," $2.00, color and black and white, illustrated; also, folder available on request at no charge.

Standard and Basic kits are offered for these precut log homes, which are available in ten models ranging in price from $4,500 to $18,500. Each includes thermopane windows, log wall material, purlins, trusses, exterior doors, 10" wall spikes, caulking compound, and construction plans. The brochure describes the construction methods and distinctive features and gives illustrations and floor plans of the various models, plus shipping information.
MO

Interior, *Northeastern Log Homes*

Prefab interiors, *Spacemakers*

Log home, *Vermont Log Buildings and Cluster Sheds*

PRESCOTT HOMES
Dept. CHC
Meredith, NH 03253

"Prescott Homes," $2.00, black and white.

If you're a do-it-yourselfer, Prescott will erect your year-round vacation home as a shell for you to finish, or they'll build you a complete ready-to-move-into home almost anywhere in New England. They'll even fabricate one from your plans. The kit shows the many styles, provides specifications and prices, starting at about $1,100 for the one-room sugar house.
MO

SPACEMAKERS
Dept. CHC
161 Forbes Road
Braintree, MA 02184

"Spacemakers," $3.00, color and black and white, illustrated.

This is a planning kit for prefab leisure homes of post-and-beam construction with redwood exteriors and Douglas fir beams, in a wide variety of styles. Each home is shown with floor plan and description. Return form is included for price information.
MO

STANMAR, INCORPORATED
Dept. CHC
Box 053
Boston Post Road
Sudbury, MA 01776

"New Directions in Home Design," $2.00, 30 pages, color, illustrated.

Stanmar designs and customizes homes and supplies such services as helping to negotiate a contract price with the builder and a mortgage with the bank. Their booklet shows in color exteriors and interiors of Stanmar homes in various styles suitable for areas from Maine to Florida and resort communities, such as traditional, saltbox, Cape Cod, and "cluster," with floor plans. There's a further-information card and a list of locations where you can view Stanmar homes.
MO

VERMONT LOG BUILDINGS, INC.,
AND CLUSTER SHED, INC.
Dept. CHC
Hartland, VT 05048

"Your Real Log Home," $3.00, published annually, black and white.

This firm offers complete prefab log construction homes for you to assemble. Each package includes two sets of working blueprints, a complete 32-page illustrated construction manual, four hours of on-site technical instruction, and list of materials to be

purchased locally to save on freight costs. Prices range from about $950 for a 10' x 10' lean-to to under $14,000 for the two-story, three-unit "Arlington" model. This company is also the manufacturer of "Cluster Shed," the individual, single-room units that can be clustered and connected to form a unique house—a new form of inexpensive, quality, do-it-yourself housing. For more information on Cluster Shed, see Carolina Log Buildings & Cluster Shed.
MO

WARD CABIN COMPANY
Dept. CHC
Box 72
Houlton, ME 04730

"There's no place like a Ward log home," $2.00, published quarterly and as new lines are introduced, black and white, illustrated.

Ward log homes encompass everything from a small "Weekender" series which starts around $4,200 or large "Vacationer" models to year-round homes and lodges in a great variety of plans and styles. Ward will also custom-design to fit your special needs. The catalogue comes complete with illustrations and plans of individual models, list of materials, question and answer form, building details, and request form for price quotation without obligation.
MO

Furniture kits, *Cohasset Colonials*

KITS AND CRAFT SUPPLIES

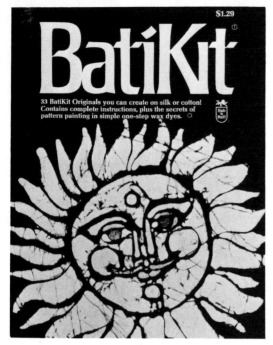

Brochure cover, *American Art Clay*

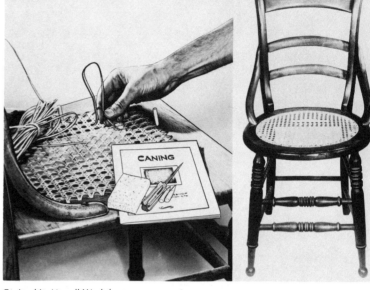

Caning kit, *Newell Workshop*

BATIK

CANING

AMERICAN ART CLAY
Rub 'n Buff Division
Dept. CHC
Box 68163
Indianapolis, IN 46268

"BatiKit," no charge, color, illustrated.

A folder describing the BatiKits
available and how you can use them to
create different batik effects such as
brilliant stained-glass effects, crackling
textures, or random veining. "BatiKit 33
Originals," $1.29, contains complete
instructions, secrets of batik technique,
as well as designs. To use with "BatiKit
33" are the BatiKit dye waxes which
come two to a card, also $1.29, in
combinations of red/blue,
yellow/green, black/clear. The "BatiKit
Complete Craft Kit" contains four dye
waxes, a warming dish, background
dye, three batik cloths, six designs, and
a technique booklet for $6.98.
MO/RS

NEWELL WORKSHOP
Dept. CHC
19 Blaine Avenue
Hinsdale, IL 60521

*"Newell Workshop," no charge, black
and white, illustrated.*

Dave Newell has worked out a
beginner's caning kit for replacing chair
seats with easy step-by-step illustrated
instructions, tools, and materials, all for
$4 (with refills at $2). He supplies
different types of caning materials—
cane webbing, fiber rush, and Oriental
sea grass are some.
MO

PEERLESS RATTAN AND REED
MANUFACTURING COMPANY
Dept. CHC
97 Washington Street
New York, NY 10006

*"Peerless Rattan & Reed Chair Caning
Handbook," no charge, published
semiannually, 15 pages, black and
white, illustrated.*

As the title indicates, this is an
instruction booklet that illustrates and
describes how to weave cane seats and
how to apply machine-woven cane
seats to chairs, easy enough if you
follow the step-by-step instructions.
The various types of strand cane, cane
webbing, and reeds are shown with the
tools necessary to complete the job. To
make it simpler for you, Peerless has
two inexpensive kits, one with cane,
the other with rush, which come
complete with sandpaper, glue, and full
instructions.
MO

TUT INTERNATIONAL ENTERPRISE
Dept. CHC
2615 El Camino Real
San Matero, CA 94403

*"T.I.E. Catalogue," 25 cents, 4 pages,
published semiannually, black and
white, illustrated.*

Suggestions for ways to use various
weaves of cane for chair seats and
backs, lampshades, screens, stereo
speakers, planter boxes, baskets, with a
list of caning kits that include
instructions and materials. Prices are
average.
MO

Mantel-clock kit, *Mason & Sullivan*

Cuckoo-clock kit, *Wilkinson Empire*

CLOCKS

COLOR PLANNING

CRAFT PRODUCTS CO.
Dept. CHC
Elmhurst, IL 60126

"Clocks and Clock Movements," 50 cents, 98 pages, black and white, illustrated.

Craft Products has a series of clock case kits, completely cut out with front and side frames, door frame, and break-arch assembled and sanded, such as the Greenwich Hall Clock Kit, about $158 plus glass kit and movement. A decorative barometer case kit in walnut is about $18 with barometer, thermometer, hygrometer, and wood inlay as extras. There is a wide variety of styles and sizes to select from. Also of interest is the history of clock-making and a selection of books on clocks.
MO

EMPEROR CLOCK COMPANY
Dept. CHC
Emperor Industrial Park
Fairhope, AL 36532

"Emperor Grandfather Clocks," foldout pamphlet, no charge, published annually, color, illustrated.

Emperor's grandfather clocks are available in kit form, without movement, from about $100.
MO

MASON & SULLIVAN CO.
Dept. CHC
39 Blossom Avenue
Osterville, MA 02655

"Imported Clock Movements," 50 cents, 24 pages, black and white, illustrated.

You can either order complete kits or plans and assorted parts to make your own reproductions of antique clocks. The blueprint with full-size details, bill of materials, and assembly instructions for making the case of an octagonal school clock is just $1; for under $300 you can obtain all the parts needed to make an 89"-high replica of an Aaron Willard case clock; or you can buy a completely assembled and finished mahogany grandmother clock case for about $235 and a choice of clock movements and chimes, ready to run, from $115. There are also ready-to-assemble kits of small clock cases (English carriage, steeple, and octagonal school), no movement, around $30.
MO

WILKINSON EMPIRE
Dept. CHC
9850 Park Street
Bellflower, CA 90706

"Decorative Gifts for the Home," color folder, 50 cents (refundable with purchase), published annually.

Clock kits, among them a variety of cuckoo clocks, are mailed directly from Europe to the customer at very reasonable prices.
MO

LIFE STYLES GROUP
Dept. CHC
Box 361
Irvington, NY 10533

Color scheming kit, $4.95 plus 50 cents postage.

To pre-plan your color schemes this exciting kit offers 64 interior-designer color schemes, each with an offbeat color accent. The kit contains color swatches, text explaining how and where to use each color, worksheets to let you experiment for professional results before setting out with paint, paper, and fabric.
MO

Paperback book cover, *Berkshire Traveller*

Pages from "Craft Horizons," *American Crafts Council*

COMPENDIUM OF CRAFTS

CRAFT PUBLICATIONS

LEE WARDS
Dept. CHC
1200 St. Charles Street
Elgin, IL 60120

"Lee Wards Creative Crafts Center," no charge, published quarterly, 72 pages, some color, illustrated.

Kits galore for fun, recreation, and do-it-yourself profit, with full instructions for everything from sand painting and doll-making to quilting, spinning, weaving, and needlepoint. Inexpensive.
MO

AMERICAN CRAFTS COUNCIL
Publications Department
Dept. CHC
44 West 53rd Street
New York, NY 10019

List of publications, no charge.

The American Crafts Council will send you a list of their publications—crafts exhibition catalogues, directories of crafts courses in colleges, universities, museum schools, etc. ($4); a two-part directory of craft suppliers ($3 for each part); or the magazine *Craft Horizons* ($3 per issue, special subscription rate available). There is also an excellent "where-to-find" guide covering every type of craft from batik to wood carving, "Contemporary Crafts Market Place," published annually for around $14 plus postage.

THE BERKSHIRE TRAVELLER
Dept. CHC
Stockbridge, MA 01262

"Berkshire Traveller Press," no charge, 12 pages, black and white, illustrated.

The catalogue lists two books of special interest to the amateur furniture craftsman or collector: *Shop Drawings of Shaker Furniture and Woodenware,* Volumes I and II, $3.50 each. The former contains 80 measured drawings for reproducing original Shaker pieces. The latter contains 76 more scaled drawings and photographs of selected Shaker pieces.

DOVER PUBLICATIONS, INC.
Dept. CHC
180 Varick Street
New York, NY 10014

The Standard Book of Quilt Making and Collecting, $3.50, 276 pages, some color, illustrated.

This paperback tells you just about everything you need to know about quilts—their history, the techniques of quiltmaking, how to draft patterns of famous American designs, collecting quilts—and contains 483 illustrations of quilts, full-scale patterns, design elements, and quilting equipment. Dover also has two other books on quilting: *Traditional Patchwork Patterns* for $2 and *One Hundred and One Patchwork Patterns* for $2.50.

EMERSON BOOKS, INC.
Dept. CHC
Reynolds Lane
Buchanan, NY 10511

"Book List," 25 cents, published semiannually, 12 pages, black and white, illustrated.

Emerson lists at least a hundred books for the craftsman, repairman, and hobbyist. Net making, string art, mobiles, origami, paper sculpture, candlemaking, leatherworking, pottery, and woodwork are some of the offerings. Prices are included.

Curio cabinet kit, *Baroness Curio Cabinets*

Mirror and wall bracket kit, *Bartley Collection*

CHIPPENDALE LOOKING GLASS
This handsome solid mahogany mirror reflects Chippendale design at its best. The molding and scroll work are copied from an original made in Philadelphia about 1765. As Chippendale mirrors were made both plain-edged and beveled, our Bartley reproduction also offers this option. Ready for assembly in two sizes, no tools required. Complete instructions and Bartley finishing kit included.
Small: overall size: 18¾" x 35½" Model SLG-20
   Unassembled, ready-to-finish $59.00, beveled glass $10.00 extra
   Assembled and hand finished $125.00, beveled glass $10.00 extra
Large: overall size: 21½" x 40¾" Model LLG-10
   Unassembled, ready-to-finish $69.00, beveled glass $10.00 extra
   Assembled and hand finished $140.00, beveled glass $10.00 extra

MIRROR SHELF/WALL BRACKET
Used in conjunction with a mirror, or by itself, this shelf is extremely handsome with its eighteenth century mirror-molding rim and graceful slipper foot support. Of solid mahogany, the shelf is very easy to assemble. No tools are required and finish is included. Model MS-13 is 7½" x 14", Model MS-14 is 9½" x 20".
Unassembled ready-to-finish:
   Model MS-13 is $26.00, Model MS-14 is $29.00
Assembled and hand-finished:
   Model MS-13 is $60.00, Model MS-14 is $65.00

FURNITURE

SELECT BOOKS
Dept. CHC
P.O. Box 626
Pacific Grove, CA 93950

Folder, no charge.

The folder lists and describes eight books, priced from $2 to $6, on hand-spinning and hand-weaving, yarn dyeing, designing on the loom, and building a loom.

THE UNICORN
Dept. CHC
Box 645
Rockville, MD 20851

"Textile Craft Books," 50 cents, published annually, 48 pages, black and white.

An extensive alphabetical listing of craft books (American and imported) under subject headings: appliqué, quilting, patchwork, basketry, embroidery, lacemaking and tatting, macramé and knotting, rug hooking, spinning and dyeing, and weaving. Separate catalogues on 18 other crafts from batik to woodworking are available on request if you send a large, self-addressed, stamped envelope for each one. A $2 annual subscription entitles you to the quarterly "Guide to Craft Books," plus the specialty catalogues.

AMERICAN CONTEMPORARY
Dept. CHC
P.O. Box 634
Simsbury, CT 06070

"American Contemporary," 25 cents, two 6-page brochures, black and white, illustrated.

Contemporary furniture kits, assembled in minutes, contain precut, drilled, smoothly sanded pieces with instructions and finishing tips. Clean-lined tables of solid wood in several sizes, some with glass inserts which you provide to save shipping costs, stacking wall units with adjustable shelves, and a cabinet that doubles for stereo or, on ball casters, as a bar. Prices are reasonable. A 30" x 30" x 10" modular shelf unit is under $35, a stereo or bar cabinet with four doors is $130.
MO

BARONESS CURIO CABINETS
Dept. CHC
P.O. Box 9122
Mobile, AL 36609

Single color sheet with assembly instructions, no charge.

This mahogany collector's cabinet in kit form for under $140 is three-sided, 68" high x 12" deep and 27" wide (back), 13½" each front side, and comes ready to assemble and finish. An interior light fixture is also available.
MO

THE BARTLEY COLLECTION, LTD.
Dept. CHC
747 Oakwood Avenue
Lake Forest, IL 60045

"Antique Furniture Reproductions," $1.00, 16 pages, black and white, illustrated.

Replicas and adaptations of original 18th-century furniture in ready-to-assemble-and-finish form, with each piece handcrafted in solid cherry or mahogany. The kits include everything for assembly and finishing, and no tools are needed (not even a brush). The brochure pictures such items as cabinets, mirrors, wall brackets, stands, tables, chairs, lowboys, footstools, and a rocking horse. Finished pieces may also be ordered; they cost about twice as much as the kits, which range in price from about $26 to $350. A separate kit for other home wood-finishing projects is available.
MO

212

Collector's table kit, *Classic Crafts*

P.V.C. tubing chair kit, *Pipe Dream*

Swiveling table kit, *Yield House*

CLASSIC CRAFTS
Dept. CHC
P.O. Box 12
Point Clear, AL 36564

"Mahogany Pieces," series of leaflets, no charge, black and white, illustrated.

Small pieces of solid Honduras mohogany furniture—collector's tables, vanity tables, fern stands, gout stool, and footstools—available in do-it-yourself kits with instructions for assembling, or ready-finished. Kits range from $17 to $65, finished pieces from $30 to $185.
MO

HAGERTY CO.
Dept. CHC
38 Parker Avenue
Cohasset, MA 02025

"Cohasset Colonials by Hagerty," 50 cents, published annually, 32 pages, some color, illustrated.

Hagerty offers a wonderful selection of kits of 17th- and 18th-century furniture copied from originals in museums or private collections. A pine blanket chest kit (from an original in Old Sturbridge Village) comes complete with handmade nails for under $70. With a Color Pack kit, $3.50, it can be painted and stenciled with an eagle motif taken from a Vermont mantel. A simple octagonal maple top candle stand like one in the Metropolitan Museum of Art, 13" across, 25" high, is just under $16. Other interesting pieces include Windsor chairs and settees, Shaker tables and benches, a Bible-box desk, a butterfly table, and a Pilgrim box stool.
MO

PIPE DREAM
Dept. CHC
1121 East Commercial Blvd.
Ft. Lauderdale, FL 33308

"Pipe Dream," $2.20 (refundable with purchase), published annually, 8 pages, swatches, black and white, illustrated.

Easy-to-assemble indoor/outdoor furniture kits of P.V.C. tubing with polyester cushions of brilliant yellow, green, or blue. Each kit comes complete with all necessary parts and assembly instructions. A dining set with 36"-diameter table and four armchairs with seat and back cushions is under $275. An étagère, 78" high x 34" wide x 16" deep, is about $62. Frames are easily cleaned with scouring powder and paste wax, and won't chip or peel.
MO

YIELD HOUSE
Dept. CHC
North Conway, NH 03860

"Yield House Country Pine Furniture and Furniture Kits," 25 cents, 50 pages, some color, illustrated.

When you buy a furniture kit from Yield House, you will save money and have fun finishing the piece. The kits come ready to assemble with all instructions for a finish in your choice—either stain or paint. The kits are so numerous only a few can be mentioned. A reproduction of an early bedroom commode for ewer and basin, with base cupboard, single drawer, and lift-up top, ready to stain, or paint and stencil like the original, is under $80. A classic hunt table, 55' long x 25" high x 15" wide, with tavern legs, ball feet, stretcher base, and scalloped apron, is under $70. A wall-hung or floor-model holder with five shelves that can hold up to 45 magazines is just under $25.
MO

Shaker furniture kits, *Hagerty*

Magic Mural kit, *Double M Marketing*

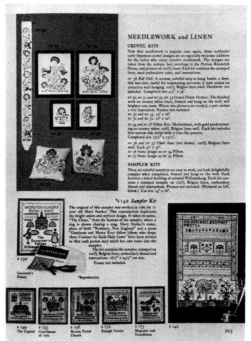

Williamsburg needlework kits, *Craft House*

MURALS

NEEDLEWORK

DOUBLE M MARKETING COMPANY, INC.
Dept. CHC
P.O. Box 8500
Fountain Valley, CA 92708

"Magic Mural," 35 cents, 32 pages, updated as needed, color, illustrated.

With the Magic Mural paint-by-the-number kit you become the artist and decorator. There are mural designs to fit any wall space and decorating scheme, from mini-murals a mere 8" wide to panoramic murals nearly 12' wide, in more than 100 different color combinations. The kits, which include a numbered pattern, paints in numbered containers, and brushes, range in price from $2.95 to $49.95.
MO

EMILE BERNAT & SONS, CO.
Dept. CHC
Uxbridge, MA 01569

"Bernat Needlecrafts," $1.25 (refundable with purchase), 48 pages, color, illustrated.

Bernat offers complete needlepoint "paks"—kits with 12-mesh canvas, needle, wools, and charts from about $3.50 to $8.50. There are petit-point kits on ten-mesh canvas, patterns for wall-hung tapestries, such as the famous Unicorn or 17th-century Flanders "La Chasse Aux Canards," from $125 to $250, or printed canvas only. Other examples are crewel kits; Rya "paks" for a wall hanging and pillows; super-bargello "paks" for director's chair seats and backs, under $14. Bernat also sells its Tapestria wool yarns.
MO

BRUNSWICK WORSTED MILLS, INC.
Dept. CHC
Rickens, SC 29671

"Brunswick Needlepoint," $1.25, 47 pages, color, illustrated.

A wealth of illustrated instructions on various stitches, framing, blocking, mounting, as well as special pointers. Painted needlepoint designs are available, both as open stock or as complete kits with yarns. There is also a 50-cent catalogue for do-it-yourself hooked rugs, made with either wool or acrylic yarns. General instructions and price lists are given.
MO

CRAFT HOUSE
Dept. CHC
Colonial Williamsburg Foundation
Williamsburg, VA 23185

"Williamsburg Reproductions—Interior Designs for Today's Living," $2.95, 232 pages, color and black and white, illustrated.

Tucked away in the section of the giant Craft House catalogue entitled "A Williamsburg Potpourri of Gifts" are some charming crewel, sampler, and needlepoint kits. The crewel designs, taken from the antique bed coverings in the Peyton Randolph House, are printed on 100 percent linen and include the stamped linen, wool embroidery yarn, and instructions; and the kits for a bell pull, flower pictures, pillows, and chair seats range from under $4 to over $10. The sampler kits are also under $4 and come with stamped linen, embroidery thread, and instructions. The needlepoint kits consist of floral designs sized to cover chair seats, pillows and stools, and handsome flamestitch patterns, some large enough to upholster a chair or large bench, priced up to $49.95. Two additional kits are a candle molding kit, with reusable tin candle mold, wicking and beeswax, and full instructions (about $10) and a Williamsburg Paintable Kit with six black-and-white sketches of popular Williamsburg subjects, watercolors, brush, and color suggestions for $4.
MO

Alaskan design needlepoint kits, *Images North*

Needlepoint footstool kit, *Creative Needle*

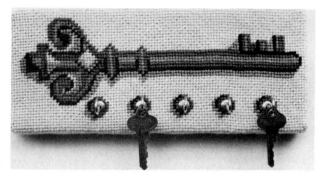

Keyboard design needlepoint kit, *In-Stitches*

CREATIVE NEEDLE
Dept. CHC
P.O. Box 8104
Dallas, TX 75205

"Creative Needle," $2.00, 24 pages, black and white, illustrated.

A catalogue of unusual needlepoint kits, hand-painted on French canvas and packaged with Persian yarns, that include Oriental designs taken from antique porcelains, Oriental symbols, and the 12 zodiac signs. Prices, sizes, and colors are included.
MO

CROSSROADS CREATIVE STITCHERY
Dept. CHC
P.O. Box 1372
Burbank, CA 91507

"Give Art the Needle," 25 cents, updated as needed, 20 pages, color, illustrated.

Needlepoint kits, yarns, and needlecraft accessories for designs that will complement any decorative style. Unusual kits include a "Remember When . . ." series, nostalgic needlepoint of the Twenties, for about $8. Also available are patchwork templates, Rya yarn, and Beatrix Potter crewel kits.
MO

GUILD OF SHAKER CRAFTS
Dept. CHC
401 Savidge Street
Spring Lake, MI 49546

"Guild of Shaker Crafts," $2.50, 28 pages, some color, illustrated.

The Guild offers three Shaker needlepoint kits complete with yarns, silk-screened pattern on backing, and instructions. Two crewel patterns are "The Tree of Life," a wall piece, at $10 and "The Tree of Love," a pillow top, also $10. "The Dove of Peace" needlepoint pillow top is $18, the pincushion $9. The Guild will also make simple pine frames for the needlework or to your specifications.
MO

IMAGES NORTH, LTD.
Dept. CHC
P.O. Box 1275
Fairbanks, AK 99701

"The Alaska Needlepoint Collection," 50 cents, published annually, 16 pages, black and white, illustrated.

The collection pictures complete kits or canvases only with about 13 Eskimo, Indian, and Aleut designs adapted from rare museum pieces. The designs, original interpretations especially created for needlepoint, are suitable for wall hangings, pillows, or chair seats and come with or without yarn. Each is described and its background, colors, size, and price given. Prices range from $13 to $50. Crewel designs and hooked rugs are being added to the collection.
MO

IN-STITCHES
Dept. CHC
325 East 18th Street
New York, NY 10003

"In-Stitches," $1.00, updated as needed, about 24 pages, some color, illustrated.

Geometrics, adaptations of famous paintings, dragons from a Chinese fan are some of the designs available from In-Stitches, who will also create custom designs for you from snapshots, sketches, or fabrics. All canvas sizes and prices are given. Kits include hand-painted canvas, yarn, needle, and directions for the continental and basket-weave stitches are given in the back of the catalogue.
MO

THE KNIT AND RIP SHOP
Mail Order Division
Dept. CHC
212 West Laurel
Springfield, IL 62704

Lists of catalogues from leading needlecraft companies, no charge.

The Knit and Rip Shop, a kind of clearinghouse for needlecraft companies, will put your name on its general mailing list, or you may, if you prefer, indicate specific subjects in which you are interested. There are many kits available for crewel, needlepoint, latch-hook, quickpoint, cross-stitch, and frames with stand or tabletop for needlework, quilting, and rugs.
MO

Astrological design needlepoint kits,
Crossroads Creative Stitchery

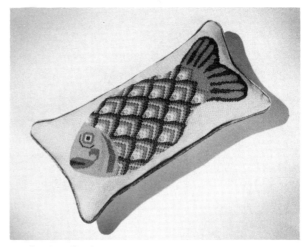

Needlepoint pillow kit, *Peacock Alley*

Norwegian klostersom needlework kits, *Norwegian-American Museum*

MAGIC NEEDLE
Dept. CHC
44 Green Bay Road
Winnetka, IL 60093

"Needlepoint Catalogue," $2.50, 32 pages, published annually, black and white, illustrated.

Included are over 125 designs in needlepoint kits, some taken from famous artists—Klee, Matisse, Chagall, Mondrian, Seurat, Gauguin—to be made into pillows or pictures; other designs are more traditional. A 1921 *Vogue* poster, 17" x 22", is smashing at $60. Offered, too, are three designs for needlepoint clock faces from about $39 to $45. The battery clock works are $18. The catalogue includes nine pages of charts describing and illustrating about 26 stitches from basket weave to web stitch and two alphabet charts. Finishing instructions are given where necessary, or the Magic Needle will finish for you. Prices quoted on request.
MO

NEEDLEPOINT SHORES
Dept. CHC
Box 123
Wayzata, MN 55391

"Needlepoint Shores," no charge, published annually, 20 pages, color, illustrated.

Specialties for every stitchery need within every price range. Kits or materials and accessories for creating your own designs in needlepoint, crewel, cross-stitch, and quick-stitch. Additional brochures are sent seasonally.
MO

PEACOCK ALLEY
Dept. CHC
650 Croswell, S.E.
Grand Rapids, MI 49506

"Brochure 2," $1.00, published annually, 20 pages, black and white, illustrated.

Interesting, original designs hand-painted on single-mesh white French canvas, Persian yarns, a needle, and complete instructions are offered in the kits from Peacock Alley. You can make straps for luggage racks with bright yellow pineapples, three straps, $27.50. A cover for a brick to use as a doorstop or book end comes with a design of asparagus in shades of green tied with red ribbon, $17.50; or mini-pillows, one, 9" x 7", of green clover leaves scattered over blue and white checked gingham, $15.50. A floral ribbon rug kit with a Louis XV motif, on five-mesh rug canvas, in mixed flower colors with soft blue ribbons on mist green ground (sounds lovely), costs $150. There are also picture frames and bell pulls and delightful coaster kits. Yarn and canvas is available separately. Although the shop does not handle finishing, they will suggest a house to do it for you. Custom designing available. Write them for estimates.
MO

NORWEGIAN-AMERICAN MUSEUM
Dept. CHC
502 Water Street
Decorah, IA 52102

Brochure, no charge.

The embroidery kits sold by the Norwegian-American Museum, adapted from early textiles in the museum collection, are designs in the traditional Norwegian *klostersom* style of needlework, which is done with wool yarns on canvas in a manner similar to needlepoint except that the stitches cover several threads and go vertically instead of diagonally. There is a variety of kits, priced from $6 to $10, which include canvas, yarns, pattern, needle, and instructions. Bell pulls, pillows, and wall hangings are just a few of the uses for the kits.
MO

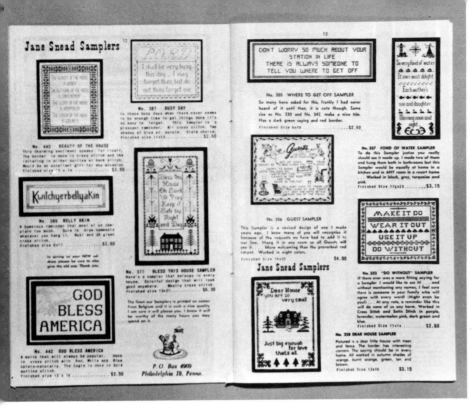

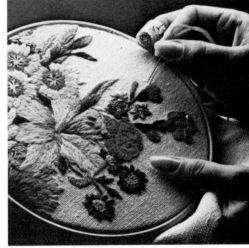

Needlework design, *Elsa Williams*

Sampler kits, *Jane Snead Samplers*

JANE SNEAD SAMPLERS
Dept. CHC
Box 4909
Philadelphia, PA 19119

"Jane Snead Samplers," 25 cents, published annually, 39 pages, black and white, illustrated.

A truly delightful and offbeat collection of samplers and sampler kits in all sizes and shapes to enliven kitchen, bedroom, bathroom, or nursery. Some are amusing, some patriotic, some inspirational, some personalized; others are one-word samplers or have long verses. The prices are average.
MO

THE STITCHERY
Dept. CHC
204 Worcester Turnpike
Wellesley Hills, MA 02181

"The Stitchery," 25 cents for four issues, published quarterly, 48 pages, color, illustrated.

A wide range of designs and materials for miniatures, pictures, pillows, cameos, pincushions, chair seats, tablecloths, and so on in various forms of stitchery—cross-stitch, embroidery, needlepoint, and crewel—and four quilts, afghans, latch-hook rugs, and Rya pillows.
MO

TOWER CRAFTS
Dept. CHC
P.O. Box 575
Champaign, IL 61820

"Tower Crafts," 25 cents (refundable with order), 27 pages, color, illustrated.

A catalogue of charming designs in pillow and picture kits in needlepoint, crewel, and cross-stitch for the home (also coasters, bell pulls, purses, belts, and tennis-racket covers). For your kitchen, a set of 4" x 5" needlepoint herbs, vegetables, or fruits, from $2.45; several amusing designs for children's rooms; a cross-stitch sampler for the entrance hall that says "Welcome" for $3.95, 4" x 5" frame included. For a traditional living room there is a lovely Jacobean design crewel pillow kit, 14" x 10", for $7.95. Also included is a selection of needlepoint books and leaflets and a page of needlework aids—canvas, pillow forms, stretcher bars, nepo markers, stork scissors, and stitch-'n-learn cards to teach yourself the basic and fancy stitches.
MO

ELSA WILLIAMS, INC.
Dept. CHC
445 Main Street
West Townsend, MA 01474

"A Collection of Original Needle Art Designs," $1.00, 75 pages, color, illustrated.

Crewel and needlepoint are the focus of this handsome catalogue, which includes detailed, illustrated instructions for stitches and for blocking. Elsa Williams stresses the fact that she uses *linen* needlepoint canvas, her yarns are a special blend of 100 percent wool, and Scottish twill and Belgium linen are used in the crewel kits. The tapestry yarns come in 101 shades—about five shades to a color family. Crewel and needlepoint accessories are supplied, and Elsa Williams also offers custom-finishing services: blocking, mounting, pillows, bell pulls, and carpets.
MO

Catalogue covers, *The Stitchery*

Quilt kit, *Ginger Snap Station*

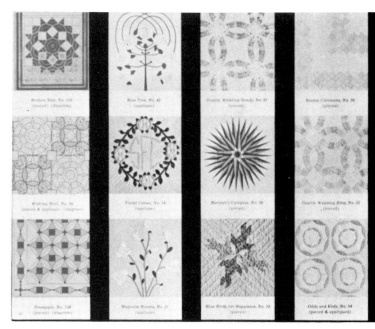

Quilt patterns, *Stearns & Foster*

PATCHWORK AND QUILTING

THE WORLD OF STITCH 'N KNIT
Dept. CHC
P.O. Box 709
Framingham, MA 01701

"The World of Stitch 'n Knit," 25 cents, published semiannually, 32 pages, color, illustrated.

In addition to the needlework, crewel, and latch-hooking kits, Stitch 'n Knit offers kits for creating pictures with nails and string, with fully illustrated instructions and everything you need except hammer and tweezers. The Owl Family and Eagle against black background are both $6. Copper wire art, made in similar fashion to string art but with fine copper wire, comes in a complete kit for under $12. There are several tablecloth kits to embroider and a quilt top kit to be appliquéd in "Tree of Life" design (under $20). Two interesting kits in the needlework group are a chess board, 16" x 16", under $8, and a blue-and-white gingham bath set—tissue box cover, $7.95, two small frames, $5.95, and a trinket box, $4.95, with full assembly instructions.
MO

Needlepoint chessboard, *World of Stitch 'n Knit*

GINGER SNAP STATION
Dept. CHC
P.O. Box 81086
Atlanta, GA 30341

"Ginger Snap Station," 25 cents, 22 pages, black and white, illustrated.
Kits for dozens of patchwork, appliqué, and quilted items ranging in price from $3 to $40. Also available: books, prints, batting, quilting needles and thread, and fabrics suitable for patchwork.
MO

DESIGN MATRIX
Dept. CHC
2424 Esplanade
Bronx, NY 10469

Price list, no charge.

In addition to their metal sculptures, Design Matrix has a $200 kit for the Bird of Paradise quilt (ca. 1854) that was valued at $12,000.
MO

LEMAN PUBLICATIONS, INC.
Dept. CHC
Box 394
Wheatridge, CO 80033

"Quilts and Other Comforts," 75 cents, published annually, 32 pages, black and white, illustrated.
A quilter's paradise, this catalogue has a huge selection of old and new quilt patterns, precut metal and cardboard templates (with pictures of block patterns that can be made from the templates), a do-it-yourself kit for plastic patterns, ready-to-sew kits, designs, stencils, and supplies, instructions for estimating yardage, even a "Quilt Library" of books. The 75 cents also gets you one issue of the monthly Quilter's Newsletter, subscription to which is $6 a year.
MO

STEARNS & FOSTER CO.
Dept. CHC
Creative Quilting Center
Lockland, Cincinnati, OH 45215

"The Mountain Mist Blue Book of Quilts," $1.00, published biannually, 36 pages, color, illustrated; *"Mountain Mist Patterns for Quilting,"* no charge, black and white, illustrated.

"The Mountain Blue Mist Book of Quilts" is beautifully illustrated with designs of all kinds of quilts from antique to modern, floral to geometric, and gives complete instructions on quilt-making, from pattern selection to finished product. Over 100 designs are offered, with all the necessary equipment and materials.

The free folder has 25 of the 100 designs for pieced and appliquéd quilts priced at 35 cents for printed, 50 cents for perforated, patterns, with complete lists of the available patterns and the quilt fillings, backings, and stuffings that can be ordered directly from the company. If you send a stamped self-addressed envelope, Stearns and Foster will also mail, on request, the name of the nearest professional quilter in your locality, should you not wish to do the job yourself.
MO

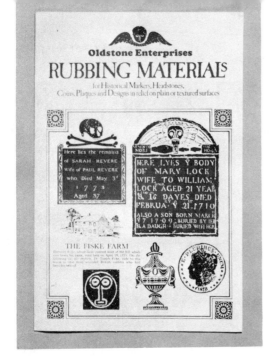

Brochure cover, *Oldstone Enterprises*

Catalogue cover, *Braid-Aid*

Catalogue cover, *Shillcraft*

ROOM PLANNING

PLAN-IT-KIT, INC.
Dept. CHC
Box 429
Westport, CT 06880

Folder, no charge, black and white, illustrated.

The 3-D Plan-It-Kit for room arrangements enables you to work out on graph paper possible furniture combinations with lightweight, styrofoam miniatures, made to scale. The kit, which costs $8.95, comes with an eight-page illustrated booklet with instructions and design pointers.
MO

Furniture miniatures, graph paper, *Plan-It-Kit*

RUBBINGS

OLDSTONE ENTERPRISES
Dept. CHC
77 Summer Street
Boston, MA 02110

"Oldstone Enterprises Rubbing Materials," no charge, published annually, black and white, illustrated.

Oldstone sells two complete rubbing kits—"The Original Oldstone Rubbing Kit" for $8.50 postpaid and a "Child's Rubbing Kit" for $3 p.p. Both are fully described in the brochure. Also available are special rubbing waxes, the rubbing paper, and slide-on hangers for top and bottom to display finished rubbings.
MO

RUGS

BRAID-AID
Dept. CHC
466 Washington Street
Pembroke, MA 02359

"Rug Braiding and Hooking Materials and Accessories," 50 cents, published annually, 65 pages, black and white, illustrated.

A complete line of kits for hooking and braiding rugs, crewel, and needlework, plus an unusual Shirret Kit, which combines shirring and crochet. With the details and descriptions of the kits comes a raft of interesting, enlightening, and unusual information.
MO

SCANDINAVIAN RYA RUGS
Dept. CHC
P.O. Box 447
Bloomfield Hills, MI 48013

"Cum Rya," $2.00, 29 pages, color, illustrated.

Over 30 beautifully illustrated do-it-yourself Rya rugs in a wide range of colors and designs are shown, with the rug and designer's names, the size, and the length of the pile given for each one. There is also a page of instructions. The kits include backing, Asborya 100 percent wool yarn, a gauge for the knotting, the required number of Rya needles, pattern, and directions. Prices are moderate.
MO

"Flying Cloud" ship-model kit, *Bluejacket Ship Crafters*

Tiffany-style glass-shade kit, *Rainbow Art Glass*

SHIP MODELS

STAINED GLASS

SHILLCRAFT
Dept. CHC
500 North Calvert Street
Baltimore, MD 21202

"Shillcraft Readicut Rugs," no charge, published annually, 48 pages, color, illustrated.

Shillcraft offers many designs in kits for hooked rugs, from traditional, floral, and Oriental-rug patterns to really way-out contemporary and a choice of 100 percent wool or wool/nylon blend yarns. The kits, complete with all necessary materials and directions, are sold only by Shillcraft, not through stores, so prices are lower. Shillcraft will draw up and transfer to canvas your own designs and supply you with materials (prices on request). There are also kits for pillows and wall hangings, using the same materials.
MO

SPINNERIN YARN COMPANY, INC.
Dept. CHC
230 Fifth Avenue
New York, NY 10001

"Deep Pile Rugs and Wall Hangings," $1.50, 55 pages, color, illustrated.

This company's kits offer choice of wool or acrylic yarns (the approximate number of yarn packages for each item is given, as well as sizes and colors) and a special feature—"add-a-square" designs (regular or jumbo) that may be used singly or in combinations for rugs, pillows, pictures, wall hangings, stair treads, or chair seats. There's also a full-page color chart and helpful hints for rug hooking and rug care.
MO

BLUEJACKET SHIP CRAFTERS
Dept. CHC
145 Water Street
South Norwalk, CT 06854

"Bluejacket Ship Crafters," 75 cents, 64 pages, black and white, illustrated.
The specialty of this family-run business with a seagoing heritage is ship models, kits of 39 clippers, frigates, freighters, schooners, tankers, with a complete line of exact-scale ship fittings, as well as plans and modeler's tools.
MO

PRESTON'S
Dept. CHC
116 Main Street
Greenport, NY 11944

"Of Ships and Sea," 25 cents, published semiannually, 144 pages, black and white, illustrated.

As the catalogue title suggests, its pages are filled with things having to do with the sea, among them a large selection of authentic ship model kits.
MO

CORAN-SHOLES INDUSTRIES
Dept. CHC
509 East 2nd Street
South Boston, MA 02127

"Stained Glass Supplies," 50 cents, published monthly, black and white, illustrated.

Manufacturers and suppliers of lead, glass, and equipment to the stained-glass artisan or buff, Coran-Sholes offers starter kits from about $10 to $50 for Tiffany-style shades and lamp bases and terrariums with all the necessary tools and supplies.
MO

RAINBOW ART GLASS CORP.
Dept. CHC
49 Shark River Road
Neptune, NJ 07753

"Rainbow Art Glass Corporation," 50 cents (refundable with purchase), published annually, color, illustrated.

Unusual Tiffany-style shades for all types of lamps, Art Nouveau wall mirrors, boxes, terrariums, a stained-glass clock, custom-made windows are packaged in kits with the glass cut to shape, ready to foil, assemble, and solder according to instructions, as well as all the other necessary materials. Prices range from $20 for a terrarium kit to about $90 for a Tiffany shade kit.
MO

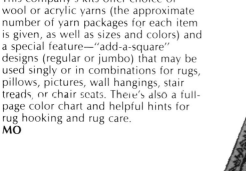

Rug kit, *Spinnerin Yarn*

220

Color TV and stereo receiver kits, *Heath*

SPIRAL STAIRCASES   STEREO

WHITTEMORE-DURGIN
Dept. CHC
Box 2065
Hanover, MA 02339

*"Stained Glass Hobby Supplies" and
"Getting Started in Stained Glass," 50
cents, folder of leaflets, updated
periodically, black and white,
illustrated.*

Everything needed for stained-glass
artistry: glass in many patterns and
colors, quality leading, copper foil,
solder, tools, glass stains, and paints.
Complete kits for making "Tiffany" and
other lamp shades, window ornaments,
candle chimneys, planters, and other
objects include patterns, precut glass,
instructions, materials. A wide variety
of prices.
MO

THE IRON SHOP
Dept. CHC
400 Reed Road
Broomall, PA 19008

*"Spiral Stair Kit," no charge, black and
white, illustrated.*

If space is limited but access to another
area is desired, the do-it-yourself spiral
stair kit is the answer. They come in
several sizes and cost from around $350
to $500 f.o.b. with complete
instructions. If you want a free-estimate
sheet and the do-it-yourself
instructions, send along 50 cents when
you write for the brochure.
MO

MYLEN INDUSTRIES
Dept. CHC
650 Washington Street
Peekskill, NY 10566

*"Mylen Industries," no charge, 30
pages, black and white, illustrated.*

Mylen makes many types and sizes of
space-saving spiral stair units, shipped
in kit form ready for installation, and
they claim no special skills are required.
If you fill out the questionnaire and
return it to Mylen, they will send you
an estimate. Prices start around $300.
MO

HEATH COMPANY
Dept. CHC
Benton Harbor, MI 49022

*"Heathkit," no charge, 88 pages, black
and white, some color, illustrated.*

Electronic kits of all kinds are the
specialty of this company. They include
complete color TV sets (table models
start at $449.95) with a choice of
cabinet styles, which come assembled
and finished. Floor cabinets are from
$154.95 to $219.95, table cabinets from
$39.95 to $89.95. One interesting
offering is a kaleidoscopic wall light
screen (22¾" square by 4½" deep) that
pulsates in color to music. It works on
any hi-fi, phono, or FM radio and costs
just $79.95. A complete
Heathkit/Thomas spinet organ starts at
$549.95. Several types of components
for complete stereo systems—amplifiers,
tuners, speakers, receivers—are
available in kit form. Prices,
dimensions, and all necessary
descriptive information are given.
MO

String art kit, *Mi-Bryn*

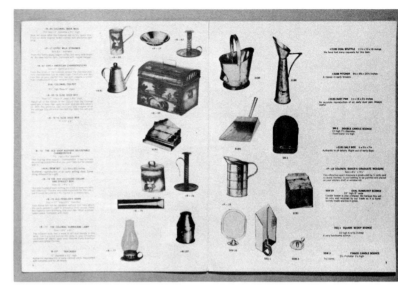

Tinware to decorate, *Carson and Ellis*

STRING ART

SUPPLIES

MI-BRYN, INC.
Dept. CHC
P.O. Box 36195
Cincinnati, OH 45236

"Kelly's String Art," no charge,
published semiannually, black and
white, illustrated.

All kinds of string-art patterns you can
make with only a pair of pliers—and, of
course, the kit, which includes fabric-
covered board, brass-plated, no-tarnish
nails, decorator string, and a pattern.
Patterns or materials may also be
ordered separately. Complete kits are
around $10.
MO

BOYCAN'S CRAFT SUPPLIES
Dept. CHC
P.O. Box 897
Sharon, PA 16146

"Boycan's Craft Supplies," $1.00
(refundable with purchase), updated
annually, 63 pages, black and white,
illustrated.

The catalogue lists and shows all
manner of craft supplies for découpage,
beadwork, macramé, tole painting,
stained glass, needlework, and more
offbeat things such as making flowers
out of artificial or dried natural
materials. Prices are inexpensive.
MO

CARSON AND ELLIS, INC.
Dept. CHC
1153 Warwick Avenue
Warwick, RI 02888

"Early American Decorating Supplies,"
75 cents, published periodically, 28
pages, black and white, illustrated.

A wide and interesting assortment of
glass, wood, and metal objects plus
materials, accessories, and tools needed
for painting, stenciling, découpage, and
decorating, all pictured and described,
with specifications and suggestions for
use. Series Three of Authentic Old
Designs is a grouping of patterns for
country tin: trays, clocks, mirrors.
Découpage and craft books are
included, as are price lists.
MO

CRAFTOOL COMPANY, INC.
Dept. CHC
1421 West 240th Street
Harbor City, CA 90710

"Craftool Catalogue," $2.00, published
biannually, 150 pages, black and white.

This beautifully designed and
handsomely illustrated catalogue has
supplies for most crafts and is ideal for
beginners as well as professionals
because it is so easy to use. Offered are
small but complete tool kits for batik,
bookbinding, ceramics, sculpture, and
other crafts, with an excellent book list
at the back.
MO

DORR WOOLEN CO.
Dept. CHC
Guild, NH 03754

"The Dorr Mill Store Catalog," 75 cents,
26 pages, black and white, illustrated.

The Dorr Mill store sells its handwoven
fabrics only through its retail shop, but
hooking and braiding supplies may be
ordered by mail. Hooking and braiding
kits are offered as well as instruction
books for both crafts and all the
necessary supplies. Wall hangings, chair
seats, pillows, brick covers are some of
the things that can be made with the
kits.
MO

Catalogue cover, *Dorr Woolen*

222

your "labor of love" afghans

Afghan designs, *Mary Maxim*

GLEN BLACK/LOCAL COLOR
Dept. CHC
1414 Grant Avenue
San Francisco, CA 94133

Folders, no charge, black and white.

Supplies and general information for batik and textile craftsmen: Procion dyes, acid dyes, methods for using dyes, color mixing hints, thickeners, waxes, and batik tools.
MO

HANDCRAFTERS
Dept. CHC
1-99 West Brown Street
Waupun, WI 53963

"Nasco Handcrafters," 50 cents, published annually, 84 pages, black and white, illustrated.

Catalogue of kits and supplies for most of the usual crafts—basket weaving, leatherworking, candlemaking, plus less common crafts such as glass art, shrink art, etching, wire jewelry, plastic art.
MO

MARY MAXIM, INC.
Dept. CHC
2001 Holland Avenue
Port Huron, MI 48060

"Your 'Labor of Love' Catalog," no charge, published quarterly, 63 pages, color, illustrated.

Mary Maxim has a large selection of designs, accessories, equipment, and supplies for such crafts as crewel, macramé, découpage, string art, needlepoint, knitting, quickpoint, crochet, samplers, quilts, hand-hooked rugs, all pictured and described. Prices and order forms are included.
MO

ROBERTS INDIAN CRAFTS & SUPPLIES
Dept. CHC
P.O. Box 98
Anadarko, OK 73005

Price lists, no charge.

The lists merely detail craft supplies and articles such as beads, cones, shells, skins, bells, fringe, and feathers, and it is necessary to write for further information on specific items.
MO

THE SHELBURNE SPINNERS
Dept. CHC
Box 651 HD
Burlington, VT 05401

"Shelburne Spinners," $1.00 for brochure, newsletters, and natural dye samples (refundable with purchase over $10).

The Shelburne Spinners cooperative makes several kinds of hand-spun yarn on spinning wheels from Vermont wool, but their main emphasis is on skeins of knitting wool and kits with directions, natural-dyed yarns, and personalized label. The whole process of making and dyeing the yarns is described. The prices are moderate.
MO

Folding backgammon table, needlepoint top, *Sudberry House*

UPHOLSTERY REPAIR   ## WOODEN OBJECTS

WOODCRAFT SUPPLY CORP.
Dept. CHC
313 Montvale Avenue
Woburn, MA 01801

"Woodcraft," 50 cents, published biannually, 48 pages, color, illustrated.

A complete upholstery kit to repair tired and sagging furniture with all the tools needed to do the job, plus step-by-step instruction book is yours for under $11.
MO

SUDBERRY HOUSE, INC.
Dept. CHC
Box 421
Old Lyme, CT 06371

"Sudberry House," no charge, yearly supplements, 12 pages, color, illustrated.

Wood products to complement and complete needlework, such as Queen Anne style footstools, trays, game tables, child's chair, and luggage racks, in solid cherry or selected hardwoods. Sizes are given, and modifications can be made. Prices are on request.
MO

THE O-P CRAFT CO., INC.
Dept. CHC
425 Warren Street
Sandusky, OH 44870

"O-P Craftwood '76 Catalog," $1.00, published annually, 20 pages, some color, illustrated.

Basswood boxes of all sizes, trays, candleholders, napkin rings, picture frames, plaques, and other objects to decorate either by painting or découpage. The company supplies "Flair Finish," applicators, acrylics, paint-mixing trays, and how-to booklets. Dimensions, prices, and item numbers are given.
MO

Upholstery repair kit, *Woodcraft Supply*

Basswood boxes to decorate, *O-P Craft*

Indoor garden under fluorescent lights, *Duro-Lite Lamps*

GARDENS: INDOORS AND OUT

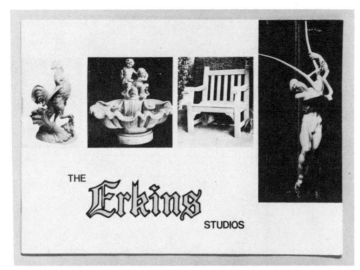

Catalogue cover, *Erkins Studios*

GARDEN ORNAMENTS, FOUNTAINS, AND FURNITURE

Indoor-outdoor fountains, *Product Specialties, page 233*

ERKINS STUDIOS
Dept. CHC
8 West 40th Street
New York, NY 10018

"The Erkins Studios," $1.00, 34 pages, black and white.

For over 60 years the Erkins Studio has offered a distinctive collection of traditional and contemporary fountains, figures, planters, sculpture, and decorative ornaments for garden and home. A beautiful carved stone 6' tier-upon-tier of shells fountain for the wall costs about $875; a tall carved stone St. Fiacre, patron saint of gardeners, is $260; and a pair of handsome 20''-high fluted lead urns is $500. There are also other urns and planters in all styles and shapes, several sundials, and garden benches of stone or teak.
MO/RS/ID

FLORENTINE CRAFTSMEN, INC.
Dept. CHC
650 First Avenue
New York, NY 10016

"Florentine Craftsmen," 50 cents, black and white, illustrated.

A distinguished collection of unusual wrought-iron, cast-iron, marble, limestone, and lead statuary, indoor and outdoor furniture, fountains, planters, and other garden and terrace ornaments. In the fountain group there are lead fountain heads of animals or gods from $40 to over $100 and wall-hung unit of a dolphin with shell, including pump and motor, under $500. A complete garden ensemble with circular pool, goose fountain, pump, and motor, ready to operate, costs less than $1,000. Dimensions and prices are included.
MO/RS/ID

LITTLE GIANT PUMP COMPANY
Dept. CHC
3810 North Tulsa Street
Oklahoma City, OK 73112

"Decorative Water and Light Products," no charge, published annually, 15 pages, color, illustrated.

Everything needed to transform your outdoor garden into an even lovelier area: waterfall and fountain sets, fountain ring sets, submersible lights, even a little waterfall designed for indoor use. Products are described, with specifications. Write for nearest dealer.
RS

REAL FOUNTAINS, INC.
Dept. CHC
264 West 40th Street
New York, NY 10018

"Fountains," no charge, published quarterly, some color, illustrated.

Anyone for fountains? The newest kind of decorating is with water—indoors and outdoors—using fountains that require no plumbing, recirculate the water, and are completely portable, as the bowls are made of reinforced fiberglass. Price range is from about $50 for a small indoor fountain to about $2,300 for Satellite II, one of the Waterama models. There is a full description of the fountains, kits, and components.
MO

Garden ornaments, *Florentine Craftsmen*

Bronze sundial, *Sundials & More*

Small attached greenhouse, *Lord & Burnham*

GREENHOUSES

SUNDIALS & MORE
Dept. CHC
P.O. Box H
New Ipswich, NH 03071

Catalogue, no charge, 32 pages, some color, illustrated.

A fascinating, if limited, selection of about 29 sundials, ranging in price from a mere $7 to $385. The sundials are made in various materials—bronze, copper, brass, pewter, cast iron, hand-carved stone, and acrylic and many are imports or reproductions of antique sundials from different parts of the world. There is a fetching little windowsill sundial that doubles as a paperweight.
MO

WILLIAMS-SONOMA
Dept. CHC
532 Sutter Street
San Francisco, CA 94102

"A Catalog for Cooks," no charge, published biannually, color and black and white, illustrated.

Williams-Sonoma doesn't only cater to cooks. They also sell charming things for the garden and patio, such as an amusing rustic bark bird feeder from North Carolina and flowerpot candles that won't blow out and burn for five hours. A post-paid order form is included.
MO

ALUMINUM GREENHOUSES, INC.
Dept. CHC
14615 Lorain Avenue
Cleveland, OH 44111

"Everlite Aluminum Greenhouses," no charge, 28 pages, black and white, illustrated.

Descriptions of these prefabricated aluminum, glass, and fiberglass greenhouses with advice on selecting your unit. Structural and installation details, sizes, weights, prices, foundation data, accessories, and order forms are included. A free gardening book comes with each order.
MO

GOTHIC ARCH GREENHOUSES
Dept. CHC
P.O. Box 1564
Mobile, AL 36601

"You never stop growing when you have a Gothic Arch Greenhouse," no charge, color, illustrated.

Designed in the shape of a Gothic arch as opposed to the usual gable design to take advantage of a curved surface's ability to transmit more light and heat, the greenhouses are precut, for do-it-yourself erection. Complete information includes owner endorsements, specifications, price list, accessories, order form. Greenhouse price range: $109 to $2344, according to size. All models have add-on feature and are made of redwood and fiberglass for long maintenance-free life.
MO

LORD & BURNHAM
Div., Burnham Corp.
Dept. CHC
2 Main Street
Irvington, NY 10523

"Your gateway to year-round gardening pleasure," no charge, reprinted periodically, 23 pages, color, illustrated.

The catalogue describes and shows the two basic lines of aluminum and glass greenhouses manufactured by Lord & Burnham—free-standing and attached—both in a wide selection of models. Price list and shipping charges and information are included, along with available accessories for possible later addition.
MO

Birchbark bird feeder, *Williams-Sonoma*

228

Backyard greenhouse, J.A. Nearing

Polyethylene and aluminum greenhouse,
Peter Reimuller–The Greenhouseman

McGREGOR GREENHOUSES
Dept. CHC
P.O. Box 36
Santa Cruz, CA 95063

*"McGregor Greenhouses," no charge,
published annually, 6 pages, black and
white.*

The McGregor redwood-framed and
fiberglass greenhouses bolt together for
strength and portability and come free-
standing or attached, starting at about
$160 for the small "Green Room"
attached model. They are available
either precut and ready to assemble, or
as a kit with a simple cutting plan that
shows you exactly what lumber to buy
and how to cut it (with a kit, you can
save as much as $50 by buying the
lumber locally). Greenhouse heater,
humidifier, exhaust fan, and thermostat
are also offered.
MO

J. A. NEARING CO., INC.
Dept. CHC
10788 Tucker Street
Beltsville, MD 20705

*"Janco Greenhouses," no charge,
published semiannually, 47 pages,
color, illustrated.*

In addition to the regular free-standing
greenhouses, Janco offers several good-
looking lean-to types and window-
garden greenhouses that will turn any
window into a small year-round garden
room. Prices range from $135 for one
33" wide x 52" high to $185 for a
window model 48" wide x 72" high.
Detailed instructions for assembly and
operation are given so that if you are
handy with tools, you can do the
installation yourself. Included are
suggestions for types of plants to
propagate.
MO

REDWOOD DOMES, INC.
Dept. CHC
Aptos, CA 95003

*"The Joy of Greenhousing," no charge,
published annually, 14 pages, color,
illustrated.*

Geodesic design, precut redwood
greenhouses in varying sizes and prices
starting at $98.50 for a complete unit,
no foundation needed are offered in a
choice of covers from fiberglass,
polyvinyl, and polyethylene to glass.
Price list and order form are included.
MO

**PETER REIMULLER—THE
GREENHOUSEMAN**
Dept. CHC
980 17th Avenue
Santa Cruz, CA 95063

*"These are my greenhouses," no
charge, published seasonally, 15 pages,
color, illustrated.*

The brochure describes the complete
line of greenhouses, which have
redwood and aluminum frames and
polyethylene, fiberglass, and glass
coverings, depending on the model.
The advantages of each are explained,
as well as the shapes and sizes that
would be best for you. Prices start as
low as $120 for an 8' x 6'6" model.
MO

STURDI-BUILT MANUFACTURING CO.
Dept. CHC
11304 S.W. Boones Ferry Road
Portland, OR 97219

*"The World's Finest Redwood
Greenhouses . . . Made for the Home
Hobbyist," no charge, 12 pages, color,
illustrated.*

Greenhouses specifically and unusually
designed for the home-hobby gardener.
Each unit has frames of redwood and is
precision-fabricated to order,
handcrafted, and packaged. Prices and
accessories folder are included.
MO

Small fiberglass greenhouse, *McGregor Greenhouses*

Interior of geodesic greenhouse, *Redwood Domes*

Terrarium gardens, *Arthur Eames Allgrove*

INDOOR GARDENING

ARTHUR EAMES ALLGROVE
Dept. CHC
Wilmington, MA 01887

"The Register," 50 cents, published annually, 24 pages, black and white, illustrated.

A fascinating newsletter with all kinds of information for the terraria-minded gardener, such as articles on how to make your own terrarium, saikei, and bonsai. Kits, plants, and garden gear are offered for sale. Of interest to garden clubs are the slide-rental programs, "Making a Terrarium" and "Beginners Approach to Bonsai—indoor and outdoor."
MO

Gazebo greenhouse, *Sturdi-Built*

DURO-LITE LAMPS, INC.
Dept. CHC
17-10 Willow Street
Fairlawn, NJ 07410

"Growing Exotic Plants Under Full-Spectrum Light," 50 cents, 31 pages, black and white, illustrated.

A complete and comprehensive guide to successfully cultivating tropical foliage and flowering plants in the home. Individual sections cover light, humidity, temperature, watering, ventilation, etc., for a host of plant families. Includes list showing types of plants to be grown under different forms of lighting. Single copies of the following leaflets are available at no charge, provided you send a stamped, self-addressed envelope: "Indoor Gardening with Indoor Sunshine," "Growing Orchids Under Light," "Natural Outdoor Light—Indoors," "Short Course on Bromeliad Growing Under Lights," "Growing African Violets Under Full-Spectrum Light," "Cultivate Your Own Rose Garden—Even in a City Apartment," "Indoor Gardening with Artificial Light."

THE HOUSE PLANT CORNER, LTD.
Dept. CHC
Box 5000
Cambridge, MD 21613

"Annual Catalog," 25 cents, 30 pages, black and white, illustrated.

All the equipment and accessories the most pampered house plant could require from lights, pots, humidifiers, plant food, planters, and misters to soil testers. Also a small selection of house plants. Prices, shipping costs, order forms are included.
MO

RAINBOW ART GLASS CORPORATION
Dept. CHC
49 Shark River Road
Neptune, NJ 07753

"Rainbow Art Glass Corporation," 50 cents (refundable with purchase), published annually, color, illustrated.

In addition to the stained-glass fixtures, the Rainbow Art folder shows a group of six amusing shapes and styles of leaded stained and clear glass terrariums, either completely hand-finished or in kit form. An octagonally shaped terrarium, 15" x 13" high, completely finished, is about $80; as a kit, it's just under $40. For some models you can buy a top mounting fluorescent lighting fixture, and for all, bags of crushed glass gravel, under $1.
MO

SHOPLITE COMPANY
Dept. CHC
566 J Franklin
Nutley, NJ 07110

"Shoplite Fluorescent Booklet H," 25 cents, 16 pages, black and white, illustrated; *"Catalog 76,"* 25 cents.

The booklet explains the kind of light that is most effective for plant growth indoors, names varieties and how much light they need. Also included: setups and propagation, use of plants and lights for decorative effects, lists of other reference books and pamphlets.

"Catalog 76" covers fluorescent kits and fixtures, growth units and plant stands, midget fluorescent units, other accessories for the indoor gardener. Price list and order form are included.
MO

Terrariums and herb gardens, *Adam Brentwood*

Catalogue cover, *Ilgenfritz Orchids*

INDOOR/OUTDOOR PLANTS

ADAM BRENTWOOD AND COMPANY
Dept. CHC
8 Dorothy Avenue
Paramus, NJ 07652

"Indoor Gardening Collection Vol. II,"
no charge, 15 pages, some color,
illustrated.

A descriptive catalogue of available
plants and accessories with
photographs, prices, order form. Among
them are cactus and foliage plants
shipped in lucite planters with
handcrafted natural sand designs. For
the indoor gardening enthusiast there
are herb gardens, uniquely designed
terrariums, even a specially created
avocado aquarium starter planter that
will convert to a lucite flower pot, for
$7.50.
MO

DESERT PLANT COMPANY
Dept. CHC
P.O. Box 880
Marfa, TX 79843

"Cacti of the Southwest U.S.A.," $1.00,
40 pages, black and white, illustrated.

Illustrated catalogue of many varieties
of cactus, blooming size, suitable for
terrariums or garden. Growing
instructions and order blank are
included. Each plant is named,
numbered, and described. Prices are
from $1 to $20.
MO

GIRARD NURSERIES
Dept. CHC
Box 428
Geneva, OH 44041

"Girard Nurseries," no charge,
published annually, 36 pages, color and
black and white, illustrated.

Everything for the home planter, from
tree seeds to mail-order-size trees,
shrubs, ground covers, pot plants,
bonsai. All varieties are described,
many shown. Also, information on
growing Christmas trees for profit and
detailed instructions for planting
broadleaf evergreens. Includes shipping
rates, prices, and order blank.
MO

GREENLAND FLOWER SHOP
Dept. CHC
RD 1, Box 52 (Stormstown)
Port Matilda, PA 16870

"Rare and Exotic House Plants," 25
cents, published annually, 6 pages,
black and white.

A listing of house plants (the shop
grows 227 varieties) by name, cultural
code, use, size, and price. House plants,
cacti and succulents, terrarium and
dish-garden plants are their specialty, at
reasonable prices.
MO

ILGENFRITZ ORCHIDS
Dept. CHC
P.O. Box 1114, Blossom Lane
Monroe, MI 48161

"Ilgenfritz Orchids," $2.00 (refundable
with purchase), 97 pages, some color,
illustrated.

The catalogue provides an extensive
listing of all types of orchids with some
information about size, color, and
blooming season. A few are pictured.
Also included: books on orchids,
cultural instructions, fertilizers,
fungicides, pesticides, nutrient
solutions, and potting materials. A
plant-of-the-month plan is offered.
Order form included and a range of
prices, which seem reasonable.
MO

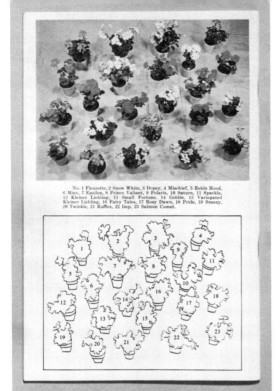

No. 1 Fleurette, 2 Snow White, 3 Dopey, 4 Mischief, 5 Robin Hood,
6 Minx, 7 Epsilon, 8 Prince Valiant, 9 Polaris, 10 Saturn, 11 Sparkle,
12 Kleiner Liebling, 13 Small Fortune, 14 Goblin, 15 Variegated
Kleiner Liebling, 16 Fairy Tales, 17 Rosy Dawn, 18 Pride, 19 Sneezy,
20 Twinkle, 21 Ruffles, 22 Imp, 23 Salmon Comet.

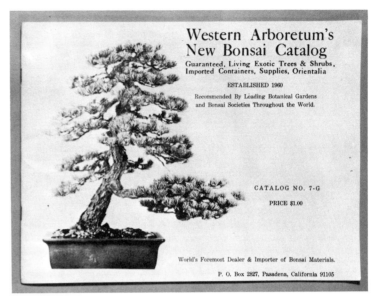

Western Arboretum's
New Bonsai Catalog
Guaranteed, Living Exotic Trees & Shrubs,
Imported Containers, Supplies, Orientalia

ESTABLISHED 1960

Recommended By Leading Botanical Gardens
and Bonsai Societies Throughout the World.

CATALOG NO. 7-G

PRICE $1.00

World's Foremost Dealer & Importer of Bonsai Materials.

P. O. Box 2827, Pasadena, California 91105

Catalogue cover, *Western Arboretum*

Miniature and dwarf geraniums, *Merry Gardens*

LOGEE'S GREENHOUSES
Dept. CHC
55 North Street
Danielson, CT 06239

"Begonias, rare plants, geraniums and herbs," $1.00, 82 pages, some color, illustrated.

Begonias, geraniums, herbs, cacti and succulents, vines, oxalis, plus section of choice plants for home and conservatory with brief descriptions and some photographs. Prices and order form are included.
MO

MERRY GARDENS
Dept. CHC
P.O. Box 595
Camden, ME 04843

"Merry Gardens Pictorial Handbook," $1.00, 36 pages, black and white, illustrated.

The booklet comprises photographs and descriptive captions of plants carried by this grower, divided into categories such as foliage house plants, flowering plants, vines, cacti, ivies, ferns and mosses, and geraniums and begonias of all types. Also a page on, "Key to care of plants indoors." Other literature available from Merry Gardens: "1975 Availability List," 50 cents, contains over 300 indoor foliage and flowering plants and vines, 200 begonias, 50 fuschias, 50 hederas (ivy), 100 cacti and succulents, 35 ferns and mosses, 35 gesneriads; "Herb and Geranium price list," 25 cents; "Herb Handbook," $1.00, contains 93 herbs, and describes their culture, uses, value as insect repellants.
MO

NOR'EAST MINIATURE ROSES·
Dept. CHC
58 Hammond Street
Rowley, MA 01969

"Miniature Roses," no charge, published semiannually, 14 pages, black and white.

Natural dwarf roses that grow a mere five inches tall—15 inches at most— have foliage and flowers in proportion to the overall size. The roses, described as very hardy, can be grown year round even in city apartments. The catalogue gives names, descriptions, prices. No additional charges for shipping or handling.
MO

SHAFFER'S TROPICAL GARDENS, INC.
Dept. CHC
1220 41st Avenue
Santa Cruz, CA 95060

Catalogue, 50 cents, 10 pages, black and white, illustrated.

Shaffer's specializes in orchids and carries many unusual varieties, including some of its own. For beginners, they recommend a $15 kit which comes complete with a phalaenopsis, which is easy to grow, complete in its pot, with fertilizer and growing instructions.
MO

WESTERN ARBORETUM
Dept. CHC
P.O. Box 2827
Pasadena, CA 91105

"New Bonsai Catalog," $1.00, published annually, 24 pages, black and white, illustrated.

Western Arboretum offers "the most complete selection of plants, containers, and tools . . . ever to be found in one place." These are exotic trees and shrubs, imported containers, supplies, and Orientalia, with about 300 bonsai plants to choose from. Also included: books, tools, supplies; tea and tea sets; dwarf citrus trees; Oriental accessories and art goods; bonsai containers, pottery, and stands. Prices are generally expensive but quality is assured.
MO

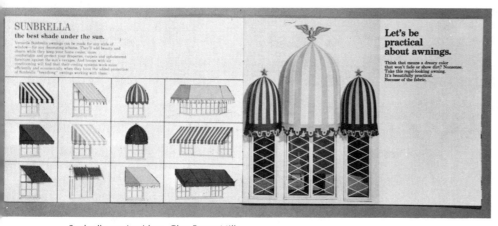

Sunbrella awning ideas, *Glen Raven Mills*

OUTDOOR DECORATING IDEAS

PLANTERS

WHITE FLOWER FARM
Dept. CHC
Litchfield, CT 06759

"The Garden Book," published spring and fall, plus three issues of notes, by subscription, $4.00 (refundable with $15 purchase), color and black and white, illustrated.

One of the most attractive, well-written, and informative of all gardening catalogues, White Flower Farm's "Garden Book" is primarily devoted to an alphabetical listing of the plants they sell, with very detailed information about culture, planting time, plant size; but there are also all kinds of good tidbits of information on things like drying flowers, forcing bulbs indoors for winter blooming, building compost heaps, thinning, and taking cuttings. The book is sensibly illustrated with sketches and photographs of plants, flowers, and gardens and schematic drawings of gardening techniques.
MO

CALIFORNIA REDWOOD
ASSOCIATION
Dept. CHC
617 Montgomery Street
San Francisco, CA 94111

"Redwood Decks, Redwood Fences, and Redwood Garden Shelters," no charge, color, illustrated.

Decorative ideas for house and garden using redwood for decks, lean-tos, fences, and many do-it-yourself projects.
RS

GLEN RAVEN MILLS, INC.
Dept. CHC
Glen Raven, NC 27215

"Sunbrella Outdoor Decorating Guide," no charge, 8 pages, color, illustrated.

The "Outdoor Decorating Guide" shows and describes various ways of shielding windows, terraces, patios, and walkways from the direct rays of the sun using awning fabric made from acrylic fibers in a wide range of solid colors, stripes, and checks, that is guaranteed colorfast, rot-and mildew-proof, and impervious to airborne chemicals.
RS

COUNTRY FLOORS, INC.
Dept. CHC
1158 Second Avenue
New York, NY 10021

"Country Floors," 50 cents, published approximately every three years, 20 pages, color, illustrated.

While Country Floors specializes primarily in imported and American ceramic tiles, they also sell sculptured terra-cotta pots and planters from Italy, based on antique designs, in a variety of shapes and sizes. As they may not always have in stock the pots shown in the catalogue, it is advisable to order well in advance to ensure delivery when a new shipment arrives.
MO

HOME PLANT DISPLAYERS, INC.
Dept. CHC
51 East 42nd Street
New York, NY 10017

"Grunmar Plant Stand System," no charge, published seasonally, 8 pages, black and white, illustrated.

Indoor plant holders and accessories of many types, including floor-to-ceiling

Hanging planters with grow light, floor-to-ceiling pole planter, *Home Plant Displayers*

Stonewood planters, *Product Specialties*

Catalogue cover,
My House Wrought Iron

pole units, floor-standing, window, wall tray, wall-hanging, and others. Some include light units. Full description and illustration of each model is given. Prices range from about $6 to $50.
MO

MY HOUSE WROUGHT IRON
Dept. CHC
417 North Robertson Boulevard
Los Angeles, CA 90048

"My House Wrought Iron," $4.00, published annually, 40 pages, black and white, illustrated.

Handmade wrought-iron planters in black or colors to hang from ceiling or wall or sit on the floor. A five-pot, 30"-high floor or wall model is under $125. The styles are traditional French and very good-looking.
MO

PRODUCT SPECIALTIES, INC.
Dept. CHC
600 East Washington
Eaton, IN 47338

"Product Specialties, Inc.," no charge, published annually, color, illustrated.

Three groups of interesting planters, fountains, and garden accessories, all of polyester resin, are offered by this firm. "Dewstone," resembling, but lighter than, concrete, has three fountains—a lion's head, jug girl, and dolphin boy; recirculating pump available for each. There are also large planters in traditional or contemporary styles, garden figures such as a horse's head or large owl, a Buddha, and two sizes of Japanese lanterns. "Grecian Fiber," of structural polyethylene, is a set of two planters in classic design in white or green; the large size, 18¾" diameter and 15⅜" high, is under $14. "Stonewood" is a group of lightweight polyester resin planters with the look and feel of wood. A large planter looks like a round log; others look like horizontal logs; some are shaped like big fish, very amusing, or owls or chickens. Of course, they can all be used indoors, too. Prices are moderate; dimensions and weight are given.
MO

TUBE CRAFT, INC.
Dept. CHC
1311 West 80th Street
Cleveland, OH 44102

"FloraCart—the Indoor Greenhouse on Wheels," no charge, 12 pages, black and white, illustrated.

Tube Craft products include FloraCart, accessories for growing house plants, and books on indoor gardening. The brochure illustrates and minutely describes FloraCart, a plant stand with all the advantages of a small indoor greenhouse. The two- or three-shelf cart has great mobility, molded fiberglass trays, "Combolite" fluorescent/incandescent fixtures, and aluminum tubing. Prices are up to $185 for complete FloraCart.
MO/RS

"FloraCart" rolling plant stand, *Tube Craft*

Family room home maintenance center (courtesy *Evans Products*)

MAINTENANCE, SERVICES, AND SCHOOLS

236

Table-setting ideas, *Fostoria Glass*

Ways to use Pacific Silvercloth,
Wamsutta Industrial Fabrics

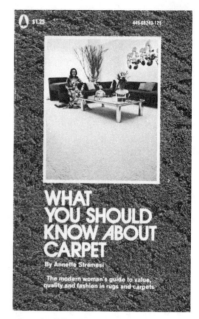

Paperback book cover, *E. T. Barwick*

CARE OF CHINA, GLASS, AND SILVER

FOSTORIA GLASS CO.
Dept. CHC-E-2
Moundsville, WV 26041

"To Have and to Hold," brochure, no charge, black and white, illustrated; *"All Crystal Is Glass . . . but,"* booklet, no charge, 6 pages, black and white, illustrated.

The brochure contains a brief history of china and crystal, the different types and qualities of each, what to look for when making a selection, tips on how to care for them, and an illustrated section on table settings with a discussion of accessories used to set an attractive table.

The interesting little booklet gives a brief history of glass, defines crystal glassware, tells you what to look for when buying it, and has tips on care.

WAMSUTTA INDUSTRIAL FABRICS
Dept. CHC
111 West 40th Street
New York, NY 10018

"Pacific Silvercloth," no charge, black and white, illustrated.

A small folder on how silvercloth can protect your silver and eliminate constant repolishing. Various ways to use it are shown with diagrams.
RS

CARE OF FLOORING, CARPETS, AND FURNITURE

AMERICAN ENKA CO.
Dept. CHC
530 Fifth Avenue
New York, NY 10036

"I'm Soil, I'm Finished!" no charge, color, illustrated.

An informative booklet describing the color value, easy cleaning, and wear-resistance (there is a five-year wear guarantee) of Enkalure II nylon. A chart on spot and stain removal is also included.

ARGO AND COMPANY
Dept. CHC
182 Ezell Street
Spartanburg, SC 29302

"Easy Carpet Cleaning," no charge, black and white, illustrated.

A booklet on how to remove spots, keep carpets looking new, and select a carpet for easy care.
MO

E.T. BARWICK INDUSTRIES
Attention Mort Kahn
Dept. CHC
5025 New Peachtree Road
Chamblee, GA 30341

"What You Should Know About Carpet," $1.25, 208 pages, paperback, black and white, illustrated.

Annette Stramesi has written a valuable guide to judging quality and fashion in rugs and carpets, with information on how to clean and care for carpeting, what to use where, a brief history of carpets, and a glossary of carpet terms.
MO

DURACLEAN INTERNATIONAL
Dept. CHC
Deerfield, IL 60015

"Housekeeping Hints," no charge, 23 pages, black and white, illustrated.

This informative booklet offers 137 ways to make housekeeping a breeze. With Duraclean "flower fresh" cleaning products, the hints include care of carpets, rugs, and upholstery; windows, mirrors, and glass; silver and other metals; plus loads of work-saving tips. The six Duraclean home services for cleaning and repair of furniture and carpets are outlined, and the name of the nearest professional dealer will be supplied on request.
MO/RS

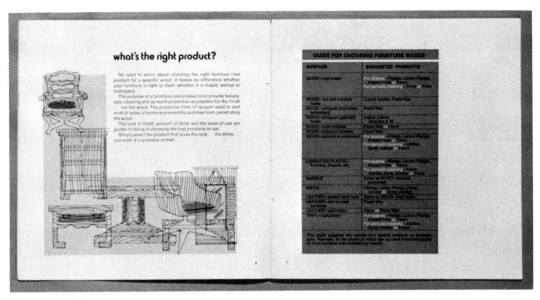

Furniture care, *Johnson Wax*

COLOR MATCHING

CONSUMER INFORMATION

THE FLINTKOTE CO.
Dept. CHC
480 Central Avenue
East Rutherford, NJ 07073

"How to Care for Your Flintkote Floor,"
no charge, black and white, illustrated.

The folder describes how to clean vinyl
asbestos flooring, how to get out hard-
to-clean spots, and proper waxing.

JOHNSON WAX
Consumer Services Center
Dept. CHC
P.O. Box 567
Racine, WI 53403

"Floor Care," no charge, 39 pages, black
and white, illustrated; "Furniture Care,"
no charge, 23 pages, black and white,
illustrated; "Rug and Carpet Care," no
charge, 31 pages, black and white,
illustrated.

Johnson Wax offers three useful and
comprehensive primers. The first covers
the care of all types of flooring, with an
assessment of different floor-care
products, the why and how of wax
removal, tips, questions, and answers.
    The furniture-care booklet tells you
quick and easy ways to protect your
furniture, when and how to clean, and
the right cleaning products for different
surfaces.
    "Rug and Carpet Care" gives a short
history of carpets and then goes into
care information under such headings
as carpets take a beating, fiber facts,
and wear and tear. There's a section on
getting rid of spills and stains and
another on selecting the right type of
vacuum cleaner.

HOUSE & GARDEN
Dept. CHC/cc
P.O. Box 1910
Grand Central Station
New York, NY 10017

Not a booklet but a set of the latest 36
House & Garden Color Chips to help
you with your color selections. A large
3" x 6" set of 36 chips, $6; the small,
purse-size set, 1" x 2", is just $2. Both
come with a complete merchandise
directory of manufacturers who match
House & Garden colors, which is very
helpful for color-coordinating your
furnishings.
MO

AMERICAN INSTITUTE OF KITCHEN
DEALERS
Dept. CHC
114 Main Street
Hackettstown, NJ 07840

"Directory of Accredited AIKD
Members," no charge, published
annually, 43 pages.

A listing, by state and city, of
kitchen/bath specialists across the
country who qualify professionally to
design, supply, and install complete
kitchens and baths. Many also give
instructions in do-it-yourself
techniques. A handy directory to have
if you are remodeling or adding to your
home.

BETTER BUSINESS BUREAU
Dept. CHC
Consumer Affairs Library
Boston, MA

"Facts You Should Know About
Mattresses," no charge, 16 pages, black
and white, illustrated.

Published in cooperation with the
Association of Bedding Manufacturers
of New England, this booklet in the
Better Business Bureau's "Fact" series is
loaded with sound information about
mattress sizes, materials, foundations,
firmness, workmanship, care, and
prices. Caveats about advertising claims
and guarantees serve to alert the
prospective buyer.

238

Booklet cover, *Brand Names Foundation*

Booklet cover, *Career Institute*

Booklet covers, *Consumer Information Division, Moving and Storage Industry*

BRAND NAMES FOUNDATION, INC.
Dept. CHC
477 Madison Avenue
New York, NY 10022

"Where to Find Out," 75 cents, revised and updated periodically, 32 pages, black and white.

Brand Names Foundation, working with Better Business Bureaus and many manufacturers, has produced an invaluable consumer-information directory that lists authoritative publications on buying appliances, clothing, food, homes, and furnishings, where to get help, and how to plan. The section on Home and Family Management, for instance, covers publications on appliance use and care, nutrition, and family finance. The listings give title, address, source, and price (if any).

"Know How to Buy Home Furnishings," 75 cents, 84 pages, black and white, illustrated.

This well-written booklet is intended to make you a confident and competent shopper by supplying you with much needed information about home furnishings before you buy. It has been put together by members of the Brand Name Foundation with the help of the major home furnishings magazines and covers everything from "case goods" (non-upholstered pieces), how to select lampshades, to what to look for when purchasing outdoor or leisure furniture.

CAREER INSTITUTE
Dept. CHC—Consumer Services
Division
Sherman Turnpike
Danbury, CT 06816

"Buy It Right," $2.95, 172 pages, black and white, illustrated.

This shopper's guide by Jan Brown has valuable information on how to judge furniture on the basis of price and quality, selecting the right store for your purchases, tips on credit buying and discount stores, decorating ideas, guides and charts on fibers, fabrics, and plastics, and take-along checklists and buying guides. Reading it could save you time, headaches, and money.

CONSUMER INFORMATION CENTER
Dept. CHC
Pueblo, CO 81009

"Consumer Information," no charge, published quarterly, 16 pages, black and white.

This is a valuable index listing the over 250 publications of consumer interest issued by the Office of Consumer Affairs. Those of most interest are "Fibers & Fabrics" (046C), 90 cents, 28 pages, about the properties, uses, and care of natural and man-made fibers; "Removing Stains from Fabrics" (049C), 40 cents, 32 pages, on stain removers and removing 142 common stains; "Floor Coverings" (273C), no charge, five pages, on the advantages and disadvantages of wood, linoleum, terra cotta, slate, mosaic tile; and "Carpet and Rugs" (149C), 55 cents, with information on fibers, textures, selection, installation, care, and cleaning. Order blanks are enclosed for subscribing to the Index and for ordering individual booklets, which are also printed in Spanish.

CONSUMER INFORMATION DIVISION
Moving and Storage Industry
Dept. CHC
10 Columbus Circle
New York, NY 10019

"When Buying a House," no charge, 8 pages, black and white; "A Guide to Do-It-Yourself Packing," no charge, 8 pages, black and white, illustrated.

The house-buying booklet provides expert ground rules for the family planning home ownership: how much to pay, additional costs at time of purchase, neighborhood, plan and site arrangement, house plan, construction features (roof, exterior materials, foundation, plumbing, wiring), where to get a home loan and the types of loans available. Each category has its own checklist.

The guide to do-it-yourself packing clearly and simply details tips that should prove valuable to the family on the move: labeling, packing specific items, last-minute items, order of packing, working with the mover. General rules and a checklist of fundamentals are included.

Booklet cover, *Gray Enterprises*

Ideas for moving kit, *Mayflower Transit*

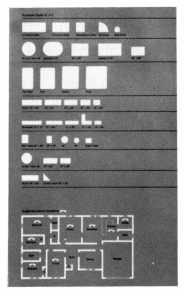

Phone location suggestions,
Phone Ideas & Moving Planner

GRAY ENTERPRISES
Dept. CHC
3611 Bridge Manor Drive
Kansas City, MO 64137

"How to Avoid Making Costly Mistakes in Buying a Home," $3.95, 47 pages.

Everything from selecting the right neighborhood to closing the deal. Guidelines on judging how much you can afford to pay, how to select the home your family needs, how to work with the realtor, how to make an offer, how to handle financial arrangements, and how to close the deal.

GUIDES BOX 183-P
Dept. CHC
Oradell, NJ 07649

"Factory Outlet Shopping Guides," one guide, $1.95; two guides, $3.50; three guides, $4.50; plus 30 cents postage per order, black and white.

Over 400 factory outlets are listed in each of the five guides, which cover the northeastern states, one each for Maryland-Virginia-Delaware; New England; New Jersey; New York; eastern Pennsylvania. Factory-outlet shopping is the smart money-saving way to buy these days.
MO

MAYFLOWER TRANSIT COMPANY
Dept. CHC
P.O. Box 107B
Indianapolis, IN 46206

"Mayflower Moving Kit," no charge, 16 pages, black and white, illustrated.

A most helpful booklet on organized moving. There are checklists of things to be done from 30 days prior to the move to actual moving day, such as sending out change-of-address cards, getting medical and dental records, checking and clearing tax assessments, plus lists to help you make complete inventory records of household furnishings and labels for cartons with instructions to load first or last or not to load.

PHONE IDEAS & MOVING PLANNER
A. T. & T.
Dept. CHC
Room 540, Residence Sales
195 Broadway
New York, NY 10007

"Phone Ideas & Moving Planner," no charge, 12 pages, color, illustrated.

If you are planning a move, this helpful booklet is full of useful information on how to pack. One suggestion is to make placement diagrams for favorite paintings or accessories on a table before packing them. So that you can preplan your move right down to the last telephone extension, there's also a grid with furniture cutouts and suggested phone locations, colors, and styles.

SIMMONS COMPANY
Dept. CHC
2 Park Avenue
New York, NY 10016

"How to Buy a Mattress," no charge, 10 pages, some color, illustrated; "The Bad Back Booklet," no charge, 12 pages, some color, illustrated.

The first booklet is designed to acquaint the buyer with the fine points of mattress buying—what to look for, how to judge firmness, the size to get. There are lists of "don'ts," an explanation of how mattresses are made, the construction and importance of box springs, and how both box spring and mattress should be cared for. There is also a handy purse-size buying guide. "The Bad Back Booklet" copes with the perennial problem by giving advice on posture, diet, and exercise—and a description of the Simmons Maxipedic mattress with built-in bedboard.
RS

the **BAD BACK** booklet

Booklet cover, *Simmons*

240

U.S. DEPARTMENT OF AGRICULTURE • EXTENSION SERVICE • PROGRAM AID NO. 1061

Booklet cover, *Superintendent of Documents*

Air-conditioning ideas, *Whirlpool*

SCHOOLS

SUPERINTENDENT OF DOCUMENTS
Dept. CHC
U.S. Government Printing Office
Washington, DC 20402

"Used Furniture Can Be a Good Buy,"
25 cents, 7 pages, black and white,
illustrated.

This government publication explains
how to inspect the framework of a
secondhand piece of furniture to tell if
it is well made and gives advice and
ideas for restyling and repairing.

THER-A-PEDIC ASSOCIATES
  INTERNATIONAL
Dept. CHC
225 North Avenue
Garwood, NJ 07027

"The Bed Game," no charge, 14 pages,
color, illustrated.

The booklet is devoted to explaining
the importance of your back and, in
direct relation, the importance of the
mattress you spend "one-third of your
life on." It also gives statistics on well-
known brands of mattresses.

WHIRLPOOL CORPORATION
Marketing Communications
Dept. CHC
Benton Harbor, MI 49022

"Question and Answers About Room
Air Conditioners," no charge, 13 pages,
black and white.

An informative little booklet that tells
what room air-conditioning is and does
by answering the most frequently asked
questions. Included are hints on
buying, installation and operation facts,
and care-of information.

WOMAN'S DAY DICTIONARY OF
  ANTIQUES
Dept. CHC
P.O. Box 1000
Greenwich, CT 06830

"Woman's Day Dictionary of
Antiques," $3.95, plus 50 cents postage.

A quick reference and authoritative
guide to antique furniture and
decorative accessories, with
information on the various periods and
styles. The book is handsomely
illustrated with detailed drawings
showing the outstanding characteristics
of each period.

CHICAGO SCHOOL OF INTERIOR
  DECORATION
Career Institute
Sherman Turnpike
Danbury, CT 06816

"Wonderful, modern and exciting way
to learn Interior Decoration & Design,"
no charge, 22 pages, some color.

An informative brochure that poses the
question "Can you succeed as an
interior designer?" and then goes on to
tell you how the Chicago School can
help you. The complete program is
outlined, with illustrative material taken
from the four-volume course. If you are
interested in pursuing a career in the
design field, this home-study course
might be of interest to you.
MO

Catalogue cover, *Chicago School of Interior Decoration*

Catalogue cover, *Emerson*

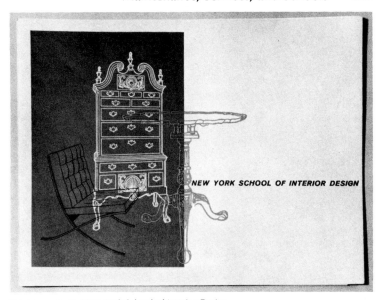
Catalogue cover, *New York School of Interior Design*

SERVICES

EMERSON AND ASSOCIATES
Dept. CHC
1225 West Barkley
Orange, CA 92668

"Professional Drapery Making, Window Styling, and Custom Decorating" and "Professional Upholstery for Fun and Profit," no charge, published annually, black and white, illustrated.

The first booklet, by the Custom Drapery Institute, details the contents of their home custom decorating and drapery course. Tuition is $123, $138 for deferred payments, and couples may enroll for $25 extra.

 The second booklet covers the home upholstery course of the Modern Upholstery Institute. Included in the 130-lesson course are six furniture kits and hand tools. Tuition for this is $300, with deferred payments arranged.

INTERNATIONAL CORRESPONDENCE
** SCHOOLS**
Dept. CHC
Scranton, PA 18515

"ICS School of Interior Design," no charge, published annually, 15 pages, color, illustrated.

The brochure describes the International Correspondence School's home-study course in interior design, with illustrations. A free demonstration lesson is included before you commit yourself to the course.

NEW YORK SCHOOL OF INTERIOR
** DESIGN**
Dept. CHC
155 East 56th Street
New York, NY 10022

"New York School of Interior Design," no charge, 24 pages, black and white, illustrated.

This well-known professional school offers an excellent home-study decorating course of 26 lessons covering such subjects as textiles, furnishings, room arrangement, color harmony, period and modern furniture, antiques, floor and wallcoverings, window and wall treatments, lighting, and accessories. The cost for the complete course, which includes materials provided, is $200.

THE CLASSIC BINDERY, INC.
Dept. CHC
Box 572 D
Mendham, NJ 07945

"The Classic Bindery," 25 cents, published semiannually, 6 pages, illustrated.

This company specializes in custom bookbinding in leather or cloth in three styles, with gold stamping and gold edges, if desired. Price is determined by the size and bulk of the book, from as little as $13, under 2", for cloth binding, to $80 for full leather binding over 3". They will also resew and repair deteriorated volumes and make slip cases.

COUNTRY BRAID HOUSE
Dept. CHC
Clark Road
Tilton, NH 03276

No catalogue.

Country Braid House has developed a rug-braiding machine that you can rent or buy on special order. They will also braid your material, make rugs to order, or sell you rug-braiding supplies.

242

WE HAVE AN
INTERIOR DESIGN
PLAN DESIGNED
JUST FOR YOU.

DESIGN ALTERNATIVES, LTD.
We take the mystery out of decorating a beautiful
home or office . . . at a price you can afford.

Brochure cover, *Design Alternatives*

DESIGN ALTERNATIVES, LTD.
Dept. CHC
146 East 56th Street
New York, NY 10022

"Interior Design Plan . . . Just for You,"
no charge, 4 pages, black and white.

Design Alternatives will "take the
mystery out of decorating a beautiful
home or office . . . at a price you can
afford." The booklet describes four
plans you can choose from, ranging
from a $50 one-hour consultation with
a designer to a complete design and
decorating job at net cost.

GUILD OF SHAKER CRAFTS
Dept. CHC
401 Savidge Street
Spring Lake, MI 49546

"Guild of Shaker Crafts," $2.50, 28
pages, some color, illustrated.

The Guild will restore or repair original
Shaker pieces, a service hard to find.
You can write for an estimate or call
them at 616-846-2870.

MODERN NEEDLEPOINT MOUNTING
CO.
Dept. CHC
11 West 32nd Street
New York, NY 10001

"Needlepoint Mounting in the Modern
Manner," no charge, 6 pages, color,
illustrated.

The brochure details the firm's service;
they will mount needlepoint on almost
anything. Illustrations show handbag
mountings plus accessories that can be
made up from needlepoint panels.
Specifications and instructions are
included.

ORUM SILVER CO.
Dept. CHC
Box 805
Meriden, CT 06450

No brochure, estimates sent without
obligation.

Antique or modern silverplate, sterling,
pewter, or any metal will be
straightened, repaired, dents removed,
spots cleaned, and replated by Orum.
Tea sets, candlesticks, trays, bowls,
resilvered; brushes, combs, mirrors, and
nail files for dresser sets, stainless-steel
blades for old knives, replaced. A
wonderful source for metal repairs.

Restorer Robert Whitley at work in his studio

Garden umbrella services, *Zip-Jack Servicenter*

SENTI-METAL CO.
Silverplating Division
Dept. CHC
1919 Memory Lane
Columbus, OH 43209

Price list, no charge.

An excellent service for silverplating or for refinishing of gold, copper, brass, or pewter. Missing parts replaced and dents removed. There is a 25-year guarantee on silver replating.

J. SCHACHTER CORP.
Dept. CHC
115 Allen Street
New York, NY 10022

No catalogue; send 50 cents for swatches and ordering instructions.

Mail Schachter your old comforter and they'll take it completely apart, sterilize and power-fluff feathers and downs, and blow them into a new interlined cover you select. The stitching is guaranteed for life.
MO

AKE TUGEL
Dept. CHC
266 Sea Cliff Avenue
Sea Cliff, NY 11579

A three-man team of expert cabinet makers, headed by Swedish artist/cabinetmaker Ake Tugel, will restore and repair fine antiques for you. Write him for advice and estimates.

THE ROBERT WHITLEY STUDIO
Dept. CHC
Laurel Road
Solebury, PA 18963

"Robert Whitley Master Craftsman," $3.00 (refundable with purchase), published annually, 28 pages, black and white, illustrated.

The booklet explains what a master craftsman is and, more specifically, Robert Whitley's credentials and skills. He restores antiques, custom designs, adapts, and keeps a file of over 4,000 reproductions that can be made in a choice of fine woods. Some representative 18th-century pieces are shown and described, as is the process of restoration. All prices are on request.

ZIP-JACK SERVICENTER
Dept. CHC
703 E. Tremont Avenue
Bronx, NY 10457

Brochure, no charge, black and white, illustrated.

Be it conventional or pagoda-shaped, Zip-Jack will launder, refringe, or recover your garden umbrella and send you a pre-labeled shipping bag with the location of the nearest United Parcel service station. It costs under $35 to recover a conventional-shaped 12-rib umbrella, 8' diameter with ribs up to 48" long. Also offered is a do-it yourself "E-Z-on" replacement cover in choice of colors and a zip-on protective rain or storage cover.
MO

INDEX

ABOUT THE AUTHORS

JOSÉ WILSON was born and educated in England. She joined the staff of *House & Garden* as a copy writer in 1953 and became Feature Editor of the magazine in 1961. Miss Wilson and Arthur Leaman edited *House & Garden's Complete Guide to Interior Decorating* in 1960. Her other book credits include *House & Garden's Book of Decorating and Entertaining* (1962), *The Cooking of the Eastern Heartland* for Time-Life's Foods of the World series, co-author with Betty Groff of *Good Earth & Country Cooking,* and editor of two *House & Garden* cookbooks. Since 1968 Miss Wilson has been a Contributing Editor of *House & Garden* and a free-lance writer. She spends the winters in New York and the summers in Rockport, Massachusetts.

ARTHUR LEAMAN, ASID, was educated at Haverford College, New York University, and the New York School of Interior Design. He worked in London with Alban Conway, a well-known decorator, and on returning to the United States, Mr. Leaman became Decorating Editor of *Apartment Life.* He joined the staff of *House & Garden* in 1951 and served as Decorating Editor of that magazine from 1958 to 1965. Mr. Leaman was a partner in a decorating firm for seven years and now spends the winter months running his inn, The Golden Lemon, on the West Indian island of St. Kitts. During the summers he works on interior-design books with José Wilson and designs rooms for companies in the home-furnishings field.

Miss Wilson and Mr. Leaman have collaborated on five books: *Decoration USA* (Macmillan, 1965), *Decorating Defined* (Simon and Schuster, 1970), *Color in Decoration* (Van Nostrand Reinhold, 1972), *Decorating with Confidence* (Simon and Schuster, 1973), and *Decorating American-Style* (New York Graphic Society, 1975). They are currently working on a budget decorating book.